The Conscious Whole

The Conscious Whole

William T. Kenny

Circle of Friends Press
Charleston, SC

The Conscious Whole Copyright © 2018 by William T. Kenny

williamtkenny@gmail.com
www.theconsciouswhole.com

All rights reserved. No part of this book may be used or reproduced without written permission from the publisher except in critical articles and reviews. Contact the publisher for information.

Paperback ISBN: 978-1-948796-17-0
eBook ISBN: 978-1-948796-19-4

Library of Congress Control Number: 2018944486

Book design by Colin Rolfe

Cover art and imprint design by R. Brad Abrahams, D.O., DABR
www.bradabrahams.com

Distribution by Epigraph Books.

Circle of Friends Press
6650 Rivers Avenue, Suite 100
Charleston, SC 29406
publishing@circleoffriendspress.com
www.circleoffriendspress.com

This is for anyone who believes there is no hope.

Preface

Every moment we observe reality in front of us with fluctuating levels of awareness. Throughout the course of my medical career, I have ranged from being hyper-aware to somnolent. I offer a view obtained during those attentive states that includes characters with different medical conditions, the majority of which are based on real people I have encountered, however, names and identifying information have been changed.

The ideas and hypotheses postulated in this book have been cited, where relevant, and great care has been taken with references from the literature to include original sources when possible, to maintain accuracy and truth, and to avoid perpetuating incorrect information. Some sources may seem out-of-date, as a broad spectrum of work has been cited from 1892 to 2017. Just because literature is not recent, does not mean it carries no significance. Additionally, some of the citations may not be the most comprehensive or current but have been included because I found those works to be relevant, accessible, and/or well-written. Also, credit has been given to authors who have developed similar concepts to those discussed within this book, and I have done my best to be comprehensive in this regard, however, there is surely prior work that deserves to be cited but of which I am not yet aware.

The nature of science includes constant change and flux; something that is considered true today, may be proven wrong tomorrow. Various scientific notions are reviewed, but future literature may prove some or many of the concepts detailed in this book to be wrong. Additionally, new ideas are presented, which may seem eccentric, however scientific theory and empirical evidence are used as a foundation to give support to hypotheses that push beyond the boundary of what is known. These ideas can easily be dismissed and categorized as metaphysical nonsense, but just because something is a metaphysical concept does not automatically make it true or false. Instead, it must be innocently considered and tested; true concepts should be accepted and false concepts should be rejected. Pure science does not judge or act with prejudice but instead seeks answers and often travels down a path no one could have envisioned. We must be open-minded while at the same time being critical; importantly, however, we must give science the opportunity to consider every possibility. The work presented opens doors of potential and not every one will lead to a truth, yet if only one is true our view of the world will radically change.

Medicine and health are discussed throughout this book, but ideas and treatments presented should not replace the currently accepted standard of medical care. It is my hope that hypotheses detailed in this book will be proven to be correct and may someday become accepted into the scientific and medical paradigms, but until then, we need rigorous and honest scientific work to prove what is discussed. At the very least, I hope this book will initiate discussions and ideas that may improve our world. For now, take the following to be a glimpse into our future, into a world that may change our present.

Part I

"*The man who first saw the exterior of the box from above later sees its interior from below*"

Thomas Kuhn, Ph.D.[1]

---

1. Kuhn, *The Structure of Scientific Revolutions* (1996), pg. 111.

1

Carried by a wave across a template of structures, the following is an imperfect translation of a primordial tool used by ancients to shape the universe

It was just the way things were. The way of life. The accepted truth. Accepted by everyone.

Thoughts were so powerful within the Conscious Whole they literally created reality while at the same time denying any possibility not within the scope of The One Reality. The people of the Conscious Whole were perfectly content in their world. It behaved as they predicted; it was controlled by their intentions; and it was stable by their perception. Everything was the way it was because of the way they observed it to be. Their scientists discovered the world and created theories based on their experimentation. A circular logic of fabricating reality and then confirming what was already created as if it formed de novo, outside of their control; a confirmation of their own deed.

Yet, how true is truth and how real is reality? Truth based on the ideas of the Conscious Whole was true for its people, and they followed it as such. Reality was what they lived, as real as the words you are reading.

On the surface, the cities and people within the Conscious Whole functioned no differently than those of any other society since the beginning of time. There were laws to obey, and there were jobs that had to be done. As a matter of fact, the people did not have any awareness of the Conscious Whole, for they were one with it. They did not call it "The Conscious Whole" nor did they know there was even something to name.

The Conscious Whole was the summation of every individual consciousness. Each unit of consciousness manifested as a cloud around the body: the extra-physical self. These clouds were primarily focused around the crown of the head[1] like a rainstorm over a small town. Different shapes and colors were possible. Some were bright like the sun, or as clear as a stream in a forest, while others were dark and opaque. The shades varied from every frequency of the visible spectrum extending to waves of light not discernible to the naked eye.[2] Differing in size, the clouds typically extended no further than one arm's length in every direction and assumed a disc-like configuration.

The characteristics of each cloud of consciousness were representative of an individual's own beingness. For example, a person feeling content and calm would have a tightly wrapped cloud that revolved very slowly with cool blue and green tones. On the other hand, someone who was frightened would have a scattered cloud, disbanding into the surroundings, with fiery red light spinning quickly. Further from the center of each cloud the energy dissipated as the density of the energy decreased.

The conscious clouds not only represented thoughts and emotions of an individual but also influenced physical reality surrounding each person. The particular characteristics of the clouds literally created a unique material structure specific to the cloud of consciousness. The reality created by the cloud, in turn, was perceived as the objective world and in-

---

1. Similar descriptions of energy fields: Oschman, *Energy Medicine: The Scientific Basis* (2000), pg. 77.

2. Idea of consciousness as coherent light discussed in: McTaggart, *The Field: The Quest for the Secret Force of the Universe* (2008), pg. 94.

terpreted as separate from the individual.³ Meanwhile, the cloud manipulated matter in the background, unseen to the creator. Hypothetically, one human floating on a small boat in the cosmic ocean would exist as a singularity, surrounded by their own form of reality, created solely by their cloud of consciousness.

However, this solitary life did not exist; densities of consciousness overlapped. People lived with and nearby many other people. The effect was summative, leading to larger and larger concentrations of consciousness. Each time two clouds intersected, they would co-adapt and become a single unit, no longer completely unique to each person but transformed into an average of the energy densities. Like mixing black and white paint, the unique waves of light in each conscious cloud blended. Some waves would cancel out, while others would be amplified. The new averaged, shared cloud of consciousness allowed people to live in a consistent physical reality, while still contributing their individuality to the shared cloud. This process continued with the collection of more and more units, building into the massive union of the Conscious Whole: the summation of many consciousnesses fused into one force.⁴

The people were never directly aware of their own conscious clouds, just as we are not physically aware of the electrical activity of our brain, heart, or body. Therefore, they neither challenged the formation nor the existence of the Conscious Whole. It was established without opposition or their **conscious** creation.

Long ago when the consciousnesses were being brought together, all of the people signed an unconscious contract with the ever-expanding Conscious Whole to be bound to its ways and to follow its thoughts, for its thoughts were also their own. The contract was necessary for life to

---

3. The eye has a "blind spot", where the optic nerve enters the eye and there are no photoreceptors. An object that falls into this portion of the visual field will not be seen, however, the brain fills in this blank space to give the perception of a seamless image. What else in our "reality" is the brain filling in? Reviewed in: Ramachandran, "Blind Spots." *Scientific American* (1992).

4. Similar idea discussed in: Tombazian, *The Path to the 5th Dimension* (2012), pg. 66.

proceed in a civilized and workable manner. If everyone lived under different pretenses of reality and thought, some may follow the laws of gravity, while others instead may float through the sky. Scientific experiments would not be reproducible or accurate because they would be carried out under different laws of nature. Even with two people, there must be a sameness of reality in order to have a functional life together. The creation of The One Reality was a predetermined requirement for life to proceed seamlessly under the Conscious Whole.

Yet, this relationship between people and thought had an unforeseen effect. The unity created by the summation of consciousness resulted in unique thought being surrendered for the sake of oneness. Consequently, the realm beyond what had already been established was cloaked in darkness, and thought could not advance. Before they knew it, the Conscious Whole weighed on everyone's lives preventing universal change. As if tracking through thick mud, it was impossible for people to make headway towards new ideas, and an individual nearing the darkness would be quickly shunned, with accusations of heresy threatening the ones seeking to see. The paradigm reminded its people of the boundaries, which they cherished for utmost security was found with the known.

This is not to say there were not creative individuals, for new concepts, materials, and devices were developed. However, these new ideas were merely based on the accepted boundaries of the world. The people were not aware of this limitation because of the unconscious influence the Conscious Whole had on the reality around each person. Since all were part of it, and they created it, it literally created them. A give-and-take process. A circular loop of influence that no longer had a clear beginning or end, sewn into the world and made imperceptible. Everyone contributed to the Conscious Whole, and the Conscious Whole in turn provided a stable, secure, and structured reality back to its people.

It did not take long for the Conscious Whole to become an entity of its own. Conscious in regard to itself, yet working with and through the now unconscious minds[5] of its people. It permeated every person's being like thick nectar, seeping into his or her pores. Similar to the atmosphere that holds in all breathable oxygen, the Conscious Whole existed above and contained the one and only created reality below. The only tangible trace of its existence was in the material world it produced.

Outside the wavelengths of light visible to the naked eye were energetic finger-like projections extending from the Conscious Whole. The fingers touched every piece of matter, channeled through each individual's conscious cloud, creating reality surrounding their bodies. Similar to the strings of a puppet attached to its legs, arms, and head animating life, the fingers from the Conscious Whole had dexterity to manipulate matter into virtually any configuration. The human body was not excluded as the fingers also attached to every person, every cell in that person's body, every molecule in that cell, every atom within that molecule, every electron, proton, and neutron in the atom, and even to the smallest components of matter that made up the subatomic particles and the smaller parts of those. The fingers moved atoms in space arranging them in the order it desired, using them like building blocks of a toy set.

The Conscious Whole built its people from the bottom up.[6] Beginning with the smallest facets of nature all the way to the people they would become. The creational process was the power of the Conscious Whole and made the reality scientists observed. Each individual's conscious cloud had the same capability of shaping matter. However, individual conscious clouds no longer existed independently as they had all relinquished their power to the Conscious Whole, for the sake of unity.

---

5. How much of reality are you consciously aware of? Change blindness is a phenomenon where observers do not notice large changes to their surroundings. Reviewed in: Simons and Rensink, "Change Blindness: Past, Present, and Future." *Trends in Cognitive Sciences* (2005).

6. For related concepts about a "morphic field" shaping reality see: Sheldrake, *Morphic Resonance: The Nature of Formative Causation* (2009) and McTaggart, *The Field: The Quest for the Secret Force of the Universe* (2008).

The form the world took was a direct result of the master puppeteer's plan, the Conscious Whole's plan, the collective people's plan. Despite the people's inability to know what the Conscious Whole was, its power was indirectly evident in their daily lives.[7] It caused waves in the ocean to crash rhythmically on the shore and wind to blow leaves from the trees eventually pulling them towards the ground. It developed rain in the clouds and pushed trees upward towards the sky. The Conscious Whole allowed the continuum of life to proceed as predicted and observed. The downstream force it created was thought to be many things and sought by the most prominent scientists.

They called it the "Universal force of all being. Unstoppable and impermeable in all regards. The driving force behind all life."

According to people living within the Conscious Whole, this force was not something that could be changed or created, and it was not even something they could see. Divine to them, and they treated it as such. It existed beyond their knowledge, yet unknown to them it was created by their knowledge and controlled by their intentions. The people never knew it, but by studying the universal force of all being, they were indirectly observing the power they created by forming their Conscious Whole. Seamlessly cloaked in nature, its truth evaded scientists. Just as a raindrop cannot know it is in a cloud, these people could not see the Conscious Whole.

Nature was a locomotive train barreling through the cosmos on an unalterable course. Yet, this unstoppable fate was not an issue of conflict for these people for they loved their existence and would have it no other way. Technology was developed to help overcome the less pleasant aspects of life. Homes were kept warm by burning fuel in the winter and kept cool in the summer by heat exchange devices. An army was formed to protect the land, and a sturdy economic system was established to preserve the

---

7. The idea of a metaphysical background of the physical world discussed in: Buhner, *Plant Intelligence and the Imaginal Realm: Beyond the Doors of Perception into the Dreaming of Earth* (2014).

livelihood of the people. This is not to say there was not suffering within the Conscious Whole. There was still pain, poverty, hunger, depression, and death.

Illness too. They had their ways of dealing with this though. Surgery, medication, and psychological therapy were all mainstays of treatment, which worked quite fine, healing many. However, limitations of this science were numerous. Some diseases ran rampant destroying lives and families while others were not understood and left to the most basic supportive care.

The demise of these people was their inability to realize they controlled their reality and were all equally responsible for the Conscious Whole's power.

2

As a prerequisite for entry, choices must be made that will affect your existence; realizing these were choices is what you will learn; the message was only given once as the being knew it had to make a decision

"It's a disease that will naturally progress to death caused by organ failure. Your cells will stop making proteins your body needs to survive. It will affect your whole body including all of your organs, muscles, and nerves. They will just stop working, one by one," the doctor paused, as he collected his thoughts and tried to think of how to make this news not as dreadful.

Unsuccessfully, he continued, "It will start with the muscles and nerves in your arms and legs. They will eventually stop working, but things like your heart, liver, intestines, and brain will work quite well for some time." This reassurance did not make the predicament sound any better to Andy.

In his prime, Andy Fergus was a large man, built like an athlete but currently inhabiting a body no longer fit to compete. He had a thick red beard that was starting to turn gray in some spots and his round face sat between his large beard and baseball hat. Some of his red hair flowed out from under the brim, and his dark brown eyes glistened as he attempted to process the diagnosis. He was hunched over in the chair, leaning forward, listening quietly to the doctor, eyebrows furrowed, waiting for the "good news" part of this conversation.

"Unfortunately, with your disease the end is inevitable," the doctor said in a compassionate tone; the irony of his comment would only later become evident to Andy.

Andy did not know how to react. Shock was the initial feeling. Numbness. Frankly, he did not believe what was being told to him, as if it was someone else receiving a verdict and Andy was listening in. He only took in small pieces of what the doctor was telling him, and as the physician's words flowed over Andy's low-slung head, he looked down at his arms and hands. Tiny muscles twitched under his skin. The doctor explained those were muscle and nerve fibers beginning to die.

Like shooting stars giving off their last light of life, Andy thought.

"We know your body makes this disease the way that it is. A terminal illness. There are no other ways it progresses because your body dictates how it advances. It's not your mind that controls your body's ability to turn on or off a disease like this. It's just the way your biology works. It's the reality of the situation." Frowning, the doctor continued, "Because this is a genetic disease, it's built into your genes, into your DNA. It's *who* you are."

Who I am? Andy thought. "Well, isn't there anything that can be done? Like a medication or something?" Andy replied, finally able to squeeze out a response in a trembling, barely audible voice.

"Not for this," the doctor remarked, sounding helpless in his ability to provide any real treatment. He went on to explain how they have devices to make life easier as the disease progresses and supportive therapies to help at the end, as if this would somehow comfort Andy.

Andy was sadly left to suffer. Not for a lack of effort or empathy from the people of the Conscious Whole but as a victim of its thoughts, ideas, and reality.

Like many others living under the Conscious Whole, Andy had had a life he felt in control of. A life he enjoyed. He lived alone, on the outskirts of a small town called Franklin. His house was built one hundred years before he was born, and it had a big yard and garden where Andy grew all of the vegetables and fruit he could ever eat. He enjoyed the daily pleasures of being with family and friends, spending time outdoors, and going to work.

Andy and his brother Peter grew up in a strict home. They shared a room and were more like best friends than brothers. Their parents dictated how everything was to proceed, and the two brothers became very comfortable with the boundaries in which they lived. For Andy in particular, it gave him structure and definition, a closed loop where he found happiness. Eating the exact same meal for breakfast almost everyday for the past twenty years was just one manifestation of the environment Andy grew up in. Two pancakes, two tablespoons of maple syrup, one egg with the yolk uncooked, and a glass of skim milk.

Andy's yard and garden were his prized possessions, which contained an orchard of peach and pear trees lined up in three neat rows of ten. Tomatoes marked the entrance to the garden that even had some corn growing in the back. Andy was a high school science teacher and once per year would bring students to his garden to talk about the fundamentals of biology, despite the fact it made him cringe every time his students stepped off the neatly groomed slate path within the garden. Trying not to lose his temper was a challenge for Andy. Nonetheless, he loved his job and found it very rewarding to teach young students about the beloved theories of science. The theories of the Conscious Whole.

Andy was passionate about teaching, particularly science, where the predictability and strict methodology fit well with his personality. He truly enjoyed learning on his own about the most advanced theories of biology, chemistry, and physics and went as far as teaching these new and fascinating theories to his students. They all enjoyed this extra effort that few other teachers brought to the classroom, even if they had, on occasion, to deal with Andy's potentially fiery temperament if things were out of order. The students quickly learned to sit perfectly forward in their seats and to sign in with their full name spelled neatly in cursive.

Andy did not realize he was a slave to the ways of the Conscious Whole. Bound by the ideals it created, limited by the possibilities that were only allowed to be possible. He and his students were within what they believed to be the one and only reality; taught under that pretense in order to allow belief in words they thought were truths.

In hindsight, as Andy thought about his new diagnosis, he could see the slow decline in function. The increased difficulty of opening jars. How his colleagues asked about his progressively sloppy handwriting. How he used to be able to walk up ten flights of stairs without getting out of breath. He was losing strength and precise movements of his muscles as well as losing cells in his lungs. Eventually, after a few tests and a blood analysis to examine his DNA, the doctor had confirmed the diagnosis and delivered the bad news, once again. There would be no "good news."

Andy had a hard time going back to his routine: going to work, teaching his students, tending to his yard and garden, pruning the fruit trees. None of it was the same. All he thought of was his upcoming decline. The inevitable future. The death that was coming.

"Mr. Fergus?" one of Andy's students said. "Um, excuse me…Mr. Fergus!?"

Andy was startled out of his now daily trance of perseverating on his disease. How could he not?

"The principal is at the door!" a spry, blond, boy in the back of the room called out.

Andy looked over and saw his tall, bald boss staring at him with one raised thick, black eyebrow.

"You know, Andy, parents have been calling me because their children are telling them "strange" things about you," Mr. Felson said in a tone mixed with compassion and disdain as he spoke to Andy outside of his classroom.

"Well…I'm having some personal issues…health issues more specifically," Andy conferred. His boss waited for more details, not changing his expression, again partly worried but also concerned about the well-being of the students.

"Contagious?"

"No. No, not at all," Andy reassured.

They stood silently for another thirty seconds, Andy reluctant to divulge details, primarily because he preferred to keep his personal life to himself, but also fearing he may lose his job if Mr. Felson knew the details.

"Ok, well. As long as you are doing well and being taken care of by a doctor...just let me know if I can do anything for you. But I don't want to hear from any more parents," the principal conveyed, completely unaware of what Andy was facing.

Andy knew his life was going to change. He could not keep his disease secret for much longer. People were beginning to notice. It was affecting his teaching. *There's nothing I can do,* Andy hopelessly repeated in his head for the rest of the day.

Feeling like he was watching his own demise, the world around him rushed by that day; like the tide drawing sand off a beach, he would soon leach into nothingness.

As a child, Andy had a hard time adjusting to new situations. Moving into a different house and changing schools when he was eleven upset his balance. His mother put him in therapy, but Andy buried the problems deeper. His inflexibility persisted into adulthood, and the routine associated with being a schoolteacher and the meticulousness of lawn care and gardening soothed his worried mind. Change was just too stressful. How was he to deal with an event as life changing as a terminal illness?

There was nothing Andy could do! No medications. No surgery. No cure and most notably, *no hope.*

Andy tried to handle the situation the same way he had dealt with everything else. Digest the initial shock and then store his fears in the far reaches of his consciousness, allowing them to eat away at him from the inside out. However, this disease affected him differently. He could not just store it away like the rest of his problems. It plagued him constantly, reminding him of its presence.

He could no longer concentrate on his work, he lost the passion he had for the outdoors, and he showed little interest in his family and friends.

Time is running out! What am I supposed to do!? Andy's desperate mind frantically sought for an escape. For the first time in his life he felt trapped, instead of being blissfully contained in predictability.

Over the next few months, Andy's disease progressed as the doctor predicted. His hands became weaker and weaker, and his breathing became more labored. He could start seeing tendons and bones through the skin of his palms, and every flight of stairs looked longer than before. With the encouragement of his family, Andy tried to look at the positive aspects of life. He was grateful to still have strength in his arms, allowing him to carry bags from the grocery store or move tools around his yard. Nevertheless, the disease was progressing at an accelerating rate. Andy noticed his legs were starting to give out on him, feeling like they were rubber bands. He was tripping more frequently, which embarrassed him, keeping him home more often than not.

The doctor had said it would be at least five years after diagnosis before needing a wheelchair, but Andy suddenly found himself filling out paperwork to get a power wheelchair in anticipation of his all too soon needs. At the most recent doctor's visit they found his heart was also beginning to fail.

"It's not pumping as well as it should. The contractions are getting weaker. Just like the muscles in your arms are deteriorating, the same is happening to the heart. It's a different type of muscle, but this disease is affecting it as well," the doctor reported to Andy. "The heart problems will worsen too," he said, predicting Andy's next question. It was now a usual occurrence to receive more bad news at every visit.

Despair quickly followed as hopelessness edged positive emotions out of Andy's life.

In his classroom, he stopped using the blackboard because he could no longer write well enough though he could still lecture to his students. However, despite his best attempts to work, six months after his diagnosis, Andy's condition had progressed to the point where he could no longer speak for fifty minutes at a time, the length of his classes. Still pushing for a productive life, he decided he would tutor students from his home. Yet, sadly, parents feared he could no longer think as well as he used to. They thought with the dying of his body, his mind was dying as well. They did not want their children being taught by someone who was incompetent. However, more than anything else, they feared his disease.

As his body thinned and his beard became long and ragged, Andy looked twice his age. His appetite was not what it used to be, he could no longer finely trim his beard, and apathy moved into his life, filling the void passion had once occupied.

Andy came to know oppression better than many others. Physically bound by the reality forced upon him. Locked in a body on its own course. The universal force of all being had determined what he would become. His genetic disease dictated where his body was headed, and he could not separate himself from this; like being on a runaway train moving too fast to jump off. Andy felt the burden of illness daily. Starting when he was thirty-seven, it took less than a year for the disease to advance to this point: on a path towards complete immobility ending with a painful death.

It was the tail end of summer and Andy still found pleasure in driving his car around town; enjoying the independence and mobility he retained while in his vehicle. Feeling the summer air flow past him with the windows down allowed him to briefly forget the disease ravaging his body. Momentarily, he would feel free again. Almost forgetting where he was going that day, he pulled into the doctor's office for a short-term checkup. The doctor was worried about Andy's mental state during the last appointment.

Walking into the examination room where Andy was slouched down in a chair that appeared oversized, the hopelessness on the doctor's face could not be hidden. Nearly one year ago, a much healthier, stronger man sat in the same spot. Now, Andy's body was half of what it used to be.

"Did you drive yourself here?" the doctor asked, surprised Andy was able to function independently and clearly not taking his prior advice of having his family more involved with his care.

"Well…yeah. I didn't walk," Andy spat back sarcastically, resenting the doctor's underestimation of his remaining physical abilities.

"I think this is a good time to talk about other living arrangements. You know, it's the best for you…"

Andy stopped listening. The high from the morning had been washed away by the doctor's bleak outlook, and it brought Andy back down to the science of his condition. It did not matter how he was feeling that morning; the world was moving forward, and it was dragging him with it. He knew what the doctor was going to say: he was going to die soon and needed somewhere to croak. He needed to be stuck in a corner and forgotten about.

Every time he visited the doctor a small part of him felt like there would be a new drug or treatment. *Nope. Not this time and not anytime*, he thought. *The end is coming soon.*

Needless to say, Andy sank into a morbid depression. *I'm useless. What purpose do I serve now? I can't work. I can't enjoy anything. I'm going to die.* No longer able to fulfill his function in life, he abandoned any enjoyment he once held.

3

The being was ushered into the seeing room;
those surrounding it were cloaked and they sought to show;
they do not speak but point to what must be seen

IT WAS SUICIDE.

The pill would kill him within seconds. Sitting at his kitchen table, the dark black pill looked like an empty void contrasted against the white plastic tabletop. Andy sat for a few minutes and contemplated just ending his life. Then without hesitation, he took it.

The pill was difficult to swallow because it had a soft, rubbery shell and tasted like a burnt piece of rubber. The caustic covering blistered Andy's mouth, and he regretted not taking it with water. As he tried to swallow the pill, it got stuck in his throat, cutting off his airway! Andy then realized how he was going to be found; that he had died from choking to death as opposed to dying from the contents of the pill. How embarrassing! He could not even kill himself properly.

His throat was dry and swelled up, wrapping itself around the pill. Yet his muscles innocently gave their best effort to swallow. The muscles did not know the contents were lethal. For all they knew, they were swallowing a delicious peach from his garden, but actually they were following Andy's command and his wish to die. Eventually, the pill was pushed beyond his airway and towards his stomach. While sitting on the floor, waiting for the pill to be processed and circulated around his body, Andy had a sudden change of heart. In a last ditch attempt to save his life, he made himself throw up. What had made him change his mind?

Observing what had just come out of his stomach, now covering his body and the floor, he saw some of the oatmeal he had eaten for breakfast and bits and pieces of the fruit he had had afterwards. Andy did not see the pill, but everything was stained bright red from its poison, and there were little parts of the black rubbery shell everywhere! It had broken open! Fear rushed through his body following the poison circulating through his veins. It attacked every living cell making sure they would no longer live another day. *I didn't get it out in time!*

As he sat in his own vomit, he began to think about dying. He thought about how his family or one of his friends would find his body. They would be the first people to see him dead. He felt terrible. What a horrific thing to do to someone. They did not deserve the burden of dealing with that situation. He did not want to die, he wanted to live! But what was he to do!? There was still some of the poison in his body accomplishing its mission.

Overcome with a terrible sense of defeat, Andy realized he wanted to accomplish so much more in life. The schedule he was so used to suddenly became insignificant and useless. *What did I achieve staying in my routine? It only kept me bound on the same path.* More than anything, he wanted to see places unknown to him. He couldn't now. Those opportunities were gone forever. He was surely going to die in a few minutes. On the floor. **Having done nothing.**

When Andy awoke it took him several minutes to realize it had just been a dream! He hadn't actually taken the pill. He wasn't going to die! It seemed so real. The pill, the suicide, the emotions. He still had his illness, but he was alive!

I nearly died, but it was just a dream, Andy kept on telling himself.

It was the strangest feeling, like having the opportunity to die, to learn what it had to offer but then being given a second chance.[1]

Andy had been so scared in his dream that it made him realize how precious every moment of his existence is. Every moment there is the opportunity to change something or just appreciate the company of another. He was no longer going to be a slave to his condition or a prisoner in his own body. He was alive and still able to do so many things. Having seen death opened new doors.

It was right before sunrise and the window in Andy's bedroom faced east, displaying the new colors in the sky that would start this day. Delicate clouds hung high above the ground, touching the outermost reaches of the atmosphere. The sun reflected a pink light off the clouds and back towards the earth into Andy's eyes. He got up and made his way to the window. The crisp morning air was fresh and a few remaining stars glimmered, preparing to rest until the next night.

Thinking about nothing but the beautiful birth outside of his window, Andy had a moment of clarity. Absolute clarity. Nothing he had been worrying about over the past year mattered anymore. His pain, his illness, his job, and his life. Those were just fleeting thoughts. Fleeting fears. Andy was able to see what he really needed to do, and what he really wanted. The voice in the back of his mind, the background noise, was no longer reminding him of his tasks, his "to dos", his worries, his resentments, and his uncertainties.

An inquisitive man by nature, a dim glow of energy inside of Andy always wanted to explore the world but had been repressed by his routine, never allowing him to stray from its boundaries. The Conscious Whole nurtured this pattern, keeping Andy from disturbing the status quo. It continually reminded him he had a job to be loyal to, a house to keep clean, and a plan to adhere to.

"There is no use for you elsewhere," the Conscious Whole would say. "Remember all of the things you must do," it would remind him. "We

---

1. Conscious mystical death as a transformative process discussed in: Tombazian, *The Path to the 5th Dimension* (2012), pg. 29.

must worry and stress about what is upcoming in the future. Fear will protect us."

The release Andy felt the morning after he awoke from his dream made him deaf to those tyrannical forces. Andy wanted to see the world beyond the gloom of his everyday life. Of course he loved the life he had lived: teaching his students, working in his garden, and spending time with friends. But that life was fading away, and with the end staring him in the face, he needed to experience the world. He must move forward without regret; move beyond the Conscious Whole's plan for him.

And just like that, Andy made a decision to leave behind all he held onto and to go beyond what was known to him. The time for the movement was now.

4

You will learn, you will teach, and then you will show;
fear and doubt and people-created forms of control

ANDY'S FAMILY AND FRIENDS WERE HORRIFIED ABOUT the idea of him going somewhere else. The Conscious Whole warned them about the dangers beyond what was known. It cautioned that if Andy ventured beyond the limits of the comfort it offered, he would be risking not only his well-being but also his **life**.

"There is unknown danger," the Conscious Whole shouted into their ears. "This is the most difficult time for Andy. It is important for him to be in a place where he can be taken care of," were the warnings family and friends heard from the ever-vigilant Conscious Whole.

Andy, however, could no longer hear these cautions. Something had changed the morning he woke from his dream. His biology was altered. The influence of the Conscious Whole could not be extended into his being the same way it had been before. This partial separation resulted in the clarity he felt, no longer completely bound by the Conscious Whole's thought processes and plan. Intuitively able to see beyond the conscious density towards the horizon, his increasing bright light was like a lighthouse on the edge of the solid, known planet.

"Who is he kidding? Going off to an unknown place is reckless!" Andy's matriarchal Auntie Mum told everyone close to him, rallying Andy's support structure. Because of this crazy fantasy, Andy's family and friends believed the disease had spread to his brain causing him to think irrationally and they dragged him to the doctor's office.

"It's not 'clarity'. The disease is affecting your brain now," the doctor snidely told Andy, with his aunt and brother at his side. "It makes you think you should get away and find a better place in a far off pretend land where you can live a 'better life,'" the doctor continued, trying to hide the condescending tone in his voice.

Everyone was concerned. Their expressions shaped by the iridescent wires of reality hanging from the space above. They all **knew**, without any doubt, that Andy's thoughts were absurd and the disease was now in his brain.

"There's no way Andy could receive sufficient health care anywhere else but here." The three squabbled amongst themselves, feeding a continuous loop of manufactured information to each other.

Are there even doctors outside of the Conscious Whole to take care of him? How is he to live? What kind of quality of life will Andy have without all of the modern conveniences the Conscious Whole could supply? What about the time immediately leading up to his death? Would he suffer or be in pain? Where would he get the treatments he needed?

These questions without answers convinced Andy's family and his doctor that he could not leave. It was crazy for him to do so.

Andy sat in the middle, feeling strangely alone, as if in an isolated bubble, in an alien world where no one understood him. *Am I really losing my mind? I feel fine*, Andy thought.

The mental changes were part of the predictable course of his illness, but it had gone much faster than anyone had anticipated. Brain involvement typically happens days before the rest of the body dies. They knew Andy was closer to death than he had ever been. They wanted to keep him under their watchful eyes, to protect him and make his death as deathless as possible. Wanting to go on some adventure was completely out of the question, particularly for a man who was losing control of his body and now his mind.

The Conscious Whole

Am I becoming demented? Andy thought, as the odd world around him tried to pierce into his protected space.

The Conscious Whole deemed Andy mentally ill. The doctor saw it and diagnosed it. "Grand delusions," he called them. The doctor explained, "These delusions are caused by dying neurons. As the cells in his brain die, one by one, they will send out aberrant bursts of electrical activity. These bursts are not coordinated and cause Andy's brain to think crazy thoughts and worst of all, he will try to act them out!"

This was their understanding. The Understanding. Established by the Conscious Whole. Measured by the scientists and doctors. However, something unusual had happened to Andy; something that had never happened before within the paradigm or history of the Conscious Whole. The death of the neurons in his brain resulted in a unique biological difference when compared to everyone else in the Conscious Whole. Out of all the combinations of connections in the brain, millions upon millions of possibilities, in all of the people of the Conscious Whole, Andy's new connections were very special. Consequently, Andy gently and quietly parted ways with his connection to the Conscious Whole.

5

Woven deeply into the base of the earth,
moving like a serpent, it waited centuries to manifest;
clandestinely tracking him along his journey, its time was approaching;
it could feel the urgency of movements above and those following;
there was no time for hesitation; all was aligned for action

"I'M LEAVING," ANDY CALMLY TOLD HIS BROTHER, Peter, who was a very caring and kind sibling, the first person Andy told about his disease. They had spent a lot more time together after his diagnosis, and Peter's face still carried the worry everyone had been feeling. "You should come with me."

"Like I said before, Andy, you know the doctor doesn't think it's a good idea to leave. Besides, everyone else, including me, thinks it's good for you to stay here, where we can help you..." Peter's soft, passive voice trailed off at the end. He sincerely cared for Andy and only wanted the best for his brother.

Andy turned towards Peter, whose wrinkled eyebrows were examining Andy's physical body, searching for a solution to his condition. Peter's portly frame was wedged in the reclining chair, his dangling legs barely touching the ground, and his shiny bald head reflecting light from windows behind him.

"There's a whole other world out there! I want to see it before I can't anymore," Andy tried to explain.

Peter furrowed his brows deeper, feeling like Andy was talking another language, further solidifying his impression of the doctor's assessment.

Andy decided not to speak his mind any longer. The doubt he had felt about his declining mental capacity had left, and he was only filled with the clear and true intention of going on his journey. Reminded of his dream and the ensuing lucidity, Andy clearly saw two paths after his blinds were lifted: live the life of death at home or go into unknown possibility. He knew no one would listen to him and was absolutely positive about what he wanted to do; he wanted to leave, and he would have to do it alone, when no one else was around to stop him.

People did not leave the Conscious Whole. It was unprecedented. There was no reason to. The Conscious Whole kept everyone safe and allowed them to live as they pleased. Sleepwalking through life, their world consisted of a false infinity, like an ocean that appears limitless but has land beyond the horizon.

That night, after Peter had gone for the day, Andy packed all the food and supplies his car could fit. Even though he often got short of breath and had to rest, the thrill of leaving pushed him beyond the limits he had become accustomed to. Andy pulled the plastic wrapping off the shiny new motorized wheelchair in his garage, which he had resisted using for as long as he could and drove it into the back of the van he had traded for his truck, which was specifically customized to hold the wheelchair. He loved his truck and hated that he had to trade it for a *van*. Andy frowned for a moment at his new ride but then stopped hesitating and began driving north.

The highway turned into winding country roads as the depth of night encased Andy's car. No longer lit by streetlights, emptiness existed beyond the scope of the headlights, but Andy did not fear the unknown ahead, for he knew where darkness lay, opportunity had space to be born.

The northern lands were considered the end of earth. To drive past them was like leaping off the edge of the world. Andy, though, wanted to escape his predetermined life, the definite future the Conscious Whole had given him, and to see what was beyond what everyone else knew. His actions were a true sign the Conscious Whole had lost its grip on his being; the changes in his brain giving him insight into aspects the Conscious Whole had kept from its people. A visceral inner force pulled him northward and he followed this intuition.

The police searched for days, but no one thought to look towards the north. Everyone knew nothing was in that direction. In time, they gave up hope and sadly accepted Andy's demise with much sorrow and prolonged grief.

"His condition has worsened and has consumed his brain. He is no longer the person we once knew," Andy's family and friends said, pacifying emotions. "He's in a better place now. It wasn't Andy making those crazy decisions, it was his disease," were the words they used to comfort themselves.

In truth, leaving was a release. Previously, parting from the Conscious Whole had not been a possibility, for anyone. Anything within the bounds of the Conscious Whole was molecularly built from the bottom up according to predetermined structure established many years prior; a code intertwined into physical reality. The Conscious Whole did this for love of its beings and, more importantly, for love of itself. The fight to stay alive kept its force powerful and determined. The Conscious Whole was an organism too, in and of itself, a form of life with a need to prevent invaders of thought from changing its ways. As with any other living force, survival was paramount for the Conscious Whole.

Non-conforming influences were a threat to the Conscious Whole, and it had adapted to deal with this enemy. Like bacteria invading a body, foreign thoughts were quickly destroyed by the immune system of the Conscious Whole. Given that it was conceived and built by thoughts, it was one with all thoughts, and in essence a thought itself. It knew all ideas below it, by every being, and therefore had an enormous amount of control over its people.

The Conscious Whole

When Andy had asked Peter to come with him, the moment before Peter was consciously aware of the thought about leaving with Andy, it was generated in his brain. The idea of leaving coursed through his neuronal connections as an electrical signal, from one neuron to another, on a course to become the conscious thought of departing the Conscious Whole. This activity in the brain, the flow of energy, was a specific electromagnetic pulse. A wave of light.

The Conscious Whole knew the mechanism of energy flow through the brain creating thoughts, since it created this system, and could quite easily sense a thought not in harmony with its own paradigm. It did not want Peter to leave with Andy, for abandonment would tear apart the structure required for its life, like a small hairline crack in its armor. The peoples' primitive, instinctive connection to desperately hold onto only known reality built the Conscious Whole into the monster it had become and whetted its thirst for more stability.

As Peter contemplated a journey with Andy in pre-consciousness, his thought emitted a color of light, an electromagnetic wave, not in tune with the existing energy structure of the Conscious Whole. These two different lights, Peter's thought of leaving as the color blue and the Conscious Whole's thought of Peter staying as red, were asynchronous, and the Conscious Whole sensed disparity.

Like a cool and calm professional, the immune system destroyed Peter's rogue thought by creating and sending out a wave of energy exactly equal and opposite to the blue light in Peter's brain.[1] Peter's original thought canceled out resulting in a paucity of energetic flow and no radical ideas. Without fanfare, the creation of Peter's compliance with the party line appeared seamless and occurred outside of his awareness. Without this protection, the Conscious Whole would perish just as a body dies when invading bacteria gain the upper hand.

---

1. This phenomena is termed optical interference: Born and Wolf, *Principles of Optics: Electromagnetic Theory of Propagation, Interference and Diffraction of Light* (1999), pg. 286.

There were no gates or armed guards physically preventing Andy from leaving. Andy's brain, with its thoughts of leaving, created a very special wave of light with faint red and ivory bands wrapping around ocean blue colors that had a solid consistency. This unique spectrum of electromagnetic energy meant "escape" in Andy's diseased, different brain,[2] but in the code of the Conscious Whole, Andy's wave of light meant "complacency." The Conscious Whole's immune system was duped, only reading "complacency" in the waveform, and Andy was free to think his radical thoughts of escape and not be changed by the Conscious Whole into what it wanted him to be; since he left alone, no one surrounding him was thinking "escape", and he was free to leave without protest from the beast lurking above.

For ones within the Conscious Whole, all they knew was all there was. There was no other knowledge. No other territory. No other material world. No other reality. And most notably, no other possibility.

Andy knew his only chance of survival was escape, even if it meant being considered out of his mind, insane, by the people of the Conscious Whole for leaving the comfort and predictability in which they loved him to live. Yet, he would mostly be forgotten, the image of his dying body tucked into a far corner of the Conscious Whole. As far as the Conscious Whole was concerned, Andy died and his new, free self never existed.

---

2. Differences in brain networks influence how easily someone can be hypnotized, i.e. how easily they can detach from their surrounding reality: Hoeft et al. "Functional Brain Basis of Hypnotizability." *Archives of General Psychiatry* (2012).

6

*How different this must look to you, for now your eyes are open;
do you believe in what you see or are you going to fall into
what you used to know*

WITH EVERY PASSING HOUR, ANDY DROVE CLOSER and closer to the outer boundary of the Conscious Whole's force, with fibers of his former self ripping off anchors that had held him in place; one by one the cords retracted back into what they knew, fearing the unknown. Like pulling his body out of a spider's web, Andy could feel the freedom waiting ahead. As day broke, the plains circumscribing the periphery of the Conscious Whole displayed their monotonous beauty.

The land was remote and desolate for a specific purpose, acting as a physical barrier to protect the Conscious Whole's reality, to keep both people and thoughts from entering and from escaping; a tangible representation of one arm of its defense.

There were no houses, no buildings, no towns, and no trees. The vegetation was dry with low-lying shrubs scattered amongst seemingly well-groomed, brown swaying grass, which strangely appeared artificially maintained despite no signs of human activity; the road went on as far as the eye could see. Despite Andy's determination, he was beginning to second-guess his decision. *Maybe there's nothing up here,* he thought as the Conscious Whole's residual beliefs echoed in his mind. However, he knew he could not turn around; he would surely be put in the hospital and be forced to die there. *Better to die trying than die against my will.*

A mentally strenuous day of driving, through a landscape that appeared to be rotating on repeat, soon turned into night. This process repeated for two days. Andy rationed the food and filled up his gas tank using the three portable gas containers he had brought along. At night he slept in his car, finding safe places to pull over but fearing he would awake to someone breaking in, even though he had not seen a person or other car in days. Fear poked its way into his consciousness resulting in patchy sleep.

Road conditions worsened with each day that passed, and both the food and gas supply were becoming low. On his last tank of fuel, Andy was exhilarated and extremely relieved to see some buildings on the horizon! *Finally, some life!* he thought.

The brown, dilapidated structures blended into the earth, eroding into where they came from. Uninhabited by the looks of them, the tall square buildings seemed to be from an era long ago. Uneasiness simmered in Andy's body, now worried he would never find anybody or, more importantly, food or gas this far from his home. *I can't possibly turn back, I would never make it.* Besides the few buildings, nothing else was in sight, and Andy's brief excitement turned to panic.

He slowed down as he passed by but feared to look into the haunting, deep dark cavities of each building. Despite the unkempt appearance, each building strangely had blinds painted on the boarded up windows. Andy looked more closely and noticed that each painted blind had a corresponding perfectly painted drawstring. His hair stood on end; he felt like someone was watching him. He pressed forward in a blur of panic and alarm.

Andy did not know how much time had passed, but he began seeing more buildings popping up, rising out of the plains. To his tremendous relief, this time they looked alive and vibrant. A small brown wooden sign read "Millrift."

Andy slowed as he approached this alien town, floating out in the middle of nowhere, like an island in a vast sea.

With each passing mile from its center, the influence of the Conscious Whole became more diffuse and fragile. People were simply too far away to completely fall within its grasp. The energetic finger-like projections weakened and thinned as Andy traveled further and further north.

The Conscious Whole occupied an area of two million square miles of both land and sea, and people from the outermost edges of this territory were at the cusp of the dark shadow: somewhat in the sunlight, yet still under the created reality. Because of the weakness of the Conscious Whole in the plains, people were different in some regards but importantly still preserved the interests of the unified whole.

They were guardians. Living in a hybrid world of their creation and the Conscious Whole's. The first defense to outside invaders.

Satellites of the Conscious Whole, the strange people in these remote towns were detached and unaware of current events. Living solitary lives, they farmed the land to sustain their microworld and only on occasion made the arduous journey to less isolated places of the Conscious Whole to replenish supplies.

Protectors of reality the Conscious Whole sustained, yet separate from both the whole and the outside, they knew no better, and the Conscious Whole wanted it as such. Like the immune system, these people absorbed incoming foreign ideas cushioning the impact of unwanted outside influence. With its powers weakened so far from its source, the Conscious Whole depended on towns like Millrift to act as military outposts, able to broadcast signals to the center.

The long, straight road went right into the middle of Millrift. There were only five buildings in the town. The first one Andy passed was a two-story restaurant with brown siding and a green roof. A three-legged dog hopped around in front and gave Andy an inquisitive look.

Next, were four, perfectly rectangular six-story houses, all painted white with red trim lining the road. Andy slowly rolled through the small town, fully aware of the eyes peering through each of the windows of the four homes. The last building was a gas station, littered with derelict cars and farming machinery. Desperately needing gas, Andy hesitantly pulled next to a fuel pump. A rough looking boy slowly approached Andy's car. He looked about ten years old and had a missing eye Andy caught himself staring at.

The boy spoke in a childlike voice with a dialect that made him difficult to understand. "I'm living here now. Being a boy, I talk to a man who is driving in that direction," he said pointing to the north. "He is not come back now. He says it's nice there. He is returning now, and I am a teenager."

Andy was baffled by this boy's odd, nonsensical way of speaking and did not know how to reply. It then occurred to him the boy did not speak in the past or future tense!

Millrift operated under a subset of the Conscious Whole's reality. The people did not see the world broken up into discreet units of past, present, or future. They saw all of time at once, like looking at an enormous painting of every event that has ever occurred, all tied together onto one canvas. This unique view of time allowed them to see incoming threats from the future.

An evolutionary adaption built for protecting the Conscious Whole, the small town of Millrift did not need force in numbers for their advantage spanned the fourth dimension. While those closer to the center were more laden in the laws of physics of the Conscious Whole, on the periphery the fourth dimension of time was not an impermeable boundary. Instead, it was a cloak that could be lifted to see across time. As such, there was no concept of the past or future in Millrift. It simply did not exist. Like having read a book of the events that will happen, they knew the beginning, middle, and end of the tale for all intruders who will try to enter. It also gave them an upper hand on anyone who would try to leave.

So then, why did they allow Andy to leave? Did they not see him coming? Or was his passage part of a bigger picture, something that Millrift was going to allow against the will of the Conscious Whole?

The peculiar boy continued, "You don't have enough gas to go there."

Andy interjected, leaning out of the car window, "Wait, wait, wait… enough gas to go where?"

"The place you go to and are coming from," the boy chuckled, amused by Andy's silly question.

"And where exactly is that?" Andy persisted.

"The road go north and the road turns east and you are driving and you can't drive anymore. This is where you are!" The boy smirked, revealing he seemed to know more than he was saying, never really answering Andy's question.

Andy tried but could not get any more information from the boy about this seemingly secret place. He bought as many portable gas cans as the tiny gas station had in stock, filled them up, and topped off the van's tank. Just before pulling away, the boy came running out with an armful of small cardboard boxes.

"These are good. Dinner pies. A specialty of our town." The boy opened Andy's passenger door and eagerly filled up the passenger seat with food Andy desperately needed to continue on.

The strangeness of Millrift detached one of the many strands that held Andy to the Conscious Whole. He looked down the road from behind his dusty, insect-smeared windshield and for a brief moment had an overwhelming feeling of déjà vu and familiarity. *This has to be right*, he thought, feeling an empowering sense he had made the correct decision. Panic and fear no longer plagued his mind, and he felt like he was no longer alone, as if cradled in a supportive network. Andy drove on, chasing his future along the plains.

7

*Movement of his journey sparked and paralleled the beings movements;
they felt the fervor of his actions and were likewise traveling
from the far reaches to assimilate for the purpose of change*

THE SHALLOW UNDULATING PLAINS, WITH THE YELLOW grass blowing in the wind, looked like small rolling waves on an ocean as Millrift disappeared back into this solid sea, like it never existed. The grass turned green as Andy drove further away from everything he knew. The road gently went up and down, ever so slightly turning to the left and then to the right. All Andy could see for miles was tall, green grass blowing in the wind. He felt like time had stopped, as if he could drive on forever.

Why didn't Peter want to come with me? What a fun and adventurous trip it has already been! Andy thought. *I was going to die in the same life, in the same place I have always lived,* his thoughts continued as he drove through one of the most beautiful landscapes he had ever seen. Andy had no idea what to expect in these unexplored lands. No one had ever spoken about them. And why not? *What were they hiding from me? Why were they holding onto me and preventing me from leaving?* Andy's thoughts raced through his mind as he questioned the world in a way he had not done before.

The shallow waves of the plains grew into larger and larger hills covered with the same tall green grass for as far as the eye could see. Day turned into night, concealing the surroundings, and Andy drove until fatigue forced him to pull over. He enjoyed one of the dinner pies before once again sleeping in his car on the side of the road.

The following morning he awoke to giant oak trees dotting the landscape. In the distance, hills morphed into small mountains covered by forests, growing steeper and steeper towards the sky. The road undulated with the mountains, going up to the top and then gradually bringing Andy down into a valley. The process repeated, and he felt familiar comfort in the steady flow of life around him. Yet, as the landscape become more rugged and untamed, the road followed suit and narrowed, at points barely paved well enough to drive on. It had been built decades ago when the people of the Conscious Whole were convening into its center and had scarcely been used since.

A thick fog rolled in just as Andy needed to concentrate on the road, which now hugged the side of a mountain. Before long, he was driving only three miles per hour, trudging through the thickest fog he had ever seen. *I could be falling off of a cliff right now and not even know it!* Having lost all orientation, he had to be very careful to follow the road as closely as he could.

After a few grueling hours of mind-draining concentration, he could see the sun shining overhead, like a big light bulb hanging above an all white room. Andy slowly rose out of the fog, released from its grasp and continued further until the road began turning towards the east, just as the boy at the gas station said it would. *East it is*, Andy thought.

Daylight again fell into night, obscuring the treacherous environment surrounding him. He stopped for much needed sleep and again had dinner pie, an amalgamation of grains cooked in root vegetables. Memories passed through his mind as he tried to sleep.

His thoughts fixated on his former wife, Leah. She and Andy had met in college and lived life like two intertwined vines, growing together. To say they loved each other would be an understatement. One weekend, Leah went to visit a friend but never returned. The selfish act of another took Leah from Andy. A car accident when she was on her way home. Seeing her dying in the hospital was the worst experience he could have imagined: tubes protruded out of her body, machines kept her breathing, the floor was covered in blood. None of the nurses or doctors would make eye contact with Andy. They all knew what was going to happen.

Andy approached her body but did not recognize it, refusing to believe it was his wife, someone he had spent nearly every minute with for the last eight years, someone he had planned to be with for the rest of his life. The loss was imprinted upon his being, now part of who he was, entangled into his core just as their lives had been. He had never released himself from the grief and suffering. The pain and loss remained despite leaving behind everything he once knew.

When the sun rose over the mountains, it was like a beacon of light directing him where to travel. However, recollections from the night before lingered and Andy felt depression and uneasiness weaving into his emotions and noticed his physical deterioration more so this morning. His lungs felt heavy, and he needed a few minutes to catch his breath after waking. His legs felt extra stiff and at first he needed both arms to turn the steering wheel of his car, a task he could previously do with one hand. Leaving the Conscious Whole provided a small respite, but thinking about Leah brought Andy back to the physical reality of his life. *What am I doing? Is this some kind of crazy suicide mission?*

He drove on for hours, back into the routine of the last few days, half aware of the surroundings but also thinking about his physical decline. Eventually the narrow crumbling road rose from the bottom of a valley and climbed up the side of a very steep mountain. The road was no wider than the car itself and was without guardrails to protect him from driving off the cliff. This small dose of fear suppressed the background thoughts seeking to bring down Andy's mood and sparked some inner energy.

As he crested the mountaintop, on the opposite side of the range, he saw the most amazing sight he had ever seen: deep, blue ocean went on endlessly, blending into the horizon. White caps spotted the turbulent blue blanket covering the earth as waves crashed on the shore below, spraying up pure white mist. A strong wind blew across the mountainside, hissing inside the car as it found its way through cracks in the doors. Small seabirds skated on the wind. Andy had never seen the ocean before, having lived his whole life landlocked in Franklin.

I knew I was missing something by staying at home. This is exactly what I wanted to do! The endlessness and possibility surrounding Andy penetrated his core. Instead of being drained and feeling like he was fighting to stay alive, he felt the world giving back to him. It was energizing him, nourishing him, sustaining him; a small part of Andy became aware of a physical force entering his body, stoking his core.

Andy stepped out of his car and took a deep breath. The fresh salty air filled his struggling lungs. The landscape wrapped itself around him, enveloping him in its beauty and serenity. All was good.

8

*A white brick house will appear in the woods as you look in the distance,
the being explained; not separate from but growing out of the woods;
the inner room is far too large for the outer dimensions of the container, the
instructions continued; this must be remembered for this is where you enter*

FAR OFF IN THE DISTANCE HOUSES DOTTED the landscape. Boats floated in a protective cove next to a larger cluster of homes. *A booming metropolis compared to Millrift,* Andy thought. The pleasure of seeing a normal appearing town made him excited to find out what lay ahead.

Andy inched along the dirt road that hazardously wound down the steep slope. Approaching the town, the valley grew deeper and darker as natural walls formed on either side. He felt like he was going through a portal, being transported into another world, separated even further from the Conscious Whole than distance would portray. *This must be the only way in and out.*

Arriving at last, like the boy at the gas station had said, the road simply ended, and Andy emerged from the other side of the claustrophobic mountain into a bright and open square. Protected on three sides by walls of earth and in the front by an endless ocean, this town was naturally built like a fortress.

To the left and right were two-story, brown and gray, cedar plank houses lining the town square. Some were stores selling food out of large open windows, whereas others looked residential. Behind the first row of buildings, walking trails led up to other houses scattered on the slopes of the mountain. Even higher on the north side of the village, one house sat on top of a ridge resting at the edge of a cliff. *A perilous perch*, Andy thought. Bright blue waves crashed on the rocks below in slow motion, firing white spray high into the sky. The northern and southern cliffs marked the boundaries on either side of a harbor that was no more than a few hundred feet from the town square, filled with fishing boats. *I wonder what this place is called?* Entirely removed from the rest of the world there was no need for a sign. Everyone there already knew the name.

The few dozen people in the town square all seemed frozen in space, staring at Andy; the sight of a strange car rolling into town unsurprisingly caught everyone's attention, as Andy stared back at an equally peculiar scene. People began cautiously approaching Andy's car, treating it like an alien spacecraft, and others followed. A crowd eventually surrounded Andy and they asked a flurry of questions through his open car window wanting to know who he was, where he had come from, and why he had traveled to Meat Cove. Suddenly, everyone parted as a woman approached Andy's car.

She was tall, a few inches over six feet with fair skin and short blond hair. The sky seemed to brighten as she entered the space, making him squint his eyes. This woman held a long walking stick that looked centuries old with a large, black volcanic rock affixed to the top. Her turquoise collared shirt had an intricate hieroglyphic pattern sewn into the front, and at least a dozen different necklaces hung from her neck. The most prominent was a string with one black polished mussel shell, *holding the ocean's depth*, Andy thought.

A dog named Coco followed closely by her side. A stout animal with broad shoulders, wide gait, and gray and black coat, appearing more like a wolf than a dog; born in the wild, she was the fearless protective guardian of the town's leader. Her ears curiously perked up, just as interested as everyone else.

Andy had the strangest experience as the woman and Coco came closer. The form of their bodies did not appear fixed but rather physically in multiple spots; separate reflections of many different forms all lined up on top of one another, each slightly off-center and translucent. The perception was transient, and then all of a sudden they looked "real" again. Permanent.

The duo approached Andy's car much more guardedly than the rest. However, seeing his wheelchair in the back seat made the woman a little more comfortable.

"If you are here to change us, we can not be changed," she calmly but affirmatively told him, her words speaking of past encounters.

The people of Meat Cove had experienced the Conscious Whole. Years ago, a mission was sent to convert them, to incorporate them into the whole; the Conscious Whole was recruiting strength and unity, wanting others to be like itself for the sake of conformity. It feared difference, sweeping through the northern lands taking anything in its path. Most were coaxed into its epicenter to start their new lives. The people of Meat Cove, on the other hand, would have nothing of it and revolted. The missionaries of the Conscious Whole never made it back. They got stranded in the mountains during a brutal winter storm.

Andy quickly explained his intent, "I mean no harm. I just need a place to stay. I traveled a long way to find a better life." He pleaded his case, sensing he could not just check into a hotel and that he had entered a tightly knit community.

After a long period of silence, the leader of Meat Cove, whom Andy came to know as Sandra, invited him to dinner to not only learn more about her new guest but more importantly, to figure out his motives.

Her home was at the top of the cliff overlooking the whole village and coastline; the same one Andy had noticed when he first arrived. A perfectly groomed, winding trail, illuminated with violet and brilliant yellow flowers, led up to the house. Andy looked up at the steep trail and knew his weak legs and lungs would not be able to endure the short journey and gave in, taking out his electric wheelchair for the first time and navigated up the trail, which at times was so steep, he did not think the wheelchair could make it.

Eventually, they arrived at Sandra's house, and she led him into the dining room where at least twenty other people sat at a large circular table full of food. Andy felt uncomfortable as he realized he had interrupted everyone's dinner and tried not to stare at the gourmet feast while his stomach growled. Strangely however, Andy had a sense they were all waiting for his arrival, but his mind was promptly distracted by the otherworldly view out the windows revealing the coastline, which extended for miles as its tall cliffs stretched indefinitely north and south.

Feeling welcomed but also under the scrutiny of Sandra, Andy described his circumstances in more detail, as if on trial at the large dinner table. He explained he was looking for a new home where he could live without the normal cares of his old life and to explore a new land. However, he left out the details of his illness: how he was going to die soon, how his body and mind would quickly deteriorate. Yet for all the people of Meat Cove knew, Andy was just disabled and did not have a terminal illness.

Fully aware of the harmful effects of the Conscious Whole, the decision to let Andy stay would not come without much questioning. Some of the town's people feared Andy was sent to convert them, while others felt he would seed unwanted beliefs into their culture.

One of the elders, a man of short stature and tanned from a working life on the sea, asked Andy directly, "Do you have any intention of changing us?"

"Changing you?" Andy responded. "No, not at all! I am the one who is looking for a change. For a new place. I left my home because I wanted to get out of the routine I was stuck in," Andy said, imploring his case.

"What do you know of the missionaries?" another senior member asked, with his long grey mustache seeming to do all the talking. He looked like the oldest in the room, and his eyes reflected the past encounter, showing the strength he subsequently gained.

"I…I don't know anything about missionaries," Andy said, confused by the question. "I came here alone. No one even wanted to come with me!"

"Here in Meat Cove," a tall man sitting to the right of Andy said, "you are free to do and think what you please. However, we do not tolerate forcing ideas onto other people. We all welcome learning and expanding knowledge. There is much you can learn by living here, and I am sure there are things you will teach us as well," he said, reassuring Andy, as well as the others, of Andy's future place in the community. Other questions were exchanged across the table, side conversations were started, and eventually everyone focused on enjoying the meal, while Andy felt relief no longer being the center of attention.

Sandra sat quietly, sensing there was another motive for Andy's visit he was not divulging. She knew people did not leave the Conscious Whole and would keep him under her watchful, vigilant eye. "Do you need a place to stay?" Sandra said sarcastically, knowing very well Andy had no place to go or sleep.

Andy nodded, but before he could speak, Sandra continued, "You can stay with a man named Jeremy. He lives down by the ocean. We'll take you there."

After dinner, the tall man accompanied Andy and Sandra back down the trail with Coco leading the way. They headed towards the southern precipice, where Jeremy's house was perched one hundred feet up the side of the mountain facing the ocean, also on the cliff's edge, looking like it was growing out of the mountainside, which was completely covered by yellow, purple, and red wildflowers.

With no other houses in this part of the community, Jeremy's home looked like a temple where people went to find peace. A trail meandered up to the house, and as they approached, the vibrancy and tranquility was palpable. Wooden sculptures were scattered amongst the lawn; abstract representations of people and animals that Andy found odd. The house had large windows facing the ocean, bright blue cedar plank siding the color of the sky, and a copper roof stained green from salty air topping the one-story home.

This place is perfect! Andy thought, already feeling more relaxed and comfortable than he ever had.

A large swell came crashing on the cliff, and Andy felt the ground vibrate. *The land is so alive!*

"You'll get used to that," the man accompanying Andy said smiling.

As he looked towards the ocean, Andy could see sets of waves rhythmically making their way towards land, originating from the other side of the horizon. *The water looks like it stretches to another world…where anything is possible,* he thought. Following Sandra and Coco, he entered Jeremy's home.

9

They all looked up in anticipation, hoping the connection would yield results as they had intended; yet, despite the beings not knowing doubt, they harkened to past times knowing that all may not go to plan

Jeremy was sitting in a dark wooden chair with intricate patterns engraved into the armrests and legs carved into lion paws. He was facing a pair of windows that stretched to the ceiling, overlooking the ocean, writing in a small book. As they entered, Jeremy turned around and approached them with a big, warm smile.

"Hi, my name is Jeremy," he said enthusiastically.

"Jeremy, this is Andy. He will be visiting us for a while. Do you mind if he spends some time with you?" Sandra politely asked.

"Of course not, I have plenty of extra room."

"Thank you very much for giving me a place to stay," Andy graciously said in a hoarse sounding voice. After the long day of speaking, his voice had become weakened, and a sudden, sweeping fear overtook Andy's body, starting from his head and spreading to every corner of his being. The doctor said the illness would eventually affect his vocal cords making it difficult to speak. His disease was getting worse.

"Not a problem. It will be great to have some company."

Suddenly, Sandra's dog Coco bolted out the front door, ears perked up, eyes focused on a point off in the distance, as if there was a postal worker on the other side of the town she needed to dispose of. Sandra excused herself so she could take care of the trouble Coco was getting herself into.

Jeremy was a thoughtful, considerate, and welcoming man who was very loyal to Sandra. Twenty-five years old, with a slender face, sharp nose, and bright blue eyes, as if the color from the ocean had seeped into his core and reflected back into the world. His long jet-black hair covered his ears and neck and looked like it had been blowing in the wind all day. Jeremy invited Andy to come by the front window, and they spoke superficially for a few minutes about the weather while Andy's mind was preoccupied with his worsening medical condition.

"What brings you to Meat Cove? We really don't have many visitors," Jeremy inquired in a voice as smooth as silk and equally as delicate.

"Well, I just wanted to get away from my old life," Andy replied with a scratchy forced voice. "I guess I felt repressed in a way. Forced into believing I had a certain path to follow..." he paused, "...a destined future. A fate I didn't like. Being far away from there will allow me to live as I want to. Or that's the plan at least..."

Jeremy looked confused as he had lived in Meat Cove his entire life and was not familiar with the oppression Andy dealt with. The people in Meat Cove lived freely, worked their jobs, and functioned well in a peaceful, self-sufficient community. They harvested countless varieties of fish and shellfish from the sea and hunted game in the mountains. The items they did not fabricate were recycled from leftover cars and equipment the missionaries left behind. As far as modern day equipment and technology, there was not much; the farm equipment was made from a piecemeal of parts from other machines and the fishing boats used wind for propulsion; the people were well-adapted, shaping their lives based on the surrounding natural resources.

In spite of the fact that Jeremy lived by himself, his house was quite large, and Andy could easily navigate the four bedrooms, the spacious living room overlooking the ocean, and the open kitchen in his wheelchair, which he used increasingly as days passed.

Over the next few weeks, Andy adjusted to his new life spending most days exploring the small town and making new friends. The citizens of Meat Cove were very friendly and always had time to sit down and simply be present in the moment[1] without constantly thinking about their jobs or worrying about chores for the day. Yet, in the background there was still apprehension about Andy's presence, which seemed to subside as people became more familiar with him. Sandra, however, remained guarded.

She asked Andy to do some work while living in Meat Cove as a way to contribute to the society. Andy's job was to monitor the weather as the ships left the harbor. He kept watch on top of the northern cliff, near Sandra's house, for four hours every morning on the lookout for approaching storms and rough seas. Andy would relay this information by raising different colored flags. Blue if the conditions were good, red if a storm was approaching, and black if it looked treacherous out at sea.

Quite often at Jeremy's home, he and Andy would sit outside on a small deck overhanging the cliff below, facing the ocean. A small railing was the only thing between them and a one hundred foot drop. The two men would spend hours watching waves as they crashed on the rocks below and observing the calming, meditative patterns created by the water. They made note of small ships leaving port, sailing off in different directions searching for the day's catch. Jeremy taught Andy about where each ship was heading, how they fished the sea, and the weather patterns, honing Andy's skill as the new watchman.

Jeremy had come to know Andy quite well with the exception of one issue: the illness. Andy did not divulge his fate, fearing the situation would be handled as his doctors and family had wanted. Having traveled out of his known world to escape his disease, the last thing Andy wanted was to discuss what was going to happen to him. One morning, however, out of curiosity, Jeremy felt comfortable enough to bring up the issue, not knowing the extent of Andy's terminal illness.

---

1. For an excellent guide about "being present in the moment" see: Tolle, *The Power of Now: A Guide to Spiritual Enlightenment* (2004).

"So, when did you start using a wheelchair? Have you always needed one?"

"No, I haven't always…more recently though…it just makes it easier to get around, you know," Andy paused for a few moments caught off guard by the question. He felt anger beginning to simmer beneath his skin. He did not want to talk about it.

"Oh, well, did you get hurt or something?" Jeremy innocently asked.

"Kind of…I mean, yeah it's something that happened to me a while ago. I got hurt and it makes it hard to walk," he evasively answered.

Jeremy looked towards Andy who was staring off in the distance, avoiding eye contact.

"It's really none of your business!" Andy fired at Jeremy sensing his peering gaze. "It's getting late and I'm tired. Goodnight." He abruptly ended the conversation and went inside, leaving Jeremy to wonder even more about his condition.

Sandra had tactfully chosen Jeremy to host Andy and had asked him to keep a close eye on Andy to ensure he did not have ulterior motives. Andy was clearly hiding something, and Jeremy reported it to Sandra.

"Do you think he's a threat?" she asked Jeremy, the one person in the village who knew Andy the best.

"He seems harmless. I think it's just something personal, something he doesn't want to talk about," Jeremy replied sincerely, feeling Andy had no ill intentions.

"These attacks can be very subtle, Jeremy. He may be here to infect us with something. Here to spread some sort of disease, or worse, disseminate an idea from the other side. Something that we can not easily disinfect, like we can a virus."

Jeremy heeded Sandra's increasing wariness but felt torn. His loyalty to Sandra burned strongly, yet, Jeremy sensed Andy needed his help and that Andy's true purpose was pure.

10

Truth may be found by visiting Mirror Lake; it lies over the pass, nestled in a valley of newborn growth that never ages; the path is dark and dangers lurk off the trail, but every being must travel there once to find their truth within; Mirror Lake shows but does not tell; Mirror Lake points but does not blame; Mirror Lake carries the burden of knowing but not being able to speak; all beings know the journey to Mirror Lake must precede transformation, but not all beings choose to look into the mirror

The next morning Andy awoke early and was putting together breakfast. He felt badly for being rude the night before, as Jeremy had only been kind to him.

Jeremy sat at the breakfast table nibbling on some toast, carefully observing his guest, who may be an enemy.

"The doctor said I have a disease that basically kills all of the cells in my body. One by one," Andy said frankly as he cooked some eggs. "Eventually it will kill me."

Jeremy was surprised by Andy's candidness considering the night before and did not know exactly what to say. After a long silence he asked, "What does it feel like?"

"I wake up with it every morning and go to sleep with it every night. Even during sleep I can't escape it," Andy paused for a moment. For the first time, he was consciously facing his illness. Before, he was standing by, an observer, as if watching a movie of his life unfolding. As he continued speaking, Andy realized how dramatically his life had changed.

"It started in my hands at first, and then it affected my legs. They were not painful in the beginning; I just started to lose strength and control to the point where it had become difficult to do precise tasks. The pain started recently, and now it hurts where the cells are dying. I notice it mostly at night, a dull ache; during the day I try to ignore it." Andy reflected on his prior life: how he ran a marathon, how he played rugby, how he could walk without losing his breath, how he could lecture in a strong voice, and how he was not always in pain. Trying not to let himself get caught up in his past, he continued, "Recently, I noticed my voice has changed too. It sounds raspy, like I need to cough, and it's starting to get harder to swallow liquids…everything seems to be happening so fast."

Jeremy nodded, trying to comprehend what Andy was describing.

"It's hard to breathe because my lung cells are dying. I usually wake up a few times each night feeling like I'm suffocating."

Insulting his condition even further, the muscles controlling his breathing were beginning to fail, just like in his hands and legs. When awoken at night, Andy would try as hard as he could to cough up debris accumulating in his lungs, but it seemed to be getting worse, not better.

"The doctor diagnosed me when I was in my prime. I loved my job and my life; it was all so perfect. I exercised and was a great rugby player! I kept my yard and garden in top shape, taught the children in my classes…" Andy sobbed for a minute. Tears ran down his cheeks. Jeremy felt the rush of emotions escaping from Andy's core that had been locked up with no intention of ever leaving. Knowing it was better for him to talk about his illness than to repress it, Jeremy allowed Andy to mourn the losses he had faced.

Gaining enough composure to speak again Andy continued, "The worst part, though, was being told I was going to die…"

Jeremy reflexively chuckled and then hastily tried to shove the laugh back into his mouth. Andy furiously glared back with a confused and resentful look.

"Oh, I'm sorry. I didn't mean to laugh at you," Jeremy said. They both paused for a moment in an awkward silence. "It's just the last thing you said about dying was kind of funny," Jeremy tried to explain, feeling badly he upset Andy even further. He looked at him from the corner of his eye trying to gauge Andy's reaction.

Andy, not amused but emotionally distraught, did not see the humor in his illness.

Sensing tension, Jeremy continued, "Well, you do understand everyone is going to die. It's not just you," he paused for a second. "You know that, right?" somewhat unsure if Andy actually knew that fact.

"Well of course I know!"

"No, but do you really know that everyone is going to die or are you just saying you know?"

"Of course I know that!! Can't you see me? Are you blind! I need a wheelchair to get around, and I'm going to either suffocate or choke to death very soon!" Andy was irate and had the urge to physically attack Jeremy. Jeremy though, remained calm, knowing Andy was not expressing personal hatred towards him but releasing accumulated anger.

Jeremy's voice again broke the silence with its calm and certain words. "There are many lessons in life: those that come easily and those that you must attain. I can teach you what we know here, in Meat Cove. I think it may help you deal with your illness and gain a different perspective of your disease."

Andy sat quietly, clenching his jaw, staring at the now overcooked, burnt eggs. He looked out the small window towards the ocean. Slowly, it transferred its soothing rhythm to him and allowed him to be present in the moment. As the minutes passed, so did the wave of his emotions, swept out with the current in the sea. Andy went out onto the deck, trying to catch his breath after expending almost all his energy towards Jeremy. Jeremy met him outside and sat in his worn wicker chair. Andy looked toward Jeremy with a hard-hearted expression revealing his determination to hold onto the past and what he knew. Jeremy sensed this stubbornness but decided to start talking anyway, if for nothing else than to break the silence.

Part II

"Your connection to all those things around you literally defines who you are"

AARON D. O'CONNELL, PH.D.[1]

---

1. O'Connell, "Making Sense of a Visible Quantum Object" TED Talks, March 2011, 7:29.

11

The seer does not use eyes; the seer does not judge; the seer looks beyond; but most importantly the seer must show others how to see

WITH THE SEA IN FRONT OF THEM and infinity on the horizon, Jeremy began speaking, "Do you ever wonder what the percentage is of everything we see, touch, and know compared to *all* there really is?"

Andy gave Jeremy a puzzled look, not quite sure of what he meant.

"I would say it's a few percent."[1]

Andy did not respond, still overcoming his anger.

"We consciously know of only a few percent of all of reality, but our bodies are under the influence of it all, one hundred percent of reality," Jeremy firmly asserted. After a brief pause, he continued, never looking at Andy but keeping his eyes on the horizon, "You will come to appreciate this idea, but first you must understand us, the people of Meat Cove."

"Who? You?" Andy said, still confused.

"Well, yeah, and everyone else who lives here."

Andy, though, could not convince himself he noticed anything unique about them. "Well, what's so special about you people?"

Jeremy laughed but was eager to answer Andy's inquiry, "We're not special. I didn't mean it like that. The difference I'm talking about, however, is the foundation for everything we experience in Meat Cove."

---

1. A related idea discussed in: *Green, Love Without End: Jesus Speaks* (2002), pg. 248.

The Conscious Whole

Andy gave Jeremy another bewildered look. *What kind of experience is he talking about?* he thought.

Jeremy's tone of voice indicated the wisdom he was about to convey had come from the general field of knowledge, which everyone in Meat Cove had as a part of their consciousness.[2,3,4]

"The human body is composed of many different organs that, when put together in a certain order, make a functional body. Organs are themselves formed by particular cells that work in unison and define the type of organ. Inside of the cells are organelles, which function to keep the cells working and alive, like small farms that produce food for a town. The organelles are made up of molecules, that when put together in the proper orientation create the organelle, like the seeds, animals, and workers that compose a farm. The molecules that create the organelles can be further broken down into atoms, which are in specific assemblies to create the exact type of molecule. Amazingly, even though we are talking about very small things, the atoms can also be dissected into smaller components, called electrons, protons, and neutrons. The precise arrangements and numbers of these components determine the specific atom and its characteristics. Believe it or not, we can scale down the size ever further; the pieces making up the atoms can be reduced to smaller constituents, and on an unimaginably minute scale, even those can be reduced to smaller pieces of matter," Jeremy paused, collecting his thoughts.

---

2. Collective memory discussed in: Sheldrake, *The Presence of the Past: Morphic Resonance and the Memory of Nature* (2012).

3. Similar to but uniquely different than Carl Jung's collective unconscious since Jung's idea is centered around an innate unconscious knowledge that is not learned or obtained through experience but one we are born with (Jung, *The Archetypes and the Collective Unconscious* (1981)). Conversely, the Meat Cove collective consciousness is readily accessible and consciously known by the people.

4. Panpsychism is the view that literally all things are conscious; a philosophical concept that is not new, but a recent publication describes an empiric way to measure such effects: Matloff. "Can Panpsychism Become an Observational Science?" *Journal of Consciousness Exploration & Research* (2016).

"So, when you put it all together, our body is made from intimately connected layers of structure built upon each other, starting with something very, very small."

Andy understood these concepts since it was well within the scope of the Conscious Whole's knowledge.

"Now, considering what I just said, let's think about two main areas of physics. I promise, this will help you understand what I said before about the percentage thing. There is the large-scale, classical, Newtonian theory, which describes objects in the big world,[5] things we can see and feel like an apple falling from a tree, by using equations for acceleration, velocity, and friction. However, there is also a theory called quantum physics,[6] which describes the very small world.

"These two theories are very different while at the same time both being real and true. The difference, however, is the scale at which the two seemingly operate. Quantum effects of nature have typically been found to be significant at very small sizes, like that of the atom, electron, neutron, proton and all of the smaller pieces of matter that make up these particles. There are many bizarre properties of quantum physics; for example, the location of an electron in an atom at a specific time is described by the probability function, represented by phi, Ψ. It is also called the wave function. This probability function is a mathematical way of describing where the electron may be at one given time. The important thing to take from this equation is there is the possibility for an electron to exist absolutely anywhere in the universe![7] However, based on its probability function it is only likely, or probable, that it exists somewhere within an atom, in its own electron orbital. The probability is based upon statistics, analogous to

---

5. Einstein's theory of relativity also describes the large-scale world.

6. For a more complete and thorough explanation of theoretical and experimental quantum physics two very useful and accessible resources are: Gribbin, *In Search of Schrodinger's Cat: Quantum Physics and Reality* (1984) and Gribbin, *Schrodinger's Kittens and the Search for Reality* (1995).

7. Gribbin, *In Search of Schrodinger's Cat: Quantum Physics and Reality* (1984), pg. 119.

the different probabilities, or statistics, associated with the flip of a coin. Still keeping up with me?"

Andy gave a quick nod, as he had read a little about quantum theory on his own. Quantum physics was an accepted theory within the Conscious Whole. Yet, Andy was still trying to figure out how this information was going to change anything in his life.

Jeremy paused briefly and once again began speaking in his silky smooth voice that sounded like it was in rhythm with the movements and flow of the earth surrounding them. "You can extrapolate quantum theory to say the electron can be somewhere in an atom in a beaker in a chemistry lab or the same electron can be somewhere on one of the rings of Saturn. Of course though, the probability of the electron being on a ring of Saturn, far away from its atom, is very unlikely. But very importantly, there is still a chance!"

Reiterating this vital concept, Jeremy continued, "Remember at least one point, Andy, even though it is very unlikely for an electron to be far away from its high probability location, there is a very real and strange process occurring at the level of the atomic world that is not readily apparent to us during our daily lives! Electrons and other subatomic particles are not as stable as you may think. They are not just a fixed part of an atom but can be in two different places at once![8] This possibility is very important, and I do not want you to miss this point," Jeremy said with a seriousness that caught Andy's attention.

"Delve deeper and the quantum world loses even more similarities with the macroscopic realm. Wave-particle duality, a core component of quantum physics, describes light behaving as a wave and a particle at the same time but is dependent upon our observation, not isolated or separate from us.[9]

"This discussion brings forth one interpretation of quantum theory that can be demonstrated by a paradox Erwin Schrodinger, a physicist,

---

8. Myatt et al. "Decoherence of Quantum Superpositions Through Coupling to Engineered Reservoirs." *Nature* (2000).

9. Expertly explained (including experimental evidence) in: Gribbin, *In Search of Schrodinger's Cat: Quantum Physics and Reality* (1984), pgs. 81 and 163.

thought of involving a cat in a box.[10] Now, suppose a cat is placed in a metal box, such that you cannot see inside. Also, assume a machine containing a radioactive particle is set up inside the box whereby the random decay of the particle triggers the release of a poisonous gas, killing the cat. As such, the poison is released at a completely random time and you don't know when by looking at the outside of the box. So, the question is, when the cat is placed inside of the box, the machine is activated, and the box is closed, when has the cat died?"

Andy was fond of cats and the idea of purposefully killing a cat bothered him. He had read a little about this paradox before but never in enough detail to fully understand it, so he let Jeremy continue without interrupting.

In a very excited voice Jeremy said, "The answer is the cat is both dead and alive until you open the box and look at the cat! Before you open the box, it exists in a superposition of states at the same time. One dead and one alive. The cat is **both** dead and alive!" Jeremy could not contain his passion.

"You see, every possibility always exists," he continued. "The creation of reality occurs when the person opening the box observes and passes a judgment. They either made a judgment that the cat is alive, because it purrs and jumps on their lap, or it is dead because it is not breathing. The person's judgment chooses the one to see. The act of observing and making a judgment is called collapsing the wave function resulting in the creation of one reality.[11] Which reality would you choose, Andy?"

"Keep the cat alive!" Andy fired back with an enthusiasm he hadn't felt in a long time.

---

10. The cat-in-the-box paradox, thought of by Dr. Erwin Schrodinger, attempted to help explain the classic understanding of quantum theory, the Copenhagen Interpretation. However, there are many other interpretations of quantum physics (including among others the de Broglie–Bohm theory and the many-worlds interpretation), all of which help to explain principles of quantum theory but none of which work perfectly. Reviewed in: Gribbin, *Schrodinger's Kittens and the Search for Reality* (1995), pgs. 23 and 220.

11. Quantum experiments show what scientists/observers are looking for and are evidence for the creational reality of the world.

"Erwin Schrodinger developed the cat in the box paradox because he thought this interpretation of quantum physics was ridiculous.[12] However, the scientific theory he was trying to invalidate was only the tip of the iceberg. Many important pieces of the puzzle were missing. It is one of those things that is hard to explain with words; you'll have to experience it."

Andy had no idea what Jeremy meant by he would "have to experience it," but before Andy had much time to think about the comment, Jeremy continued.

"However strange and absurd the paradox of the cat in a box seems to be, it is one of the interpretations of quantum theory, and it does help to illustrate proven laws[13, 14, 15, 16] of quantum physics: the world is not as fixed as you may think and is based upon all possibilities, some with a higher and some with a lower probability, until the one reality is observed with consciousness[17, 18] being a key component of creation![19, 20, 21]

---

12. Gribbin, *Schrodinger's Kittens and the Search for Reality* (1995), pg. 19. Schrodinger was referring to the Copenhagen Interpretation of quantum physics with the cat in the box paradox.

13. Certain aspects of quantum theory, including decoherence, nonlocality, and superposition have been experimentally proven and can be found in the literature. Some of the more monumental experiments are in the following footnotes.

14. Aspect, Dalibard, and Roger, "Experimental Test of Bell's Inequalities Using Time-Varying Analyzers." *Physical Review Letters* (1982).

15. Myatt et al. "Decoherence of Quantum Superpositions Through Coupling to Engineered Reservoirs." *Nature* (2000).

16. O'Connell et al. "Quantum Ground State and Single-Phonon Control of a Mechanical Resonator." *Nature* (2010).

17. Consciousness and quantum mechanics discussed in: London and Bauer, "La Théorie de l'Observation en Mécanique Quantique." (1939), pg. 41.

18. Eugene Wigner was a proponent of consciousness being fundamental in quantum mechanics, although he later changed his view: Wigner, *The Collected Works of Eugene Paul Wigner* (1997), pg. 247.

19. Anaxagoras (500-428 BC): «the mind created the cosmos».

20. Idealism in philosophy describes the principle that objects of knowledge are in some form dependent upon the mind; several examples include absolute idealism, subjective idealism, and pluralistic idealism.

This theory holds true for really small things, like atoms, that only become real, in terms of the reality you experience, when they are observed. Until that point, every one of their possibilities exists! Your one reality is then a manifestation of an infinite selection of potential realities that *you choose*!

"Everything surrounding us, even our own body, is built from the small pieces of matter, electrons, protons, neutrons, and atoms. Atoms make molecules, that make organelles, that make up cells, which then make organs in our bodies, all coming together to form who we are; everything resting on the foundation of quantum molecules. These quantum molecules are only real when we are present in their moment! And we decide how present to be!

"The important point, Andy, is that our bodies are also quantum bodies in addition to being bodies that follow large-scale physics! Most importantly, the atoms and molecules that govern and lead to higher-order structures and processes, like the functioning of our organs and brain, are dependent on quantum probabilities and quantum laws!"

"Wait, so are you saying the cat in the box stuff happens with all of the small stuff in our bodies, like molecules in our cells?" Andy asked.

"Yes! That's exactly right. Pieces of matter bigger than the very, very small electrons, protons, and neutrons have also been found to obey the laws and strange rules of quantum physics including atoms,[22] molecules,[23] and even objects visible to the naked eye![24] This is very significant because of the small scale on which the biology of our bodies operates. For example, there

---

21. The effect of consciousness on the outcome of random physical processes has been experimentally explored by a team of researchers at Princeton University with interesting and controversial results: Dunne and Jahn. "Experiments in Remote Human/Machine Interaction." *Journal of Scientific Exploration* (1992).

22. Kurtsiefer, Pfau, and Mlynek. "Measurement of the Wigner Function of an Ensemble of Helium Atoms." *Nature* (1997).

23. Arndt et al. "Wave–Particle Duality of C60 Molecules." *Nature* (1999).

24. O'Connell et al. "Quantum Ground State and Single-Phonon Control of a Mechanical Resonator." *Nature* (2010).

are little factories inside of our cells that make proteins. The proteins are built from small molecules called amino acids, which are themselves made from atoms arranged in a particular configuration. Amino acids are put together in a specific sequence and folded in a specific arrangement to create a specific type of protein. These proteins can do many different jobs depending upon which type they are and where they are made in the body. They keep us alive. Amino acids, and their inner atoms, are so small they obey quantum laws and behave as quantum molecules! Like the cat in the box!

"DNA is no different and just like every other molecule made from very small atoms, obeys the same laws of quantum physics! Our bodies not only follow the classical laws of Newtonian physics but the foundation of our bodies, atoms and molecules, behave quantum mechanically!"

The idea of DNA being a quantum molecule, considering its size, was also accepted by the Conscious Whole's paradigm to a certain degree. [25, 26, 27, 28, 29, 30, 31, 32] The Conscious Whole, however, decreed the quantum world as a peculiarity of very small atomic particles; something artificially created by experiments; separate from their own world, having no influence in their lives; beyond their grasp, and therefore, beyond their influence.

---

25. This is a constantly evolving topic with a wide variety of prior and emerging work of varying degrees of quality in the literature. To put it succinctly, DNA is like any other molecule and can be described by the principles of quantum chemistry, which uses quantum theory to illustrate chemical phenomena (Priyadarshy, Beratan, and Risser. "DNA Double-Helix-Mediated Long-Range Electron Transfer." *International Journal of Quantum Chemistry* (1996)).

26. There is also a sizable amount of literature describing how quantum effects relate to DNA and biology in a broader scope than described by quantum chemistry, some of which is controversial. At the time of publication of this book many of these articles are theoretical with a paucity of strong experimental studies, however, there will likely be more work published in the future. The following citations are a few examples for reference; many more are published and many more will be published in what is being called quantum biology.

27. Rieper, Anders, and Vedral. "Quantum Entanglement Between the Electron Clouds of Nucleic Acids in DNA." *arXiv* (2010).

28. Davies. "Does Quantum Mechanics Play a Non-trivial Role in Life?" *Biosystems* (2004).

29. McFadden and Al-Khalili. "A Quantum Mechanical Model of Adaptive Mutation." *Biosystems* (1999).

"Let me give you an interesting scientific example of quantum physics at work," Jeremy said.

Andy was pleased to hear about an experiment, as he found comfort in the steadfast laws and rules of science as opposed to the fanciful discussion as of yet.

"An experiment was done where a piece of metal, visible to the naked eye, was cooled to a very low temperature. The piece of metal could be in one of two states: stationary or vibrating. To help confirm laws of quantum physics the scientists were able to make the one piece of metal both stationary and vibrating at the same time; a superposition of states; just like the cat in the box, which is both dead and alive before being observed, this piece of metal was both moving and not moving![33]

"The amazing part about this experiment is that the quantum effects of nature were observed on a scale that is visible to the naked eye!

"Even though we may not be consciously aware of the manifestation of quantum laws surrounding us, they are still present in our lives and influencing us! Our bodies and the world around us must follow quantum laws and the laws of the cat in the box," Jeremy paused, sensing confusion in Andy's expression.

"Andy, do you want to be observed in the box and have your illness created based on judgments made by you and others, just as you observed and judged the cat to be dead?"

Andy did not believe the body could change, especially by judgments made by him or others.[34] He was taught the course of biology was deter-

---

30. Home and Chattopadhyaya. "DNA Molecular Cousin of Schrodinger's Cat: A Curious Example of Quantum Measurement." *Physical Review Letters* (1996).

31. Electronic properties of DNA mutations: Shih et al. "The Interplay of Mutations and Electronic Properties in Disease-Related Genes." *Scientific Reports* (2012).

32. A more mainstream publication: Vedral. "Living in a Quantum World." *Scientific American* (2011).

33. O'Connell et al. "Quantum Ground State and Single-Phonon Control of a Mechanical Resonator." *Nature* (2010).

34. A related and similar discussion on the interaction of DNA with our minds: Rudd, *The Gene Keys: Unlocking the Higher Purpose Hidden in Your DNA* (2013).

mined at birth by DNA. Andy was not sure where this discussion was going but continued to sit quietly and take in all of the knowledge Jeremy was pouring out. He had not thought about a correlation between quantum theory and the human body.

Jeremy continued, "In order for me to show you what we know in Meat Cove, I would like to explain something else to help expand your understanding, another strange property of the very small world, where particles communicate with each other over vast distances. Two interrelated concepts are involved, called 'nonlocality' and 'entanglement'.[35, 36, 37, 38, 39] These theories have been proven by complex experiments, but you can get the idea by an analogy. There are things called quarks, the constituents of subatomic particles like electrons, which have specific properties. One way of describing a quark is by defining its spin. For the purpose of the analogy, you can think of the quark's spin as the way it moves in space, like a top spinning on a table.

"So, take for example, a case where one quark has a clockwise spin. Now, if this quark has a partner quark, which they often do, the partner will have the opposite spin, in this case a counterclockwise spin. Therefore, we have two quarks that are related, like a twin brother and sister, paired since birth. However, similar to the way a brother and sister are

---

35. Idea originally devised by Einstein, Podolsky, and Rosen in an attempt to show the incompleteness of quantum physics (Einstein, Podolsky, and Rosen. "Can Quantum-Mechanical Description of Physical Reality be Considered Complete?" *Physical Review* (1935)). This became known as the EPR paradox.

36. John Bell conceptually developed a method for an experimental test of the EPR paradox (Bell. "On the Einstein-Podolsky-Rosen Paradox." *Physics* (1964)).

37. Freedman and Clauser experimentally proved Bell's theorem (Freedman and Clauser. "Experimental Test of Local Hidden-Variable Theories." *Physical Review Letters* (1972)).

38. Alain Aspect as well as others also experimentally proved Bell's theorem in multiple experiments (for example: Aspect, Grangier, and Roger. "Experimental Realization of Einstein-Podolsky-Rosen-Bohm Gedankenexperiment: A New Violation of Bell's Inequalities." *Physical Review Letters* (1982) and Aspect, Dalibard, and Roger, "Experimental Test of Bell's Inequalities Using Time-Varying Analyzers." *Physical Review Letters* (1982)).

39. Nonlocality and entanglement reviewed in: Aspect. "Quantum Mechanics: To Be or Not to Be Local." *Nature* (2007).

different genders, these quarks must have opposite spins as part of their nature.

"Now, let's say someone separates the two quarks in space and is able to alter the spin of one of these paired quarks to make the clockwise quark spin counterclockwise. Like putting a dress and lipstick on the boy. A strange phenomenon then occurs: the other quark that started counterclockwise alters its own spin to become a clockwise quark in order to maintain its complementary nature, and it does this completely on its own! Since the brother is wearing the sister's dress, she must wear her brother's overalls and boots. The complementary, paired nature is called entanglement and the communication between particles that were once related but have become separated is termed nonlocality. Weird, huh?"

Andy nodded and forced a smile. "I don't get the nonlocality thing. How do they communicate?" he asked.

"Right! So, there must be some type of force connecting these two quarks allowing them to know what the other is doing. Yet, the most interesting part of this fundamental aspect of nature is these two quarks, even when separated by light years across the deserts of the universe, will still know what the other is doing! Like the mother telling the sister that her brother is wearing her dress, the quarks do not need to be next to each other to communicate, and therefore their interaction is not localized to the same region. They are able to converse with each other through a bridge that skips across space and time for instantaneous communication: the Mother Connection. The quarks in this example, in nature, and in our bodies are no different. Our Mother is constantly keeping communication open between all related particles that exist in the cosmos."

Jeremy stopped speaking for a few minutes and Andy glanced over waiting for him to continue, but he could tell Jeremy was deep in his own thoughts. *There must be some quarks way off on the other side of the universe Jeremy was communicating with and were talking back to him. Maybe Jeremy's mother was sending him her love through the Mother Connection,* Andy thought. He wondered if the people in Meat Cove were more sensitive to this property of nature, allowing them to tune in and communicate with particles that have since lost their immediate physical connection to the people.[40]

Andy thought of Leah and focused on the memories he had of her. He concentrated on the theory Jeremy had just taught him and thought about her quarks and particles he used to be connected to. The particles that made her previous body must still be somewhere in the world, for Andy knew the most basic property of matter and energy: that it can neither be created nor destroyed. Despite the fact she was not physically next to him, Leah and Andy were still connected. He still felt a special bond to her and now knew there was a scientific reason for his feelings. For the link he had with her.

Andy's thoughts then drifted to his mother. She had left the earth long ago, but he must still be connected to her former particles and quarks. Her particles originated from the birth of the universe and explosion of stars. Eons after the particles settled onto the planet, Andy's grandmother nourished her body with them to give her the building blocks to create a new life. The particles assembled together to create larger and larger structures finally resulting in the child Andy's mother became.

All of the particles making up the body of Andy's mother communicated through their quarks and the Mother Connection, exchanging signals and details from previous bonds with their current ones. The particles themselves were ancients and had access to information they acquired ages ago. Information about previous entanglements, previous interactions, previous structures, and previous forms they were part of. This information was transmitted nonlocally across space and time as a code, dictating the formation of small structures and the assembly of the larger physical whole. Physical eyes see it as new life in the world. A child.

---

40. "In quantum mechanics, particles are delocalized (i.e. nonlocal). Are we therefore delocalized? Is our consciousness delocalized?" Paraphrased from: O'Connell, "Making Sense of a Visible Quantum Object" TED Talks, March 2011, 6:30. So, is delocalization of consciousness occurring when we see, feel, or think about things that are far away in space and time?

Throughout a child's life, particles are ingested and create more and more structure resulting in a larger, adult body. Each particle communicating and connecting to other particles, forever changing the characteristics of the complementary particle, just as the quarks changed each other's spins. Constantly being recycled, re-entering the earth from where they came, every particle with an imprint of the past forged on its surface like handprints written on the inside of caves by humans of the past.

Andy was mesmerized by the ocean in front of him, mentally seeking particles of his mother's life. Particles he was still connected with. The memories he had of her making delicious peach pies and teaching him invaluable lessons. All of this information written onto particles that only now were in Andy's conscious awareness. The memories he was having were not random connections of brain cells but rather the brain cells' ability to tap into the Mother Connection and read templates of all the particles that made up the past.[41]

Andy focused on the vast connectedness of the world, permitting his busy mind to rest. He was very present in the moment, not allowing unrelated thoughts to come into his current awareness. He felt as if he could hear quarks in his body talking to other quarks around him. The ocean in front of him, filled with an innumerable amount of matter, was in harmony with his own body. Both men sat on the deck for what seemed like an hour, allowing their bodies to become in sync with the meditative forces of nature.

Just as suddenly as he had stopped speaking, Jeremy began again, "The big question with quantum versus classical Newtonian laws of physics is at what point does one become the predominant influence, given that they seem to contradict one another and work on opposite ends of the size spectrum?"

He paused and looked at Andy waiting for a response. Andy shrugged.

---

41. Similar concept detailed in: McTaggart, *The Field: The Quest for the Secret Force of the Universe* (2008), pg. 95.

"The transition from quantum to Newtonian is called decoherence.[42, 43, 44] Typically quantum mechanics describes the very small world of subatomic particles whereas classical physics describes macroscopic objects we can see and touch. Yet, there are certain things visible to the eye that follow the laws of the quantum world, but this observation is only made if we remove outside influences, like other molecules and high temperatures. So, why does decoherence occur?"

Andy, just trying to keep up, didn't really have a good answer for Jeremy but was able to squeak something out, "Well, I'm not really sure. I guess at some point it either just switches over or it blurs from one into the other."

"Well, the specifics of decoherence are not certain, but one thing seems for sure: decoherence occurs due to external influences on an object. A combination of all surrounding influences on an entity. A summative force of the whole that creates the universe. As such, effects of the whole system, all of the observers and powers, lead to a classical appearance of the observed world!

"A large object interacting with many other molecules will behave classically but so will a single molecule when interacting with other molecules or outside influences; in which case, the wave function collapses and infinite possibilities become one, once the outside influence exert its effect on an object. This means that entanglement, the nearly unavoidable connection to the surrounding world, is key to creation! The communication and resultant change between quarks is happening an infinite number of times, over and over at every moment keeping the world in check.

---

42. Joos et al. *Decoherence and the Appearance of a Classical World in Quantum Theory* (2003).

43. Zurek. "Decoherence and the Transition from Quantum to Classical." *Physics Today* (1991).

44. Zurek. "Decoherence and the Transition from Quantum to Classical-Revisited." *Los Alamos Science* (2002).

"Everything is entangled, Andy. It's what constructs us, and it's how we build the world around us. This turns into a dominant force: the conscious mediator, which is the key to the quantum puzzle!"

Andy gave Jeremy a sharp glance, lifting his eyebrows with a quizzical expression.

"Nothing is isolated. Molecules swim in a bath of other molecules and interact with many other molecules. This is why we can't really see the quantum world. Decoherence is happening at every second obscuring the quantum effects of nature, collapsing the wave function. In order to measure quantum effects, outside influences are removed.[45, 46] When reintroduced, the outside influences collapse the infinite number of possibilities into one.

"This is very important, Andy. Remember, outside influences act on the quantum world and create the observed universe. Yet, there is more to 'outside influences' than other molecules,[47] temperature, or gravity.[48] Our minds and intentions[49] are powerful influencers too.[50] They cause deco-

---

45. In O'Connell et al. "Quantum Ground State and Single-Phonon Control of a Mechanical Resonator." *Nature* (2010), as previously cited, the causes of decoherence (temperature and other molecules) were removed to observe pure quantum mechanical behavior. However, when external influences are reintroduced, quantum physics transitions to classical physics because the outside influences determine one of the many possibilities of the superposition of states.

46. When anything interacts with a system, the outcome is altered and the wave function collapses. "Anything" includes a measuring device, a person, or an atom of carbon. Does this mean we (people) change the outcome? We do in a way, but is it conscious, subconscious, or independent of consciousness? This is a question that needs an answer and presently does not have definitive, supportive scientific evidence one way or another.

47. The moon appears permanent for very long periods of time because of its size and number of associated molecules, as opposed to the instant quantum properties of a single atom: Gribbin, *Schrodinger's Kittens and the Search for Reality* (1995), pg. 150.

48. Penrose. "On Gravity's Role in Quantum State Reduction." *General Relativity and Gravitation* (1996).

49. Intention as a force in reality discussed in: McTaggart, *The Intention Experiment: Using Your Thoughts to Change Your Life and the World* (2008).

50. In my opinion, the energetic field/conscious cloud also masks the behavior of quantum mechanics and acts as another external influence resulting in decoherence, i.e. the "observer" collapsing the wave function.

herence as well! They choose the world from unlimited possibilities! But it's bigger than just our minds. The whole of the universe is responsible for its outcome. This is the conscious mediator.

12

Bellowing deeply below earth, in a realm never seen or explored by humans, the ancients gathered; one would think that because of its size the meeting place must be the origin; yet, it was merely a throughway, a place to collect before implementation; many different routes were used to congregate; the massive primordial workers entered down the backs of open, golden channels, personified by those they passed through, taking the form of larger-than-life Neanderthal-like beings and buffalos stampeding through the plains, they transmuted during the passage; the high-energy synthesizers of the Seven Sisters coursed in the zero resistance space between solid matter, easily making the journey; whereas guardians of the bounds of space rode on tattered wisps of light carried centuries through the universe with barely enough strength to complete the arduous voyage; others were strangely marooned but took part in the task as payment for future passage; finally, the few who originally manifested on the planet, growing in parallel, were surely present not having to travel far; they waited the longest out of all and had accrued the most potency of character; like any assortment of unique beings there were leaders and those who followed; those who were passionate and those who labored for secondary gains; nonetheless, all were equally invested in the duty before them, in those they were responsible for; typically, at any given moment the gathering place contained a handful of beings, fleeting in time and space, constantly changing, however, now they all assembled; a very rare occurrence; words were not spoken, but thoughts and intentions were exchanged; they all knew what was going to be done and preparations had begun; like the connection between a parent and child, a seamless bond was formed to the surface world, fixed in place by the workers and crafted by the descendents of the Seven Sisters; it provided support for interactions to follow

"DNA. Deoxyribonucleic acid. A bunch of molecules inside of our cells. Small molecules. Really small molecules. Do they fall from the cliff just as Newton's apple fell from a tree? Bound to the earth by gravity? Obeying the classical laws of physics? Driven by fate with nowhere to go but down? Down generations to create new humans? DNA, the building block of life, the blueprint of the body we occupy, creates new structures by the second. Remember, DNA is in the same box the cat occupied, obeying the laws of quantum physics. It is part of the cat's body, isn't it? What is the probability function of DNA, Andy?"

Andy was no stranger to DNA. The Conscious Whole had studied its structure and composition over and over, a double helix of molecules called nucleotides, with four different types arranged in a specific sequence: the order creates the code. In fact, the doctors of the Conscious Whole attributed Andy's illness to one misplaced nucleotide in his DNA resulting in a coded sequence for disease. Andy's nucleotide only differed from the correct one by a few hydrogen, nitrogen, and oxygen atoms. The grand result was that Andy's cells could no longer make the correct protein needed for survival. That was DNA's job anyway, to make proteins to nourish the body and supply tools for cells to use for their lives. Andy's DNA, however, no longer made the protein in the correct way. It was malformed. Misshapen. Out of its inherent order. No longer able to do its job, death was the consequence, and Andy was systemically feeling this effect.

The cells in his muscles were dying; he was bound to a wheelchair. The cells in his lungs were dying; he was having trouble breathing. The cells in his heart were dying; blood was not getting pumped. The cells in his bones were dying; his bones were weak and brittle.

Jeremy continued speaking, "Atoms in DNA are arranged in a specific orientation to create nucleotides, which are in a certain sequence to produce the uniqueness we know as individuality. DNA, the nucleotides that form DNA, and the pieces that make up the nucleotides are so small, Andy, that DNA is in the box with the cat! Therefore, every combination and every possibility must exist with its respective probability. Some combinations are less probable than others, while others are more likely. Once the DNA molecule is observed, its probability function collapses, and only one of its many possible conformations becomes real!

"The observer, just as with quantum laws, has no way of becoming truly objective. Instead, a perspective or judgment is always layered on top that influences creation of one reality! According to principles of the quantum world, there is no objectivity and as such, no separation of us from other parts of the world![1, 2, 3, 4, 5]

"The one form of the world we see at every moment is there solely because we are observing and acting on it. The cat is not objectively alive or dead, it only has a subjective reality and a subjective life based upon the observer. When the observer adds a perspective, he or she generates a reality of the cat as dead or alive. The large-scale environment we are living in now, as we hear these words, does not appear to be a quantum world because we tangibly experience only the end result. Our consciousness does not naturally tune into the prequel of reality, quantum reality, it just sees what it creates and not the raw materials. Reality is the subjective creation

---

1. Stapp. "S-Matrix Interpretation of Quantum Theory." *Physical Review D* (1971).

2. Stapp. "The Copenhagen Interpretation." *American Journal of Physics* (1972).

3. Stapp. Correlation Experiments and the Nonvalidity of Ordinary Ideas About the Physical World. Lawrence Berkeley Laboratory (1976).

4. d'Espagnat. "The Quantum Theory and Reality." *Scientific American* (1979).

5. The world is as objectively real as a rainbow is real; we can all see a rainbow, but you can never get to the pot of gold: Herbert, *Quantum Reality: Beyond the New Physics* (1987), pg. 162.

of the world. It does not exist in an objective, separate sense. The chair we are sitting on is only there and real at the present moment because we are observing ourselves sitting on it!

"Factors, including the number of atoms involved, the force of gravity, external influences, and the elusive conscious mediator prevent the unpredictability and strangeness of the quantum world from being present before our eyes. These forces establish the chair as being present, under us, creating the false impression of objectivity. Meaning, if objectivity were true, the chair is present without you being in the room. In contrast, a quantum, subjective chair is only there because you are sitting on it.

Andy had a baffled expression on his face and frankly did not believe what Jeremy was telling him. He knew a little about quantum physics, but Jeremy was taking it to a new level. None of it made any sense in terms of what Andy had learned or experienced before. *Things are not only there just because you look at them*, Andy thought. *How could that be?*

The veil placed over Andy when he lived under the Conscious Whole was not going to be completely removed by the simple act of coming to Meat Cove; it was ingrained into his being. Yet, Jeremy was trying to pull off the shroud and show Andy what was behind the curtains.

"I know one thing your world has not taught you, Andy," a determined Jeremy continued. "The people where you come from fully believe the true origin and central cause of many medical conditions is DNA. On one level, it is true that a variation in the sequence of DNA molecules is one of the many ways in which a biological problem can result. However, the pertinent question, and what your world does not fully accept, is whether or not DNA is a quantum molecule and behaves as such. Is it permanently fixed, immovable? Or is it as prone to the observer as the cat in Schrodinger's box? Remember, it all comes down to the scale of the object we are observing. The doctors of your world do not appreciate that DNA is a quantum molecule, even though it is known to be such in their scientific literature!"

Andy had always believed his DNA was what made him who he was. DNA was the one thing that created, without a doubt or outside influence, his illness. It was not a question of his DNA being "real" or not, as Jeremy had said. It was surely real. The doctor measured and studied Andy's very own DNA in a lab and found a mutation. The mutation was, they thought, the ***origin*** of his disease.

Jeremy looked towards Andy and could see he was having a hard time believing all he was hearing.

"What I know…" Andy paused for a moment, "…is that my DNA is faulty and makes bad proteins that kill cells in my body."

"Yeah, well, that is correct to a degree, but important information is missing. As I have explained, DNA is not as real as you think. It is too small to be objectively real and requires your subjective perspective to make it function. Without your perspective, it can be in any form. Once again, Andy, since DNA is a quantum molecule, it belongs in Schrodinger's box! And, if DNA creates your body and if all of your DNA is in the box, then you and your disease belong in the box as well. Therefore, you and your illness have the same fate as Schrodinger's cat! A fate determined by the observer and peculiar rules of the quantum world! As I eluded to before, what makes us, the inhabitants of Meat Cove, different is how we apply and harness the inherent energy of the quantum world."

Andy looked to the horizon thinking deeply about the world he came from, confused about what was real and what was fanciful.

13

It slept soundly waiting for its time; when awoken, its lessons would be shown; in time it would be summoned

"Maybe a story will help," Jeremy said, trying to facilitate Andy's understanding of the paradigms known in Meat Cove. "It is about a giant; a human-like creature the size of our planet. This being travels around the solar system as easily as we travel to the corner store. Going to a far-off galaxy for him, one hundred light years away, would be like us taking a trip to our favorite vacation spot one hundred miles away. The giant can easily manipulate and move planets in whichever direction he pleases like rocks in a garden and has a proficient understanding of gravity. He is able to tangibly experience this force as it tugs him towards larger planets and suns; similar to the force of magnetism we feel when a magnet is attracted to metal. The giant has even created mathematical equations to better his understanding of gravity.

"Being a curious creature, the giant has probed the contents of many planets and looked closely at the matter creating them. When studying our planet, the giant first saw clouds and observed their movements around earth. He developed a theory about their motions and created a paradigm about weather. Digging deeper into the earth, the giant found three substances: a solid material, a liquid material, and a gaseous material. He concluded they are the sole constituents of earth and based upon his theory, putting these three materials together on another planet would create an identical planet, exactly like the one he was observing.

"This was the limit of the creature's understanding. Not because of intelligence but because of the scope of his work, the scope of his abilities, the scope of his understanding, and most importantly the scope of his perception. Only able to comprehend what is within the realm of his beingness and limits of his size, the giant knew the absolute basics about earth. The concepts we take for granted, like different types of solids, were far beyond his envelope of knowledge, mostly because he was not physically able to see different types of rocks that make up the 'solid' part of earth. Beyond that, he was not even aware there are different types of solids and assumed the solid component he isolated from earth was indivisible. However, this does not mean what the giant does not know is not affecting him in some way.

"As the giant hovered above earth, sticking his large fingers and strange instruments into oceans, lakes, mountains, and fields, the people on earth were terrified. However, there was a keen and brave scientist who created a device allowing him to communicate with the giant looming above. Both creatures were very curious about each other, but without the communication machine the giant would have never known about people, whom he previously grouped into the solid substance. The scientist and giant talked for many hours a day and shared details about their seemingly separate realities. It took some time for the giant to grasp the concept of little creatures called people living within the three basic elements he had discovered." Jeremy paused and looked over at Andy, "You still following me?"

"Yeah, but this is just an analogy, right? There aren't really giants roaming around space, are there?" Andy asked kiddingly but also not entirely sure considering the bizarre theories Jeremy had been explaining earlier.

"Yes, it's just an analogy. The giant hasn't been to visit us recently..." Jeremy said chuckling. He continued, "Once the giant understood that people were a separate substance, the scientist tried to explain the microscopic world of living creatures called bacteria, amoeba, and cells. This information blew the giant away. He could not believe the scientist and thought he had lied to him, simply making fun of his ignorance. With time, however, the scientist convinced him the microscopic world did in fact exist! It was not that the giant could not intellectually understand what the scientist was talking about; he was just not able to perceive the microscopic realm. It was unimaginable, as the giant was born to understand how gravity moves planets and how forces mysterious to humans pull galaxies away from one another.

"Well, the scientist, already experienced with building a machine allowing communication between the giant and himself, built a massive microscope that stretched from the earth all the way through the atmosphere to the giant's large eyes, allowing him to see these so-called bacteria, amoeba, and cells.

"The very determined scientist used all of the resources available to him to successfully create a microscope for the giant. When it was finally complete, the giant approached and peered inside, very excited to finally see the microscopic world that was beyond his imagination. Yet, as he looked through he was extremely disappointed! He saw nothing! It looked like empty space. Nothingness. The scientist spent endless days and nights attempting to fix the microscope, adjusting the lenses, reworking the mirrors, and recalculating the equations. However, it was to no avail. It wasn't the construction or design of the microscope, which was perfect; on the other hand, one very important fact was not accounted for in the scientist's equations and engineering of the microscope.

"The giant's brain. It's not wired to see the cellular world. The cells at the bottom of the microscope were there, but the giant could not perceive them. If a human were to look into the huge microscope, they would surely see the cells, bacteria, and amoeba. The ability to see the microscopic world was beyond the giant's scope of perception, despite the fact that cells existed at the bottom of the microscope. When the giant probed the earth and collected all of the matter, bacteria and cells were present in the mix, and even though he did not see them, they still influenced the nature surrounding the giant, albeit he would not consciously feel their actions.

"After the scientist had confirmed the equations and microscope as perfect, he was evermore curious why the giant could not see the cells in his microscope. His inquisitiveness motivated him to study the giant, and he found the giant was much like a human with similar organs functioning to keep him alive. Like humans, these organs were composed of smaller parts that lay structure to sustain their function. The scientist even found smaller parts and pieces, at a scale the giant could not imagine: the giant's cells. Very similar to the cells that make up the human body, the same size as the cells the giant was trying to view in the microscope.

"Even though the cells in the giant created his body, he was not able to see them; they were beyond his perceptive ability. Yet, this would not change the fact his cells were playing a vital role by keeping him alive. He was, of course, composed of the same matter that makes up the planets and universe he observed and studied.

"The scientist became obsessed, spending all of his time thinking about every facet of the giant and his life. He wondered what would happen if the giant were to become ill, infected with extraterrestrial bacteria, could he be treated like us?" Jeremy paused, looking towards Andy making sure he was still paying attention.

Andy, caught off guard, said "Um, well. I'm not really sure."

"Well, of course he could! They would just need to give him antibiotics like they do for us. Except, they would have to develop a new antibiotic to fight the extraterrestrial bacteria and make a huge pill for him to take. This would not be impossible as novel drugs are developed all the time to kill newly evolving[1] strains of bacteria."

---

1. Don't believe in evolution? It occurs all of the time in bacteria and viruses. That is why antibiotics and vaccines that used to work no longer do because microorganisms develop a defense mechanism against the prior drugs or vaccines. New variations of bacteria and viruses then exist. The influenza virus mutates and evolves into a slightly different form every year! That is why a different vaccine is used every year. Evolution does occur. Perhaps the question that should be debated is, "What controls evolution?" Science would say the force of nature and random occurrences. Religion would say God. I argue the force driving evolution is the Conscious Whole!

"So, I still don't understand why the giant couldn't see cells through the microscope," Andy interrupted.

"Well, the situation was analyzed thoroughly by the good scientist; maybe it had to do with the change in the thickness of the atmosphere from where the giant was and where the cells were, like trying to look at the bottom of a lake from the shoreline; maybe the sun's glare interfered with light refraction in the microscope; maybe solar flares interfered with the electronics in the microscope.

"The scientist even conferred with colleagues from all different areas of science: physics, astrophysics, chemistry, biochemistry, astronomy, meteorology, biology, medicine, geology, and anthropology. He even asked a psychologist to speak with the giant and see if he was subconsciously seeing the cells but suppressing their image. No one found anything wrong or amiss. Then, one day the scientist had an idea. What if the giant's eyesight and neurons in his brain are not capable of seeing something as small as cells?

"Despite his intelligence, the giant's mind could not grasp the very small; he evolved in the extraordinary large-scale world of the universe after all, never interacting with or even thinking about small cells that made up his body. Evolution selected him to develop a brain that understood the vast scale of the universe, which is what he needed to survive. Just as the scientist's brain could not imagine traversing a galaxy in a single jump, the giant could not imagine the microscopic world of cells.

"This is analogous to our understanding of dimensions in the world. We say there are four dimensions: three spatial and one time. If we were to try to conceptualize a world made up of five or six dimensions, it would be impossible.[2] Our brains are only wired for the four we physically interact with. Always remember, Andy, despite limitations of perception, what we don't see still affects our lives!"

"Wait a minute. What's this talk about other dimensions?"

---

2. Kaku, *Hyperspace: A Scientific Odyssey Through Parallel Universes, Time Warps, and the Tenth Dimension* (1995).

"Sure, I guess I forgot to talk about multiple dimensions."

"Multiple dimensions!?" Andy said, shocked that Jeremy was seriously going to address the topic.

"Yeah, multiple dimensions. Well, it's a complicated subject, but I'll give you the brief summary. There are the four dimensions I just mentioned, but in addition there are about six or so more dimensions.[3, 4] Remember what I said about having to experience it?"

"Well, sure I guess," Andy said disappointed by Jeremy's response.

"Multiple dimensions will make more sense to you soon. I promise," Jeremy said smiling. He continued, "Okay, now back to our big friend. So, if the giant, with his intelligence and capability of traveling distances humans could only dream of, had a very obvious void in his ability to see the world, then what are humans not able to see, Andy?"

Andy was starting to understand Jeremy's analogy.

"We are giants when looking into the very small quantum world, Andy! Like the giant looking down the microscope at cells, our biological brains are not capable of really seeing and fully understanding the subatomic and quantum world for how it really is. We can only attempt to conceptualize it and use analogies to understand it, like the cat in the box paradox. Still, just like with the cells and the giant, the quantum world affects us even though we are not consciously aware of it!

"Do you really think DNA, with its very small size and the even smaller size of the nucleotides, behaves as we think it does with our very limited perceptive ability and understanding of the small world!?" Jeremy said with passion.

---

3. It is theorized and demonstrated mathematically that the world may in fact have many more dimensions than the four that are obvious to us! Two useful and accessible resources on this topic are: Kaku, *Hyperspace: A Scientific Odyssey Through Parallel Universes, Time Warps, and the Tenth Dimension* (1995) and Randall, *Warped Passages: Unraveling the Mysteries of the Universe's Hidden Dimensions* (2005).

4. The brain creates neuronal structures in greater than 3-dimensions; can it then perceive a multi-dimensional world? Reimann et al. "Cliques of Neurons Bound into Cavities Provide a Missing Link between Structure and Function." *Frontiers in Computational Neuroscience* (2017).

Andy looked down at his own body. At his legs, which were thin from disease and disuse. He knew there were cells within his body. He had seen them himself. One day, the students in his class took cells from the inside of their mouths and looked at them under a microscope. Andy demonstrated this experiment for the students and saw his own cells. Where his diseased DNA existed. He never thought about the smaller parts that made up his DNA. The molecules, atoms, and electrons he could never see. *What kind of properties of very small matter did I make assumptions about?* Andy thought. *What was I wrong about? What was the world I came from wrong about?*

14

A sailboat is carried by invisible wind; planets are carried by invisible gravity; the universe is carried by invisible forces; humans live within invisible fields of energy; to navigate, you must cast your sail and tack into the wind

Jeremy's soft but strong voice continued the flow of knowledge, "On the other hand, surely the massive scale of the universe is another limitation of our human mind. There is a finite distance we can observe, even with the most sophisticated telescopes. When looking up into the night sky with our bare eyes, we can see massive beauty and simultaneously begin to perceive the boundaries of our vision.

"A star. One shining, twinkling light in the sky. On a clear night you can see thousands. The light that strikes your eye travels to the retina at the back of your eye and is transformed into an electro-chemical signal that courses to the brain, allowing us to perceive the light coming from the sky above. This light may have come from millions of light years away. Even more unimaginable, is at the very instant we are looking at the star, it may have already burnt out! Died. Yet, its light is still living on, racing through the cosmos, taking millions of years to reach our planet, seemingly immortal, with no care for time or for the fact that the matter once making it up has ceased to exist. As far as we know, the star is still alive, its ray of light beaming with life. Does that make it dead or alive?"

"Well, if the sun that contains the matter is dead, then the star must be dead," Andy said with a confidence that was beginning to diminish.

"No. It is light that makes something alive. Nothing exists without its own electromagnetic energy, which is the catalyst used by everything to interact with the world. The only way we are interacting right now, Andy, is because my light is flowing towards your light. That is how you see me, and that is how I am real to you. I am both matter and light at the same time, as are you."

"Matter and light at the same time?" Andy asked, confused by Jeremy's words, figuring he must have misspoke.

"Yes! Both matter and energy at the same time!" Jeremy continued. "A photon has been found to act as both a wave of light and a particle at the same time! Scientists call this wave-particle duality.[1,2] An object's physical matter is only one facet of its reality with electromagnetic energy being the other half. Our eyes receive light and our brain then creates the perceptive world of matter around us, simply based on waves of light. Only after interpreting light do we see and experience matter!"

Andy simply did not believe Jeremy. These ideas did not fit into any paradigm he had ever lived under. The people of the Conscious Whole did not extend the realm of quantum physics to the large-scale world Andy lived within. The world was absolutely and objectively real where he came from. Matter was matter, no matter what. It was not real because "we built it" that way but only real because it was real, physically present in the world.

Jeremy continued, "186,000 miles per second. The speed of light. Traveling for one year, it has traveled 5,865,696,000,000 miles. Over 5 trillion miles. Now do that for a million years. Over 5 trillion million miles. This is a number we can only see on paper. It means nothing to us. It is

---

1. De Broglie. "XXXV. A Tentative Theory of Light Quanta." *Philosophical Magazine Series 6* (1924).

2. Aspect and Grangier. "Wave-Particle Duality for Single Photons." *Hyperfine Interactions* (1987).

beyond our perception. We can think of it and pretend to know it, but we come short of truly grasping its significance.

"A ray of light from the sky on a clear summer night has traveled to our eyes to greet us, and we just look at it with no gratitude for where it has been, what it has seen along its journey, and how far it has traveled. Starting from a point across the galaxy, passing by other suns and planets we have no idea have ever existed, millions upon millions of miles. The giant knows what it means for the light to travel the distance it has. Just as we know what it is like to sail a boat around the world nonstop.

"The colossal realm of the giants, planets, suns, galaxies, and beyond is just as difficult to grasp as the infinitesimal subatomic and quantum world. Can we really say we understand the subatomic realm? Sure, we have a concept of it just as the giant had a muddled concept of the cellular world. We also have a concept of the boundless universe, but infinity is beyond our minds. The subatomic world is another infinity. We understand it through analogies, equations, and indirect experiments. These equations and experiments are valid and do give us a glimpse into what may be there, but to say we can take hold of and understand a world we are aliens to is unwise. We have not mastered our own world; weather can destroy cities in an instant and end many lives; an asteroid can strike at any moment, and we could not do a thing about it. We are truly along for the ride. Andy, it is very important to realize that the realm of molecules, like DNA, operates on rules we do not consciously experience.

"Our perception of the small world is limited by our egos and our bodies. Even though our eyes are not capable of seeing small objects, with the help of machines we can. How small can we go though? When will our mental capacity run out as the giant's brainpower did?

"There are processes occurring in the small world of molecules, right under your eyes that you cannot see or feel. No matter how much the doctors of your world think they know, they will always fall short since some parts of nature are unknowable because of the paradigm they believe in, limiting the amount of knowledge possible for them to know. They cannot understand all of the influences on your DNA. Forces rooted deeply in the structure of your body and surrounding environment. Your doctors think your disease is genetic with an unalterable course. They called it your fate! This is not true Andy!

"Our egos are often so strong, telling us we know everything, that we forget our true potential. We mediate the world through our bodies. We see objects and structure and think they are separate from us, but they are a product of us! A creational reality, Andy. Don't you see how important this concept is for *you*!?"

Andy sat silently, attempting to grasp Jeremy's words, trying more than anything to believe what Jeremy had said but also feeling conflicted and somewhat angry, realizing that Jeremy was saying Andy was responsible for his own illness.

Jeremy let his statement be, knowing it would take time for Andy to sort through this counterintuitive and indirectly offensive information. Jeremy was not trying to hurt Andy but knew self-reflection was required. Andy needed those words and Jeremy hoped he would embrace his message, giving him optimism that was long lost. Having already gone through the pains of accepting his dying body and the unbearable transformation it brought to his life, Andy was now faced with a change that could bring him health.

Jeremy continued speaking, his voice carried on the wind to Andy's ears, "Let's talk a little about other forces in the universe relevant to our discussion on perception: dark energy and dark matter.[3,4,5] These represent energy and matter that should exist but evade direct sight and measurement. Both dark energy and dark matter account for about 95 percent of all mass-energy. Meaning, the matter we know and feel only represents about 5 percent of

---

3. Freeman and McNamara, *In Search of Dark Matter* (2006).

4. Aguilar et al. "First Result from the Alpha Magnetic Spectrometer on the International Space Station: Precision Measurement of the Positron Fraction in Primary Cosmic Rays of 0.5–350 GeV." *Physical Review Letters* (2013).

5. Ade et al. "Planck 2013 Results. XVI. Cosmological Parameters." *Astronomy & Astrophysics* (2014).

the reality we see! Dark energy is a force responsible, in part, for the expansion of the universe, while dark matter has been indirectly measured from its gravitational influence on the regular 5 percent of matter we know.

"The forces of dark energy and dark matter are very difficult to conceptualize by humans because we do not consciously feel them in everyday life. However, we are within the field of these unseen forces, so are they not influencing our lives?

"Day by day it may seem like the answer is, 'no' since these forces do not seem to push against us like a wind when we walk to work, but they still surround and permeate our bodies. Yet, other invisible forces are 'clearly' evident to us. Gravity, for example, pulls us down to the earth when we jump. It too is so integrated into our lives we don't conceptualize it as an external force unless we stop and think about it. Isaac Newton teased this force out of reality and explained its behavior, but previously no one had quantified and described this invisible energy.

"What forces are seamlessly woven into our lives that we don't know exist but affect us daily? The people before Newton knew if you dropped an object it would fall, but they did not know how this force persisted throughout space and kept our planet in orbit.

"What do dark energy and dark matter do to our lives as we carry on throughout our day? The giant can surely feel how dark energy plays into his life as the universe is stretched. He must account for it in his travels just as a sailor must correct for invisible wind when navigating across an ocean. Andy, there is unseen wind in our lives that we could be correcting for. You need to tune into this. How do dark energy and dark matter relate to the disease you are experiencing?"

Looking over towards Andy, Jeremy waited for a response. Andy did not know what to say. It was such a foreign concept, as if he was learning about the world all over again.

"Your disease is far more complicated than a strand of DNA simply pumping out bad proteins into your body," Jeremy said frankly. "That is only the biological part; an end result of something else. What is influencing your body has to do with other forces in nature. Your DNA responds to these forces, tuning in to pick up on the signals it receives like a radio antenna.[6, 7, 8, 9, 10]

"DNA is a channel for energy to flow through. The double helix structure allows electromagnetic signals to course through like a child going down a spiral slide. Energy is what mediates the structure of DNA[11] by connecting through a skeleton of fibers inside the cell,[12] which provide channels for energy, making you who you will become. It is difficult to feel these forces flowing through your DNA, but remember what I said before about us not feeling dark energy and dark matter? There are forces affecting us that we are not consciously aware of[13] and you are experiencing the end result: your disease!"

They sat in silence.

Andy was still conflicted and felt overwhelmed. *What forces are flowing through my DNA?*

---

6. For similar concepts see: Oschman, *Energy Medicine: The Scientific Basis* (2000), pgs. 67, 88, 177, and 178.

7. Solomon and Solomon, *Harry Oldfield's Invisible Universe: The Story of One Man's Search for the Healing Methods that Will Help Us Survive the 21st Century* (1998), pg. 38.

8. Similar concept in: Narby, *The Cosmic Serpent* (1999), pg. 131. This reference also delves deeper into unconventional theories of how DNA interacts with the world and discusses analogous ideas as described in The Conscious Whole.

9. Geomagnetic and solar magnetic energy may affect DNA: Ulmer et al. "Theory of Coupled Electromagnetic Circuits, the Connection to Quantum Mechanical Resonance Interactions and Relevance to Chronobiology." *arXiv* (2011).

10. Electromagnetism and ultrasound are mainstream treatments used for bone healing: Nelson et al. "Use of Physical Forces in Bone Healing." *Journal of the American Academy of Orthopaedic Surgeons* (2003).

11. Similar concept discussed in: Tombazian, *The Path to the 5th Dimension* (2012), pg. 76.

12. Oschman, *Energy Medicine: The Scientific Basis* (2000), pgs. 46, 55, and 67.

13. We do not feel most electromagnetic radiation, yet it can affect our bodies in unexpected ways: Volkow et al. "Effects of Cell Phone Radiofrequency Signal Exposure on Brain Glucose Metabolism." *JAMA* (2011).

Jeremy knew he had to impart all of the wisdom from the people of Meat Cove. He needed to inform Andy because he knew in his heart what Andy was looking for when he left in the first place: an answer for the cause of his illness and most importantly, a cure.

15

You will forget after you make the journey, but you must return to your core purpose; there is a reason you are making this journey and though it is absolutely evident now, when biology forms around your core, matter will take precedence

WAVES CRASHED IN FRONT OF THEM. The evening sun kept the men warm and content,[1] contrasting the cool, pushing breeze from the ocean rolling towards them. Boats were returning from every direction as large thunderclouds began filling the horizon. They both focused on the clouds and shapes they made, constantly changing, morphing as they pleased. Andy pictured himself as a cloud, able to change shapes with no more effort than a gentle breeze. He imagined life would be easier by emulating a cloud, constantly moving, having flexibility to be and do as you please, floating high above the ground.

Jeremy took a deep breath of ocean air. Energized, he continued, "When we smell the salty breeze and feel the warmth of the sun on our face, we are experiencing the small and large parts of nature simultaneously. Molecules from the ocean breeze get sucked into our nose and bind to receptors sending signals to our brain creating smell; we perceive the

---

1. Light therapy can be used for health benefits: Rohan et al. "Randomized Trial of Cognitive-Behavioral Therapy Versus Light Therapy for Seasonal Affective Disorder: Acute Outcomes." *American Journal of Psychiatry* (2015).

smell as salty. The deep blue of the ocean and white top of the waves are actually energetic waves of light or photons that have different energies. Our eyes pick up the light energy, which then send signals to our brain to create color.[2] We experience the depth and beauty of the ocean. It is amazing when you think about the warmth of the sun; we can actually feel heat emanating from this massive star that is incredibly far away from our planet! Yet it heats us up every day, and we take it for granted. The size of the sun is as incomprehensible as the size of the molecules we smell.

"We must be aware of the complete nature of the world around us. We are not isolated from theoretical parts of our world: the theory of the molecules floating around in space that we interpret as smell or the theory of energy the sun produces that we feel as heat. What about the theories of quantum physics? A world *seemingly* separate from our being, from our nature, and from our bodies. What secrets do these theories hold about our true self? Where is the wave function in our lives determining the likelihood of an event? Is the equation that says every possibility exists only theoretical and displaced from the individual?"

Andy looked down at his body, wanting to change his perception of his disease.

Jeremy, in a trance-like state, spilled more of the core knowledge to Andy, "There can be no separation from the nature of everything, and no objectivity if the one who is describing the world is also the one who is living inside of it. Objectivity is a created word to distance the self so the world can be described and measured, as if outside of subjectiveness. But this is a deception. The objective world, where nothing is under the influence of the mind, cannot exist.[3] It is a fallacy of thought. Our mind is the only thing that makes this world real! Without it, there is nothing!" Jeremy looked intensely at Andy. The passion in his deep blue eyes pene-

---

2. Perception of color is relative among different cultures: Roberson et al. "The Development of Color Categories in Two languages: A Longitudinal Study." *Journal of Experimental Psychology: General* (2004).

3. Discussed previously with associated citations.

trated Andy's body making it known how important this concept was to Jeremy and the people of Meat Cove. "The true fate of the cat in the box becomes real **only** when the mind observes and creates the form of the cat,[4, 5] alive or dead!"

The mind creates the cat. The mind creates the cat. The mind creates the cat. The mind creates the cat, Andy repeated in his head in a meditative state,[6, 7] like chanting an ancient mantra,[8, 9] focused on the possibility of not being as fixed as he thought he was. Not being the same structurally from day to day. *Maybe it is my mind, and for that matter everyone else's minds making the world and our bodies as we see them and the way we think they have to be. But, that's crazy because a house doesn't just disappear from one day to the next. Objectively, it is sitting on its foundation whether a person is present or not.*

Why would Andy think any differently if everything he saw was physically in the same place and unchanged all of the time, independent of an "observer?" He had never seen the quantum world Jeremy spoke of.

---

4. There has been a substantial amount of experimental evidence supporting the notion that the mind influences matter, relating to possible large-scale effects of quantum mechanics: Radin and Nelson. "Meta-Analysis of Mind-Matter Interaction Experiments: 1959-2000." *Healing, Intention and Energy Medicine* (2003).

5. Interaction of the mind with matter discussed in: Stapp, *Mindful universe: Quantum Mechanics and the Participating Observer* (2011).

6. Meditative practices can structurally change the brain: Hölzel et al. "Mindfulness Practice Leads to Increases in Regional Brain Gray Matter Density." *Psychiatry Research: Neuroimaging* (2011).

7. Conversely, harmful environments can also change brain structure: Sheffield et al. "Reduced Gray Matter Volume in Psychotic Disorder Patients with a History of Childhood Sexual Abuse." *Schizophrenia Research* (2013).

8. "DNA can be influenced and reprogrammed by words and frequencies"; this statement as well as other fringe ideas/research about DNA may be found in: Fosar and Bludorf. "Vernetzte Intelligenz: Die Natur Geht Online." *Omega-Verlag* (2001).

9. The subconscious mind is an important and powerful component that influences the conscious mind and body; more than just "positive" conscious thoughts are needed to change the body, the subconscious must be convinced as well! Discussed in: Lipton, *The Biology of Belief: Unleashing the Power of Consciousness, Matter, and Miracles* (2008), pg. 97.

Andy's thoughts and perception about life being objective, given to him by the Conscious Whole, led him to naturally think about the human body in the same objective manner. *My body is a structure too, just like a house, objectively there whether I'm present or not. Forces that can't be seen or felt do not affect DNA. How ludicrous*, Andy thought.

Countering Andy's thoughts, Jeremy continued speaking, "We live in a 'top down' causation and 'bottom up' creation world. The brain collapses the wave function to one state of atomic organization: top down causation. Atoms create DNA, which builds a body and a brain: bottom up creation. The brain exists in one configuration for only one moment, which is its physiology, biology, and anatomy. This state of neurons and neurotransmitters then builds reality and the body. The placebo effect[10, 11] is really more of a mind-atom effect."

Bouncing between his old ideas and new knowledge, Andy was confused about what he really thought and believed. Completely new to him was the idea about the body not being structurally stable without a human observer, and the concept of unknown, invisible forces flowing through the body. Andy had a vivid flashback of his grandfather's funeral when he was a teenager.

The family had decided on an open casket. Andy never knew why they chose that, but he was sure after he left he wanted to be cremated. He did not want people staring at his dead body. He remembered walking up to the casket; everybody took their turn and said a little something. Andy did not have anything planned to say, he felt like he was not even there. *That's not grandpa*, he said under his breath. *Sure, that's his body, but that's not **him**.* It was not the same man who taught Andy how to catch turtles in the lake. It was not the same man who would bake the best struffoli, covered in honey and sprinkles; that was not him in the casket. He was sure they must have changed the body. Why was the same warmth he felt when he

---

10. Harrington, *The Placebo Effect: An Interdisciplinary Exploration* (1997).
11. Mayberg et al. "The Functional Neuroanatomy of the Placebo Effect." *American Journal of Psychiatry* (2002).

was around his grandfather absent? He did not understand. This was not his grandfather. He wanted to know where he went.

Jeremy's words were beginning to change Andy's perception of the body. *We hold onto our physical self so tightly and with so much emotion that we can never see the fact that we, too, will someday leave our bodies,* he thought. He was now starting to see how he had fallen into the trap he was blindly led into, the trap set by the Conscious Whole.

It told him his disease was, "Who he was."

"It's permanently written into your DNA," his doctor had said with confidence.

"Your fate is chosen and can not be changed," Andy's dear family reminded him.

No! Andy thought. *It's not who I am. I am the one who is writing my DNA to make me who I am. My grandpa is not in his body anymore; he is not trapped by his DNA.*

Written onto the particles of Andy's grandfather's being and onto all of the particles that he had ever interacted with were entangled connections of previous contacts. His light had moved on, not with his physical body any longer but connected to particles that would go back into the earth. The memories of who he had been written onto the recycled particles. Still the same person he was when Andy knew him but transcended after death.

Do I have to wait until death to transcend my own body? My supposed hardwired piece of machinery that is permanently fixed? Does every possibility really exist? Andy reflected on Jeremy's comments. *If I could only be like the cat in the box, then every possibility physically does exist. I wouldn't have failing organs. I wouldn't have this disease. In my box, I would have two possible states: one diseased, paralyzed self and the other a healthy walking man,* Andy's positive thoughts raced through his mind toiling over his belief structure. *I just need to look for and see that healthy self.*

It was one of those summer evenings. The kind you never want to end. They both sat on Jeremy's deck that hung over the cliff, Jeremy in an old weather-worn wicker chair and Andy in his wheelchair. The backs of their chairs pressed against the side of the house, scraping off layers of paint that had been reapplied many times. Beneath the bright blue paint was another layer, slightly less bright. And below that another. The sun was setting over the hills directly behind them with its late, warm, lazy rays providing enough light for the fishermen to make it back to port, a beacon guiding them home. This was Jeremy's favorite time of year. He was always happy to just be sitting there, watching the distant clouds morph from pink, to orange, and finally to brilliant red hues. He loved losing himself in the moment, feeling as if he was staring directly into his own creation.

The sun, way out in space, felt like glowing embers during winter keeping Jeremy and Andy warm and blissful.[12] The breeze from the ocean had a thick, filling smell, full of salt.

Andy thought about his childhood, when he would play outside with friends, running around until dark, chasing lightning bugs. He missed those days. He missed being able to run and this evening reminded him of that time in his life. He closed his eyes and felt the breeze on his face.

Andy breathed in deeply.

He did this for a few minutes, thinking of nothing but air moving in and out of his lungs. He wanted to be free. He wanted to run.

Andy took another deep breath.

He focused on the energizing air flowing into his lungs and the sweet aroma accompanying it. When he exhaled, Andy felt something change. He felt invigorated, as if he could just stand up and run around again.[13] Surely the cells in his legs could remember the days of running. The cells in his brain remembered the minutest details of those nights. *Doesn't the*

---

12. Ultraviolet light exposure increases activity in the reward center of the brain: Harrington et al. "Activation of the Mesostriatal Reward Pathway with Exposure to Ultraviolet Radiation (UVR) vs. Sham UVR in Frequent Tanners: A Pilot Study." *Addiction Biology* (2012).

13. Self-healing discussed in: Sha, *Power Healing: Four Keys to Energizing Your Body, Mind and Spirit* (2003) and Petty, *Healing, Meaning and Purpose: The Magical Power of the Emerging Laws of Life* (2007).

DNA in my nerves remember how to run? Andy thought. *Why would they want to stop and become sick? Does my DNA have the only say in who I become? I want a say in who I am!*

Andy and Jeremy spent another hour watching the beauty around them. The change from dusk to night. To the west the sky smoldered, to the east stars began sparking. Andy thought how strange it would be if someone on a far-off planet was looking at his sun and calling it a star, just as he was calling their sun a star.

The cool air showed both men indoors. Lying down in bed that night, Andy thought about his life and what he wanted to do next. He slowly dozed off.

Part III

"Black Elk, a Sioux, talks about the hoop of many hoops. He says that above the people is a hoop, a conscience, the total belief of the people. If the hoop is sick, meaning dysfunctional, codependent, a lot of alcoholism, family abuse, violence, racism and sexual abuse, the people can get used to this and think this is normal. In other words, the people are asleep. If we have left the spiritual way of life, the people are asleep. If we are giving our power to another entity, the people are asleep. In most tribes, there are Coyote Clans. The job of the Coyote Clan people is to wake the people up. They need to become a nuisance and irritate the people. We must return to the spiritual walk."

VERNON COOPER, LUMBEE TRIBE[1]

---

1. Cooper. *White Bison Elder's Meditation of the Day.* (July 25, 2011).

16

Teachers walk amongst the masses, ironically unnoticed despite their differences; the masses envelope themselves in sameness and find security in their homogeneity; look into the extra-dimensional origins of those whom you judge and know they are here with a purpose

THE MONTHS PASSED AND JEREMY SET OUT to sea with other fishermen for the fall catch. They would work for three weeks on the ocean before returning with enough seafood to support the town through winter. Andy spent his mornings exploring the village, enjoying the beautiful scenery, and thinking a lot about the last few months; how he felt free from the routine he thought he needed in life; how living in a peaceful environment eased his tension. But Andy also thought of home, missing his family and friends, and considered returning. However, he knew in his condition he could not make the drive back alone.

Andy's thoughts swayed between the new ideas of Meat Cove and the paradigm of the Conscious Whole, wondering what it was like beyond Meat Cove. He had found this far-off place, supposedly non-existent to his old world. *What else was out there? What was it like on other planets orbiting stars in the sky? What about beyond visible space?*[1] The Conscious Whole conditioned its people to think within its limits. Andy, although

---

1. For a discussion on antimatter, a world of matter that is invisible and seemingly separate from ours see: Close, *Antimatter* (2009).

beyond the oppressive hand of his former life, was not fully conscious of being released from the Conscious Whole but rather was experiencing openness of mind that came with leaving the world of his past.

Yet, while some days Andy's optimism shone brightly, other days his mood was stagnant, focusing on his disease and upcoming death. The hope Jeremy's words brought was only theoretical in Andy's mind, and he could not deny his health was noticeably deteriorating. It was becoming more difficult for him to breathe, and he became even shorter of breath when speaking. Coughing was a challenge. Mucus built up in his lungs from dying cells, and he could only let out small weak coughs, which did almost nothing to clear out his lungs, no stronger than a passive exhalation. He would nearly choke to death at night and was morbidly surprised each morning that he had made it through the night.

Andy now needed the wheelchair almost all of the time, as his muscle strength seemed to be declining exponentially. He was feeling really sorry for himself and felt like he did not want to continue any longer.

It was a bad day and Jeremy was not around to elevate Andy's mood. Depression.

The inevitability of his situation, he thought, made life not worth living. Frightened by the uncontrollable fate ahead, Andy's thoughts paralyzed him; a man paralyzed psychologically and near physically by fear. Andy felt, and knew, there was no way out. Trapped in his physical body, soon he would only have control of his thoughts, leaving the body behind like a ready-made casket enclosing his mind with no way to express what he was feeling or desired. His eye movements would be one of the last bodily functions to remain, allowing him to only look around at his world. Everyday he saw this future closing in on him.

Andy decided to get out of the house and headed down the trail towards the harbor in his wheelchair; he hoped the fresh sea air would help him breathe easier and improve his mood. He remembered the vibrant wildflowers that had covered the mountain, which had passed, giving way to brown and maroon colored grass. The fall days were becoming shorter and shorter, with grayness now blanketing the sky; Andy could not help but see the correlation between the transition from summer to fall with his own life ending soon.

Halfway down the trail, he noticed another path leading directly towards the ocean, previously obscured by the tall summer grass; it seemed to come up out of nowhere. He figured he might as well explore, since the trail lead to the ocean anyway. The path dropped steeply down the face of the mountain, winding back and forth. Andy could barely navigate it with his wheelchair, but his depression and self-destructive thoughts numbed any worries of falling onto the rocks below. The trail took him south and eventually leveled out, ending above a threatening, rocky cove with the tall mountain towering behind him. Near vertical sheets of rock dropped into the sea, guarding the town against unwanted visitors. Strong fall winds from the northeast not only brought cold air but also a fierce ocean swell. The vigor of the currents and waves kept people far away from this isolated section of Meat Cove. Periodically, icy water sprayed Andy's face; the lack of sensation in his arms and legs left him yearning for some type of feeling elsewhere on his body, and the cove gave Andy what he needed at that moment.

To the south, a small house was perched on the cliff's edge; the same dark gray color as the surrounding rocks with a rusted metal roof seamlessly blending into its surroundings like a chameleon sitting on a small outcropping of rocks. It looked uninhabited, but smoke coming from a stovepipe on the roof indicated otherwise. Andy could not imagine someone actually living in that place! It looked like it was going to fall into the water! An even smaller trail than the one leading to the cove went from the perch where Andy was to the house, not wide enough to fit Andy's wheelchair.

Suddenly, an old man who looked at least ninety-five years old popped his head out of the front window, leaning over the ocean. A wave splashed up, just missing the house. *How crazy is this guy?* Andy thought. Not long after disappearing from the window, the man was walking towards Andy on the precarious path. He was hunched over using a wooden cane but walked as if strolling through a field. The man had thick silver hair, which was elegantly combed to one side, styled to perfection. As he approached, his small beady eyes peered at Andy from the depths of his head looking like perfectly polished stainless steel spheres. Andy got a sick feeling in his stomach. Strangely, he felt like he was looking at a long, lost friend.

An out-of-key, piercing voice said, "I guess you're the one I've heard about. I remember the days when I had the same thoughts, just like you. It wasn't long ago."

Andy wanted to leave immediately; get the hell out of there. Get away from the possibility of change in his future.

Russell was a watchman for the South Seas and was the first to spot missionaries from the Conscious Whole, remaining at his post with the same intention of keeping out unwanted visitors. He was the first to see Andy drive in months ago but had yet to meet the newest member of Meat Cove. Russell enjoyed the solitude of living in his remote dwelling and the satisfaction of being intertwined with nature.

He sat on a rock near Andy and began speaking in his high-pitched voice that echoed the sounds of the sea birds, "I can help you, but you have to trust me." Russell paused for a few moments, gauging Andy's reaction. Even though Andy felt so powerless, he still held onto his inner strength to a fault, not letting others help him even as his illness progressed. Andy knew he should say something, but no words came out of his mouth.

"I would like you to know that what I am going to show you is not unique to me, to this place, or to you. It's simply part of the fabric of reality." Andy suddenly noticed an elegance and articulateness to Russell's voice, sounding more like the smooth vibration of a hummingbird rather than squawking, raucous seagulls. He was looking at the ground when Russell said those words so he did not know if Russell was actually speaking or if he was imagining what he was saying.

All of a sudden, Andy noticed their surroundings felt like a lucid dream, a strange multi-dimensional awareness, where Andy could feel every square inch of his body at the same time. It was amazing since he had lost most of the sensation in his body, but he could now feel a flow of vibrating energy resonating through him. The vibrations originated from Russell's voice and connected Andy to everything around him: to the rocks on the ground, to the tiny brown plants along the edge of the trail, to the crisp ocean air, and even to Russell's body. Andy could viscerally feel the connectedness. There were no boundaries where his body ended and the rest of the world began.

Andy had heard of "oneness" in the world, but he had never thought about it in the context of the real world he lived in. Andy's state of mind had changed as well; his bad mood had abated.

Russell spoke again in the same elegant voice, "It's amazing, isn't it?"

"Yes…it is. But what am I feeling?"

"This is one of the realities of the world. One that is with every person at every moment but rarely ever experienced, explored, or thought about. I was once fraught with depression and hatred and was so angry that I wanted to kill myself, but then this was shown to me." Russell paused allowing Andy to acclimate.

"In this other reality, we can connect to our core state of being and see our true potential. I had become a black hole before, sucking in all of the energy around me, taking in every little ounce until I had created an empty universe surrounding my body. I thought everything in the world was bad, and there was no good, so I compensated by holding onto everything that happened to me. No one would get close because they could feel my emptiness and despair. I didn't even want to be with myself, but the powerful force of my black hole wouldn't let me escape.

"Where we are right now is a dimension of infinite potential, where all is possible." Russell stopped speaking, while his energetic body questioned Andy's, *'How do you think I found the health I am enjoying right now, during my later years of life?'* He paused, staring intently at Andy with his tiny eyes attempting to draw the answer from Andy's mind.

Andy was taken aback and did not know what to say.

The Conscious Whole

Russell continued, patiently allowing Andy to take it all in, "Here, all of the possibilities exist! Every possible arrangement of matter is here, with us. In the world we are used to living in, we are fooled into thinking the one permutation of matter we see is the only one that is possible. In truth, what our eyes see as the material world is one form of one reality drawn from infinite possibilities for that one instant. But matter is constantly changing! Coming into and out of our 'normal world'.[2] Every moment there are new possibilities forming matter that becomes reality for one point in time. The following instant another set of possibilities become real. A dance between worlds happening at every moment!

"What we know as time is the appearance of all the pieces of matter coming into and out of the 'normal world' in succession, observed in sequential order, interpreted by our brains as time.[3,4] In actuality, we are just seeing moments of possibility coming into reality all stacked up upon one another."

Andy thought about Millrift and how they did not speak in the past or future tense, as if observing all of time at once, instead of fractionated into discrete, chosen units.

"At one moment, pieces of an atom come into this world and contribute to the creation of the rock I am sitting on. The next moment, they leave the 'normal world' and go back into the soup of possibility only to be replaced by another form of matter representing the rock I am sitting on, contributing to the next unit of time I experience."

Just like the cat in the box is a possibility until it is observed, Andy thought.

Andy looked down at his hand and strangely saw all of the structure once making up his healthy hand overlaid on top of his current, diseased,

---

2. The 'normal world' here refers to the 4 dimensional world while the 'abnormal world' would be the other dimensions of the world as discussed and cited previously. Also, maybe the 'abnormal world' is the world of dark matter, which may represent these other unseen dimensions?

3. Walker, *The Physics of Consciousness: The Quantum Mind and the Meaning of Life* (2000).

4. Barbour, *The End of Time: The Next Revolution in Physics* (1999).

atrophic hand; a blueprint for health; a three-dimensional form composed of potential atomic positions to form a hand. Andy could see the atoms, like a blanket of translucent indigo blue covering his hand.[5, 6, 7]

Russell continued, "Right now we are sitting in the deepest realm of possibility and can see all of the potentials at once with every form of matter existing at the same time!"

Andy thought about the wave function and what he had learned from Jeremy. *The wave function must not be collapsed but still open to all possibilities, not continually collapsing as it does in the "normal world".*

The atoms around Andy's hand represented not only the atoms in existence in the "normal world" but also atoms in the other six[8] dimensions. When a single particle is isolated and viewed, it is not static but constantly going back and forth into and out of the physical, four-dimensional reality. All of the atoms making up the blueprint surrounding Andy's hand were particles that normally go into and out of reality;[9] the difference was that Andy perceived all of the possibilities at once!

This must be what Jeremy meant when he said I "would have to experience it", Andy thought, mesmerized by the blue light emanating from his hand.

The blueprint lightly covered him, waiting for the opportunity to manifest and construct what Andy once knew to be real. Andy mentally picked out the atoms needed to create the anatomic components of a

---

5. Choi et al. "Biophoton Emission from the Hands." Journal-Korean Physical Society (2002).

6. Nakamura and Hiramatsu. "Ultra-Weak Photon Emission from Human Hand: Influence of Temperature and Oxygen Concentration on Emission." *Journal of Photochemistry and Photobiology B: Biology* (2005).

7. Visualizing energy of the world discussed in: Kamm, *Unlocking Your Intuitive Power: How to Read the Energy of Anything* (2007).

8. See previous citations regarding multiple dimensions; there is debate about how many dimensions exist, maybe 10-11 in total, but it is presently not certain.

9. For concepts related to particles coming into and out of existence as matter and antimatter see: Close, *Antimatter* (2009).

healthy hand, manipulating structure, observing how the instructions fit exactly where needed.

Russell continued, "While in this realm, we can be our infinite potentials. Free from constraints and partly unbound from our earthly bodies. Through our minds we can access infinity, however, we have a very important choice to make: to permit infinity or to set limits. This can be a conscious decision, but it is often left to the power of the unconscious psyche. This moment is temporary for you. When you go back into full material form, you will once again be forced into your perishable body by *your* perceptions. Yet, in the world of possibility we are free without having to choose one path."

Enthralled by the experience but somewhat disappointed by what Russell had just said, Andy responded, "If I have seen and experienced this infinite world, why can't I use the potential to become whatever I want?"

Russell was silent, shaking his head, slightly upset by Andy's question. He said nearly shouting, "It's your mind! You create reality from the pool of possibilities! What you choose to create, whether you are consciously aware of it or not, becomes what you observe and what you live with. What are you choosing to create!?"

Andy was caught off guard by Russell's harsh response.

"The world of possibility is not a place for you to look down upon the material world. You must see it as part of the bigger picture, one component of the whole, a template for your life, and a pre-dimension of existence where we can view numerous routes for reality to follow. For years it has been known there are other dimensions besides the three spatial and fourth dimension of time. However, for some unknown reason I was shown the additional dimensions, kind of like stumbling upon a secret lake in the middle of the woods no one has seen in centuries," Russell chuckled.

"Importantly, do not denounce the material world outside of the space we are in, but instead allow it to be a teacher. It is no longer a secret from your consciousness, for you have felt its elegance and tasted its infinity.

This is where our moments begin and your mind will choose the next instant from an endless list!"

Before Russell left, he gave Andy a long hard look. His deep-set, small, silver eyes reflected the world before him. Andy had not realized that Russell was blind!

Russell stood up, pulled out a comb from his back pocket to style his now wind-blown hair, gazed towards the ocean, and then walked back on the narrow trail to his home, hanging over the edge of earth. Although he walked like someone who could see perfectly fine, he was not using his eyes to see. In fact, Russell partially lived in the infinite world, using it as a portal to see in a different way: for walking, watching the weather, and protecting the town.

This blind man of Meat Cove would only be classified as blind based on standards set within the Conscious Whole, where they solely believed in the material world. The other dimensions, even though thought to exist, were not believed to be connected in any way to the life people lived; too abstract and far off to have any influence. Therefore, people like Russell who lost their sight of the material were blind, without a doubt. The Conscious Whole set standards for sight, and according to their standards, blind people were blind, only allowed to see what the Conscious Whole saw. However, in Meat Cove people lived within their own limits and boundaries and did not establish the same definition for sight. Russell used the plane of many possibilities to see impending moments about to materialize allowing him to navigate the world.

Two hundred and sixty-three years ago, Russell believed he had nothing left. He was plagued by loneliness, even though he purposefully isolated himself on the southern cliff. Depression filled every space he occupied, as if it was the normal way to live. His health was terrible, as he did not care for his body or mind. He thought he had nothing more to contribute to the community; no purpose and no goals to strive for. One cold, gray morning he stood up on the wet rocks and prepared to jump. Blind from illness and depressed from his own intentions, Russell leapt into another world. As he fell, gaining speed, the rock wall racing by, Russell waited for impact. Yet, an unexpected variation in reality changed the course of the world forever.

Resting within solid earth, a being Russell was intimately connected with outstretched its hands catching him before the point of no return. Relative to the size of a human, this being was a leviathan and existed at the interface of the four-dimensional world and other lands. Its large eyes and smooth head gave it a reptilian-like character. As Russell lay on his back, cradled in the large weathered hands as if in a hammock, he looked into the being's eyes. Now able to see, Russell thought he had died.

The being wept as its soft soul mourned Russell's actions. It could not allow him to take his life. It would not allow him to think life was worthless; to believe there was nothing else to do. The interworld being could not only see the other dimensions but also lived within them. It innocently did not understand why Russell thought his life needed to end. Why this man who had lost perception of a fraction of the world thought there was nothing more?

Russell looked around and could see the town of Meat Cove. Vague silhouettes walked around. Weather formed far off in the distance as a storm approached thousands of miles away. He asked, "What is this?"

The being smiled but was silent. It reached its long arms upward and placed Russell back at the top of the rocks as it slipped away between dimensions and out of sight. Russell was in a state of delirium as he struggled to grasp reality. *Did I really jump or just imagine that?*

However, the truth of the situation slowly sank in as Russell worked with his newly found sight to walk back home. He worked in the physical realm for months to build back his life, make social connections, restore his health, and contribute to the community. Life was never the same after standing above the rocky cove as he went back and forth from the physical world and into the infinite, traveling on the connection shown to him by the strange being that he would never meet again.

Russell saw many things that would be invisible to the people of the Conscious Whole.[10, 11, 12, 13] Like the being had done for him, Russell held the wave function open long enough for Andy to see that the world is born from possibilities and a disease-free state always exists. Andy's perception and mind continually collapsed the wave function, choosing only one outcome: disease. A certainty still maintained by the Conscious Whole.

Even though Russell could easily navigate multiple dimensions, no one else used it with such proficiency; Andy would only get a fleeting glimpse.

Andy stayed where Russell had left him, looking down at his hand, which was still vibrating and glowing, however, the rest of his body felt like it did before. In the background, energy flowed, connected to the flux of energy surrounding Andy and contributing to a wave of light directly acting on the atoms in and around Andy's hand.[14] A gift had been given.

---

10. Just because something is invisible to some, does not mean it is invisible to all. See examples below.

11. Birds can see the earth's magnetic field: Stoneham et al. "A New Type of Radical-Pair-Based Model for Magnetoreception." *Biophysical Journal* (2012).

12. Sharks can sense electrical currents using specialized electrosensory organs: Freitas et al. "Developmental Origin of Shark Electrosensory Organs" *Evolution & Development* (2006).

13. Reindeer can see the ultraviolet spectrum of light: Hogg et al. "Arctic Reindeer Extend Their Visual Range into the Ultraviolet." *Journal of Experimental Biology* (2011).

14. Related concept and many others in regard to the interaction of the body with the energetic world discussed in: Gerber, *Vibrational Medicine: The #1 Handbook of Subtle-Energy Therapies* (2001).

17

You see her feed the man, as a mother would a child; her near paralysis supernatural compared to his inabilities; he relies on her and she provides for him; others walk by with pity on the woman's state of being and layer further pity on the man; yet, for him she is a liberator and demonstrates that disability is contextual; you think you are suffering until you see the affliction of others; you believe you can't get around until you see the immobility of some; in the context of the world you have entered, you were told of your disability and shown your path, which was their plan; be strong as the seers will show you there are others who must know your path

EVERY FORM IN THE UNIVERSE IS BOTH matter and energy at the same time,[1,2] existing simultaneously. Matter is the physical manifestation: the atoms in Andy's hand. Energy is the electromagnetic code of the matter: the light his hand emits.[3,4,5,6,7,8]

---

1. Look no further than Einstein's $E = mc^2$. Energy is equal to mass multiplied by the speed of light squared.

2. Also note wave-particle duality mentioned previously. A photon of light acts as a wave of energy and an individual photon (particle like) at the same time!

3. There is a significant body of research on light emission from living cells, called biophotons, with various points of view. Dr. Fritz-Albert Popp is one of the leaders in this area of study. Below are several citations from the literature.

4. Rattemeyer, Popp, and Nagl. "Evidence of Photon Emission from DNA in Living Systems." *Naturwissenschaften* (1981).

Andy sat in his wheelchair, bewildered by his experience. Light from the rocks, trees, sky, and even Russell had a specific and direct effect on the minute pieces of matter in the atoms of Andy's hand, affecting the strings,[9, 10] which are small units of energy, the constituents of subatomic particles such as electrons and quarks. Strings, as opposed to the particles they make up, are one-dimensional, and the unique characteristic of each string determines the type of subatomic particle they will create.

Unlike an apple, which has many defining properties, such as being round, tasty, and sometimes red, strings are only described with one dimension, as minute pieces of light. However, from one string to another, the type of light varies such as red, blue, yellow, or even light our physical eyes cannot see. The frequency of the string's light determines what the string will create; as such, strings are the basis of the physical matter we see and feel.

Many strings come together to form whole particles. The particles come together to make atoms. The atoms, formed from light, coalesce to create molecules. The molecules assemble to make sugars and proteins. The sugars and proteins conglomerate to eventually form an apple. Like adding ingredients to a soup, the countless frequencies of light, which are the strings, build a specific form of matter. One of the fundamental building blocks of nature is light. The apple is matter by the fact it exists in our presence, but it is light by the fact it is made from strings, or possibilities,

---

5. Cohen and Popp. "Biophoton Emission of the Human Body." *Journal of Photochemistry and Photobiology B: Biology* (1997).

6. Bischof. "Biophotons - The Light in Our Cells." *Journal of Optometric Phototherapy* (March 2005).

7. Van Wijk and Van Wijk. "An Introduction to Human Biophoton Emission." *Complementary Medicine Research* (2005).

8. Mayburov. "Photonic Communications and Information Encoding in Biological Systems." *arXiv* (2012).

9. Gubser, *The Little Book of String Theory*. Princeton (2010).

10. The validity of string theory has been debated; this reference discusses/addresses the issues: Duff. "String and M-theory: Answering the Critics." *Foundations of Physics* (2013).

from where the apple originates. The apple is both matter and energy, not one or the other, born from potential strings that materialize into reality.

All of the strings in existence are in Russell's world, yet only a small subset is born into the material world. Staying true to their source, traveling from the infinite world, strings become who we are. We call it dark matter, but it is really our birthplace, unseen to our eyes. Dark matter and energy are seemingly in a different realm but contain material that becomes the physical world. The expression of a string's light in our eyes is not constant. Shining and alive for us in the four-dimensional world and black to our eyes when concealed by the infinite.

The production of light is based on when and how strings are influenced by consciousness. A string must be brought to life to become real. For example, the low E string on a guitar can be a very low note if plucked alone or it can be a higher note if tethered by a finger and then plucked. Like a guitar string, the strings of particles also need to be manipulated to vibrate with light to create reality, plucked by the force of life, the force of awareness. Strings must be directed by consciousness and will not simply vibrate on their own without anyone looking at them. Strings are very, very small and therefore follow the law of quantum physics like the cat that lives in the box.

Receivers of the world's energy, strings resonate with surrounding light by harmonic resonance.[11] This process occurs when a light frequency exactly equal to the string's innate frequency, the resonate frequency, vibrates the string and brings it to life, creating a communication link and a transfer of energy from the material world to the string living in the world of possibility. The string is then brought to life and manifests into reality, contributing to a part of an atom that makes up the whole atom that makes up the molecule and so on. Structure built upon structure building

---

11. Resonance, the property of one system oscillating at a specific frequency tuning into another system with related variables allowing both systems to oscillate in sync: Pauling, *The Nature of the Chemical Bond and the Structure of Molecules and Crystals: An Introduction to Modern Structural Chemistry* (1960), pgs. 10-14.

more structure creating the reality we experience, all based on light. Matter is light and vice versa.

The human body is no exception: a summation of a nearly infinite number of strings vibrating at unique frequencies, which then build particles, and then atoms, and then molecules, and then cells, and then organs, and finally a body. As such, a spectrum of light can be used to define each being.[12] As unique as a fingerprint,[13, 14] representing every light wave from all of the strings, which can be visualized as a colorful image of the human body, including colors extending outside of the visible spectrum.

Areas of the body appear differently depending on the composition of matter and strings. For example, the heart is an organ full of strings combining to make atoms that create molecules, which form distinctive muscle fibers allowing the heart to beat in synchrony and pump blood. The unique arrangement of molecules that make the special muscle fibers are formed from a particular ratio of atoms, which are composed of a very specific spectrum of light energy of strings to make the correct proportion and types of atoms. The spectrum of light represented by the strings of the heart is solely found within the heart and nowhere else in the body, which can be detected from the spectral image of the body. From the energetic fingerprint, physical anatomy may be identified and since every person is unique, analyzing the energy spectrum reveals insight into the body structure.[15] Not only do normal differences between

---

12. There are numerous ancient and current texts, books, and publications describing energy fields surrounding the body and related effects. An additional resource not cited elsewhere that describes energy fields, as well as how electromagnetism interacts with the body, is: Rosch, *Bioelectromagnetic and Subtle Energy Medicine* (2015).

13. Similar discussion in: Solomon and Solomon, *Harry Oldfield's Invisible Universe: The Story of One Man's Search for the Healing Methods that Will Help Us Survive the 21st Century* (1998), pg. 95.

14. Analogous concept in: Green, *The Keys of Jeshua* (2004), pg. 289.

15. There have been many controversial attempts to image the energy spectrum of the body, most notably by using a technique called Kirlian photography (Kirlian and Kirlian. *Photography and Visual Observation by Means of High-Frequency Currents* (1963)) and polycontrast interference photography (PIP, developed by Harry Oldfield as previously cited).

people become apparent, but disease is also written into an individual's spectral image.

Waves of light represent the person, who they are, and what they are made of; hues of the rainbow beyond what the eye can see and beyond what instruments have measured. Light we do not even know exists. This is what makes us up. This is where we come from.

Just as the human body needs water and nutrients to sustain matter, the strings of the body need light and energy to survive. Without light, strings, and for that matter our physical bodies are only potentials in the infinite dimension of existence apart from the material world, existing as antimatter.[16]

There is a constant interaction of light energy between the human body and environment. A continuous exchange. Any condition giving energy to or taking energy from strings changes their state of existence; real or potential; health or illness. For Andy, when he was with Russell, the new flow of energy gave him health, and his new strings resonated with light from the environment and from Russell. The infinite light from Russell's strings projected from him[17] like the sun warming the earth, bathing Andy. His energy lit up Andy's dormant strings, which were once only possibilities but now shone as a blueprint surrounding his hand. Years ago, Russell had found this healthy light energy after spending most of his life deflecting it with his negative outlook on the world. He transformed into a representation of health and healing. Russell's energy spilled out of his body through the bridge between worlds. Fatefully, that morning Andy stumbled upon a pool of good, changing his life forever.

---

16. Antimatter is not a controversial theory or concept (see previous citations). Antimatter is depended upon daily in hospitals for positron emission tomography (PET) scans, which are used primarily for oncology imaging. A radioisotope is injected into the body and emits a positron (antimatter!), which then creates photons that are imaged with special cameras.

17. Biophotons are quanta of light emitted from living systems, as previously cited.

18

The beings stopped their actions temporarily and looked upward; a portal was opened and another was peering into their space

Reality is created as a result of how an individual's light signature impacts the world,[1] bringing strings to light. A power that can be used for whatever purpose the individual chooses. Consciously or unconsciously. Good intention or bad intention.

The cat's state of existence is created by the observer's emitted light, constructing the seen world. Light, coming from the strings within the body and creating reality, pools as a round disc-like spool of energy above the head as the cloud of consciousness, which has an immediate and direct impact on the contiguous environment. Within the Conscious Whole there is a compilation of many individuals' light, creating a homogenized product of all of the individual conscious clouds; the Conscious Whole assumes the role as bearer of light emitting uniform energy, creating a standardized reality across all individuals. Strings are plucked into existence based upon the collective whole with the same set of strings brought into reality at every moment; possibility is reduced, defining the physical limit.

As Andy came into a new collective whole, Meat Cove, his mind was partly released from oppression the Conscious Whole had placed over his

---

1. Optogenetics uses light to control neurons, which have been genetically modified to be light sensitive: Deisseroth. "Controlling the Brain with Light." *Scientific American* (2010).

thoughts. Whereas the people of the Conscious Whole were numb and unaware of their contribution to the collectiveness, in Meat Cove a different collective contract was formed where people were aware of their participation, understanding the inherent power of a shared consciousness. Consequently, because of their foresight, the "Conscious Whole" of Meat Cove was not intrusive, coercive, or tyrannical, but instead everyone knowingly contributed their thoughts and ideas to the whole to be widely distributed and shared. Thoughts that were different or negatively affected another person would be addressed in an open, conscious manner. Additionally, as opposed to the binary code of the Conscious Whole, in Meat Cove more than two variables were allowed to exist due to their higher dimensional awareness, allowing more variety of thought. Meat Cove's Conscious Whole was conscious by creation allowing an evolving paradigm.

For Andy, a new vibrational character became a different state of existence, leading to a new form of being for the atoms in his hand. As such, the indigo colors of light translated into new permutations of matter. The blue light, with only minute differences in frequency and wavelength, like waves on an ocean, created atoms[2] in Andy's hand in different proportions than during his diseased state. A new arrangement of atoms formed the new nucleotide his DNA needed to build the correct proteins to sustain healthy cells his hand desperately needed for survival; a process of impossibility where Andy came from.

With a new sense of reality came a different perspective of life. Connecting to the flow of energy and seeing how its potential is born in the atoms, Andy knew there was more to the world than the prison he was locked into before. For now at least, his hand was free, but not even Russell believed Andy's experience was going to last.

However, Andy built upon the bridge Russell first created, making the connection between Meat Cove and the infinite world stronger than it

---

2. The energy field "is like a…template onto which your physical molecules are strung": Solomon and Solomon, *Harry Oldfield's Invisible Universe: The Story of One Man's Search for the Healing Methods that Will Help Us Survive the 21st Century* (1998), pg. 7.

had ever been. Andy believed in it beyond any doubt, allowing him to reinforce a bond between worlds in a way no one else in Meat Cove could have done. Unbreakable belief, previously his fault by creating routine in his prior life and eventually spawning illness, was now his salvation. Andy needed to believe in the infinite world. It was a matter of life and death for him, as any morsel of doubt would dissolve the world around him.

Andy's mind was more open than it had ever been, as he did not completely leave the world Russell had shown him. He felt as if prisms were attached to his eyes that separated individual beams of light, allowing him to see colors previously obscured by his preconceived notions of what was supposed to be real. Colors were the same, but now they carried depth and movement, and he could discern the finest difference between shades of the spectrum.

Still sitting where he had met Russell, Andy looked towards the northern side of the cove and two trees caught his attention. The trees had smooth, cream-colored bark and roots that hung onto the side of the cliff, threading their tendrils deep into the rocky surface. A physical space of about fifteen feet separated the trees at the roots and about five feet separated the trees at their tops. Bright streaks of sunset red, mango orange, and iridescent purple coursed vertically within the trees. The colors nearly burned Andy's eyes, making him squint.

Like vehicles moving along a highway, the colors were contained in mosaic-like packets, reverberating with life! Most of the packets were diamonds or squares, but some were complex rhomboids or thin needle-like projections. The smaller and thinner pieces moved faster with the needle-shaped ones zipping around like shooting stars, bouncing in unpredictable directions. Conversely, the squares moped along quite sure of where they were going, pushing the smaller pieces of energy out of their way.

As his eyes drew upward, an energetic connection between the two trees was apparent, even though their tops were separate in physical space; a seamless bond from one tree to the other. At the base, the same vehicles of energy traveled deep into the earth, going through every one of the roots, with an equal amount going out as coming in. The outbound energy dispersed into the soil, coursing towards the town. It then took a sharp turn downward, into the center of the earth, mixing with other tracks of energy that looked like highways deep below Andy's feet.

Moving his wheelchair to face the sea, he saw another stratum of translucent movement superimposed on the ocean swells. Feeling like he was seeing double, Andy rubbed his eyes, but the extra layer did not go away. It was a quarter step ahead of the swells, seemingly pulling them towards the rocky coast. Further out, a bright blue light pulsated upward. Perplexed, Andy stared and then noticed a fishing boat appear on the horizon minutes later, heading towards the harbor. The blue light continued its rhythm foreshadowing the boat's path. Andy turned his chair back towards the trail that led him to the cove. He scanned his surroundings, marveling at his newly found perception. The depression and hopelessness he had been feeling during the morning had completely disappeared. He had felt like there was nothing more for him to do or see in this world.

He could not have been more wrong.

Andy had been so overwhelmed by his situation he was not able to see beyond the ground in front of him. He had thought all there was in the universe was all he had experienced; all of the suffering, pain, and despair. Now, his environment was illuminated and bursting with new life.

Even though it was only Andy's hand that was beaming with new life and the rest of his body remained in a diseased form, he had hope. Though in the Conscious Whole, hope was not allowed. It lead to misguided beliefs, they were told. It was false, they said. It would result in disappointment, they proclaimed. Yet, the importance of hope is to allow new possibilities, which can change outcomes. The power that follows hope was quelled in the Conscious Whole for it would lead to change that could destroy the structure that kept the Conscious Whole alive.

Andy now had hope. Hope for better times in the future. Hope for days filled with new experiences. Hope for relief from his suffering. He was afraid to think it, but it gave him hope for a cure.

19

You must be certain that your path will be followed by the light beings; you will not see them, but their presence will be evident in the environment; subtleness that may easily go unnoticed; they are already in route but do not know time; their travel is instantaneous and timeless, and their future actions have already been implemented

THE BRAIN FILTERS POSSIBILITY BY COLLAPSING THE wave function, only allowing one through at a time creating one moment of conscious experience.

The moment we are in right now is composed of an infinite arrangement of matter. The raven outside is calling to his companions. The sun is shining. Waves of light refract through layers of the windowpane into our eyes. There is a table in front of us holding a half-full glass of milk. The chair we are sitting on is below us.

Our body is ill. Suffocation is a continual sensation. Air is in short supply. Panic is creeping into our space.

The cells of our airways have tiny hairs on them, oscillating to and fro, keeping the lungs healthy. Molecules within the cells are being assembled to control the hairs. DNA is in a specific sequence at one moment to correctly create the components of the molecules that control the hairs. Subatomic particles of DNA are resonating at the same frequency as light coming into the room through the window and into our bodies. At this

The Conscious Whole

specific moment, particles of our DNA in the cells in our airways are connected to the sun through light-matched resonant frequencies; providing life that has traveled across an astronomical distance in space. Time, for the light traveling into our bodies, does not exist. For time, when traveling at the speed of light, ceases to move. Taking zero time to reach our bodies, distance is not a factor for light.[1]

We are directly connected and in immediate proximity to the light that is keeping our DNA in sync, allowing it to create molecules to build cells with oscillating hairs that keep our lungs healthy. The infinite dimension light carries gives us eternal life in our bodies, for we are one with light since our strings are light. An unlimited number of configurations of matter are chosen at every instant, fed by light energy, repeated over and over for every moment of conscious experience.

Illness is a temporary state of nature as is the fullness or emptiness of the glass or the calling of the raven. The body is subject to change and influenced by the surrounding world.

Matter around a being's consciousness continually comes into form giving an existence, a physical experience, and a life mediated by the conscious cloud from strings of light. Every moment, the brain sorts through all configurations of matter based on the probability they will occur, calculated by the wave function. The more likely a glass of milk is to exist on the table, the greater the chance the brain selects that specific location for the glass. Once the brain chooses a state of matter, it then becomes real but only so for that one selecting brain.

However, when clouds of consciousness overlap and a strict paradigm is established, as in the Conscious Whole, all of the brains and all of the selecting becomes a community effort resulting in a communal reality. After the agreed upon reality is created, a brain can not go out-

---

1. If time stops at the speed of light, then how long does it take light to travel one foot or one million miles from the perspective of the light? The same amount of time: zero. Distance does not matter for light. If it takes zero time to travel anywhere, distance is irrelevant. Reviewed in: Gribbin, *Schrodinger's Kittens and the Search for Reality* (1995), pg. 79.

side of this boundary and create its own physical state of nature due to probability and the collective force of others. If 999 brains decide on a glass of milk being on a table in a specific house, one brain cannot overpower the rest by trying to manifest it on a bedside table in a different house. The probability is one out of 1,000 that the collective whole will decide on the one brain's preference for reality. However, it is more complicated than simply beating probability. It would also mean overruling the other 999 brains' will-power of creation for their chosen world, for some would feel very strongly about having their glass of milk in front of them. In addition, the collective power is not linear but exponential. Ten brains are not ten times as powerful as one but one hundred times more powerful.

As such, the communal reality is the same for all contributing brains and real to them, but there is no sense of anything being created or chosen by the whole; this power is hidden from view but is the driving force and movement experienced in the world.

If physically separated from a group, an individual may create on their own by removing the influence of others and hence undoing the power of collectiveness. Yet, the only way to overturn the collective whole is by numbers or strength. Within the brain, selecting of reality is like a computer circuit board, designed to analyze probabilities through on and off switches: yes and no answers, electrical impulse versus no electrical impulse. In doing so, it calculates the quantum equation to come up with a solution to the wave function. The brain then follows probabilities generated by the equation, abiding by the results, which then becomes reality for its field of consciousness.

Computation of the wave function is a product of an innumerable number of neuronal connections, which manifests as electrical activity in the brain. The field of consciousness, or the conscious cloud, is in part created by this electrical activity of neurons.[2,3] Each calculation is different from the one before and produces a unique code of electrical frequency and light, contributing to the total light frequency of the cloud and being. The rest of the conscious cloud is made from light emitted from the body's strings inside matter. This "light" energy is not just in the visible spectrum but also includes invisible light and magnetic energy. Light in the cloud in turn plucks corresponding strings into existence, thereby selecting reality, recreating existence at every moment.

As an example of this process at work, there may be a 94% chance a glass of milk will be on a table, a 3% chance the glass will be empty in the sink, a 2.999% chance the glass will be clean and in the cupboard, and a 0.001% percent chance the glass will be in outer space orbiting our planet broadcasting a pro-lactose television station.

Calculation of probabilities for the state of nature occurs in the cerebellum of the brain at the thoroughfare of major neural tracts. Each possibility is then filtered for selection, to create one reality, in deeper, less conscious areas of the brain called the reticular formation[4,5] and reticular activating system.

The reticular formation and reticular activating system do not rule it all; they must agree with signals coming from higher functioning areas of the brain called the cortical hemispheres where conscious awareness

---

2. The Electroencephalogram (EEG) is widely used in medicine to measure electrical activity of the brain, for example when assessing seizure disorders.

3. Another device is the Superconducting Quantum Interference Device (SQUID), which detects the magnetic field of the brain: Zimmerman, Thiene, and Harding. "Design and Operation of Stable rf-Biased Superconducting Point-Contact Quantum Devices, and a Note on the Properties of Perfectly Clean Metal Contacts." *Journal of Applied Physics* (1970) and Zimmerman. "Josephson Effect Devices and Low-Frequency Field Sensing." *Cryogenics* (1972).

4. The reticular formation is responsible for maintenance of consciousness and is, in part, involved with processing/filtering incoming sensory stimuli: Bickford, Luntz-Leybman, and Freedman. "Auditory Sensory Gating in the Rat Hippocampus: Modulation by Brainstem Activity." *Brain Research* (1993).

5. The reticular formation and sensory input filtering also discussed in: Buhner, *Plant Intelligence and the Imaginal Realm: Beyond the Doors of Perception into the Dreaming of Earth* (2014), pgs. 26-27.

arises. Electrical activity containing encoded information about possible states of nature, and the probabilities of each, goes from the cerebellum to the reticular formation and activating system, where probabilities are filtered and cross-checked with incoming sensory stimuli that also passes through the reticular sieve; fibers of the reticular system then communicate with the cortical hemispheres. At the same time, the cortical hemispheres are sending signals to the overworked reticular system about what the conscious observer believes to be the correct state of nature based on sensory stimuli and previous experiences. This influences the selection process and reorders probabilities against the already calculated probabilities made by the cerebellum and already once-filtered incoming sensory stimuli from the reticular system, during a second round of sorting.

Like bribing a referee at a sporting match, the cortical hemispheres alter probabilities calculated by the more objective cerebellum and persuade the pushover of a reticular system into filtering what is possible for the individual, erasing the possibilities of the glass of milk being clean in the cupboard or floating around earth, while adding numbers to the higher probability outcomes. Ninety-nine percent chance the glass will be on the table and a 1% chance the glass will be dirty in the sink. Like a slot machine at a sleazy casino skewing the odds, one configuration of nature is eventually released into the conscious cloud as an electrical code of energy generated by the brain, and strings are brought into reality; the world is seen by eyes of the being and falsely confirmed as existing independent of conscious experience: the individual creating reality.

Each brain and conscious cloud contribute to the whole. Many brains add their light energy together on a massive scale building an immense conscious cloud, the Conscious Whole, luring everyone into its trap of an independent existence from the world formed by its power of creation.

Parts of the brain are obligate calculators of reality and form developmentally during the object permanence phase of childhood,[6] signifying

---

6. Object permanence discussed in: Piaget, *The Construction of Reality in the Child* (2013).

formation of the brain as a calculator of the wave function. This stage is apparent when a young child plays "peek-a-boo". Before object permanence develops and when an object is hidden from view, the child will believe it has disappeared. When removed from hiding, the child is amazed at how the object suddenly came out of thin air. Yet, as children grow and mature, they soon realize hiding something does not mean it has ceased to exist, despite their inability to see it.

Object permanence has developed in the brain to accept an independent real world, where reality is stable and does not simply exist because it is being observed but real and true without an observer. The brain is wired during this stage to collapse the wave function, making the world appear permanent; a necessary function in order for life, as we know it, to exist. Prior to this state, the child is predisposed to live in a quantum world, which is not amenable for existence in how society evolved.

Despite the seemingly pre-programmed fate of the brain, infinity lies within; there are immeasurable outcomes for every situation, which are all possible, as well as other layers of existence that are equally as real as the words you are reading and as the inner sound of your voice. Your body is draped in additional layers of form, habitually not perceived but instead filtered and discarded by the brain if they do not fit into the chosen paradigm. The world is not just made from the brain's conditioned response to only see the physical four-dimensional realm, as there are at least six to seven other dimensions, containing other bodies and other layers of existence.

Connecting infinity to the physical body is via the core being. Woven into physical matter, it does not live as the brain does but uses the body as a bridge to connect to the physical, where this life experience occurs. Unlike the brain, the core does not calculate because it is not burdened by strict obligations the brain dogmatically follows. It lives in the world of infinity and multidimensionality and as such operates according to different principles, where all possibilities are possible; even the physically impossible!

20

Your core being traveled to its life and chose what it wanted to see; yet, dormancy is too often the outcome of such journeys

Racing thoughts served little purpose but to distract Andy from the present; always planning future actions and events, continually drawing him away from reality occurring at every moment. A very useful tool that at times needs to be silenced in order to listen to the present. With Russell's help, Andy toned down his brain's dominant influence over his reality, bypassing unconscious circuits hard-wired by the Conscious Whole. New possibilities were brought to life as the probability function was being calculated by novel statistics; Andy's cortical hemispheres did not alter results of the probability function as before by planning the future based on prior occurrences. The Conscious Whole had gone as far as building Andy's cerebellum to tailor the outcome of the wave function with specific regulations and limits. Brain cells assembled by the Conscious Whole only allowed certain "yes" and "no" answers. Other manifestations of reality were unavailable because particular neuronal connections were never established; the people of the Conscious Whole did not know any other way and continually experienced impossibility.

Statistics of the probability function are not absolute or real but instead a manifestation of creation, based upon outcomes in the created world. Every outcome is bound to its constructed subjective foundation with results mistakenly believed to be external and independent. "Objective" equations further veil and externalize the outcome, overshadowing the fact that statistical equations do nothing more than describe created results.

For example, it is widely considered impossible to walk through a wall, which is based on people examining walking-through-wall behavior. With zero events of people walking through walls, the likelihood or chance of someone walking through a wall is zero, which is then applied universally to everyone, everything, and everywhere morphing into a scientific fact. The statistics say there is a zero percent chance of a person walking through a wall. It is impossible! Yet, this "objective" science is purely based on **experience**! Interestingly, electrons are known to channel through solid surfaces[1] and it is technically within the realm of possibility for a person to also channel through a wall.

A more tangible example can be demonstrated with human behavior. If a patient has a poor diet and lack of exercise, they are at an increased risk for heart disease, stroke, and many other medical conditions. In this case, blood tests would demonstrate an abnormal metabolic profile, prompting intervention by the patient's physician.

"First, you must improve your diet by eating less processed foods, particularly those high in sugar," the doctor tells the patient. "But you must also exercise more by at least walking and lifting weights."

"Sounds like a plan," the patient responds.

Months later at a follow-up visit the patient's physician asks, "Have you changed your diet and exercised more since we last met?"

"Of course, I eat better and exercise more," the patient reports.

"Well, unfortunately your blood tests show you are still at an increased risk for a heart attack and stroke. We will have to more aggressively manage your health, as conservative treatment was not enough. I can give you medications to improve your metabolic abnormalities."

---

1. Robinson and Oen. "The Channeling of Energetic Atoms in Crystal Lattices." *Applied Physics Letters* (1963).

Unfortunately, the patient did not diligently or completely follow the doctor's original advice. He ate one more apple and one more banana per day than before but otherwise did not reduce his intake of processed foods. Instead of increasing his exercise significantly, he went on several walks following the initial appointment but none thereafter. The patient was truthful as he ate better and exercised more than before, but predictably only after taking medications did the patient's blood tests become more normalized.

The above scenario was repeated thousands of times, and scientists studied these patients. They found medications almost always improved health outcomes, whereas lifestyle modifications only benefited the minority of patients. For the tens of thousands with suboptimal diet and exercise regimens, there were a few hundred that successfully managed their health by positively changing their lifestyles.

The prudent scientists, steeped in the ways of the Conscious Whole, knew the rigors of the scientific method would answer their questions. The data was clear and obvious. Only a small percentage of people improved their health with lifestyle modifications. The statistics did not lie. Lifestyle modifications did not work for most people, therefore most people needed medications. This was science. This was fact. This was the world created by the patients and reiterated back to them, as if beyond their control. Mathematics demonstrated absolute and objective data and the collective power reinforced this created reality.

For Andy, a disease-free state was not allowed to manifest from the infinite world. Light corresponding to Andy's healthy strings could not exist within the Conscious Whole. While speaking to Russell and connecting to his conscious cloud within the world of all possibilities, Andy's brain was rewired and remodeled, allowing unknown states of nature to become real. The cerebellum changed its circuit board, following new statistical laws. His cortical hemispheres released their preconceived notions about how his hand should exist. His more permeable reticular formation now allowed these possibilities through to his conscious experience. His cortical hemispheres relaxed, allowing reality to come into existence. He emitted new light frequencies, light that created a new state of being.

What the brain calculates, using the quantum equation, are the probabilities of quantum particles, which ultimately create finite matter, including DNA. Within the Conscious Whole, Andy's DNA had a certain configuration and order. It determined his hair color, the shape and size of his skeleton, and the presence of disease or health. DNA built Andy's physical body and life. The misunderstanding within the Conscious Whole was the permanence of DNA[2, 3, 4, 5, 6, 7, 8] in a fate-driven deterministic paradigm of biology. The collective conscious cloud of the Conscious Whole thought

---

2. DNA can change by "spontaneous" mutations or external damage (i.e. ionizing radiation or carcinogenic substances), which may lead to disease or advantageous adaptations. For a description of spontaneous mutations see: Griffiths et al., *An Introduction to Genetic Analysis* (2005), pgs. 518-525.

3. The majority of mutations leading to cancer, for example, are from "spontaneous" errors during DNA replication, whereas one third of cases are due to inherited or environmental influences: Tomasetti and Vogelstein. "Variation in Cancer Risk Among Tissues Can be Explained by the Number of Stem Cell Divisions." *Science* (2015).

4. Epigenetics describes environmental/external factors altering the activity/expression of genes without changing the inherent genetic code; yet, variation in genetic code allows for different susceptibilities to environmental influences. Reviewed in: Nestler. "Hidden Switches in the Mind." *Scientific American* (2011).

5. Jumping genes change the DNA sequence in certain cells (particularly in specific parts of the brain) by inserting short segments of genetic code into the genome. Exercise (i.e. environmental influence) increases the rate of jumping gene activity. Reviewed in: Gage and Muotri. "What Makes Each Brain Unique." *Scientific American* (2012).

6. RNA, which is a type of messenger molecule that carries the code from DNA for protein creation, has been found to undergo editing in cephalopods, functionally changing the output of the genetic code from DNA: Liscovitch-Brauer et al. "Trade-Off Between Transcriptome Plasticity and Genome Evolution in Cephalopods." *Cell* (2017).

7. Effects of the mind on epigenetics discussed in: Lipton, *The Biology of Belief: Unleashing the Power of Consciousness, Matter, and Miracles* (2008) and Church, *The Genie in Your Genes: Epigenetic Medicine and the New Biology of Intention* (2014).

8. Peruse the literature and you will find mounds of research describing genetic etiologies for a plethora of diseases, conditions, traits, and emotions, to name a few, illustrating the focus placed on DNA.

DNA was permanent and so it became; but only within the Conscious Whole was this true.

When scientists discovered DNA, they found it carried orders and commands to build life. This, they thought, was the origin: the beginning of all life. The instructions to make a human being.

True.

However, scientists thought DNA and life could be reduced no further. When broken apart, DNA was nothing more than molecules and atoms. Thought to be blank pieces of matter, one atom of carbon no different than another. They paid no attention to the intricacies taking place in the subatomic world, to the connections among particles, to the communication between two quarks, and to the bizarre laws followed by cats in boxes. They ignored these scientific principles in relation to biology, for if they were accepted, people would have to recognize they were in part responsible for their diseases. But by reducing body and disease to a humanless molecule of DNA, responsibility could be relinquished and blame placed solely on defenseless DNA.

What individuals of the Conscious Whole did not yet understand was that DNA, like any other molecule of its size, is a quantum structure. It follows the laws of quantum physics, not Newtonian physics of an apple falling from a tree. DNA does not fall but exists in a transient world of superimposed forms selected by the subjective observer and the Conscious Whole. The Conscious Whole created reality, including DNA within their reality.

The scientists proclaimed, "See here! Look! Faulty DNA causes the mental illness of Attention Deficit Hyperactivity Disorder.[9, 10] We found it! Even at birth, alterations of brain structure are a result of diseased DNA!"[11] What they created, they found, ignoring their responsibility.

---

9. Khan and Faraone. "The Genetics of ADHD: A Literature Review of 2005." *Current Psychiatry Reports* (2006).

10. However, there is literature supporting environmental influences causing ADHD symptoms: Kabir, Connolly, and Alpert. "Secondhand Smoke Exposure and Neurobehavioral Disorders Among Children in the United States." *Pediatrics* (2011).

11. Knickmeyer et al. "Common Variants in Psychiatric Risk Genes Predict Brain Structure at Birth." *Cerebral Cortex* (2014).

The subjective observer ultimately holds the ability to create DNA. However, within the Conscious Whole, DNA's form was held by the collective thought. Hence, everyone within the influence of the Conscious Whole must have their DNA structured according to previously set rules. This did not allow Andy's DNA to be anything but diseased, simply because that was how the Conscious Whole's light brought strings into existence, which formed improperly ordered particles in his DNA. Disease was created for Andy.

Now, with Andy's DNA outside of the grasp of the Conscious Whole, he was able to completely see his DNA and body.

Possibility. All possibilities.

Under the influence of his own quantum-determined state of nature, his DNA could be anything. Quantum molecules coming into and out of existence, both there and not there. Existing only because they are being observed. Andy was now experiencing the new destiny of his hand, flowing from the bridge of light connected to Russell's world.

21

Nestled deep within, like a newborn bird in a nest, it opened its eyes; awoken from its slumber it felt ashamed, for in its recent absence chaos ensued; the path had been lost, but now the being could see

ANDY WAS NEAR THE OCEAN, THE SETTING sun cast a sheet of fluorescent pink clouds on the roof of the sky. He was amazed as the new blueprint on his hand acquired a more physical, solid form. His hand tingled, like the pins and needles of an appendage regaining blood supply, but he experienced no pain. Andy could feel small packets of energy shooting out from his fingertips, corresponding to miniature, thin pieces of blue light, like shooting stars, flying out and disappearing into nothingness.

The DNA was different within the cells of his hand. Like a newly opened factory with correct assembly instructions, his cells were producing nourishing proteins, bringing them back to life!

Hope was emerging, coming out of hiding, peering around the corners of his being, making sure doubt and fear had left. Hope does not cease to exist even though at times it may appear absent. Previously obscured by Andy's false perception of reality and his disease, hope had now found its place. Andy's breathing was in sync with the waves. The wind blew through his hair, and the sky reflected in his eyes.

Over the next few days, Andy spent less time dwelling on what he used to be and where his fate and DNA were supposedly heading. Jeremy had come back from his fishing trip and had plenty of great stories to tell Andy, and Andy to tell him.

Jeremy went on and on about life on the ocean as the two men sat in the living room in front of a warm fireplace. "It comes alive when you get a few miles offshore. The porpoises seem to come from nowhere and jump out of the water at the bow of the boat. Sea turtles casually float along, every once in awhile sticking their heads above water to take a breath. Schools of fish as big as islands! You have to come out next year."

"Wow, that must have been amazing!" Andy said, cognizant of the fisherman's tale but excited by the notion that he might be around long enough to see all those creatures.

"Yeah, it was great, but storms quickly reminded us we are aliens at sea," Jeremy said as his eyes grew wide. "On the second day, waves began building. We worked all day and then took a break for a late dinner. Below deck we felt the boat climb up a wave that did not seem to end and then like falling down a mountain, the boat slid down the backside of the wave and rolled on its side! Slowly, the boat righted itself, but before we knew it we were climbing up another swell. It was a close call and could have ended another way..." Jeremy trailed off.

"I'm grateful you made it back safely," Andy said, now feeling like a trip at sea would not be such a great idea.

"We always end the trip at a group of islands called the Three Tombs. Many boats sink there because waves crash on shallow reefs, but fishing is the best! The islands are part of an active volcanic hot spot, so the reefs are different every year.

"However, the most awe-inspiring part about the Three Tombs is the sunsets. The islands look like tall spikes coming out of the water, covered in bright green vegetation. That far out, the water is warm and turquoise blue because of tropical currents from the south. One evening we were fishing directly east of the three islands, and the sun set in perfect alignment. The most eastern island sat between the northern and southern islands directly in line with the westward sun as it was going down. The middle island is so tall and thin it split the sun in half making it look like two parallel sunsets from two suns! Most days there is a rainy mist on the islands teasing out every color of the sun. Once, I saw seven full rainbows, stacked on top of one another, containing colors outside of the visible spectrum."

Andy now knew of the colors Jeremy spoke of in a way he had never known before.

"You can feel oneness with light on the sea," Jeremy paused for a moment, "like being part of the sun with rays passing through you, providing nourishment[1] and then continuing towards their destination."

"I think I know what you're talking about," Andy said, nodding his head.

After Jeremy had settled back into Meat Cove and equilibrated to life on land, he and Andy once again met outside on the deck facing the ocean. The air was warm for such a late fall afternoon, so the men took advantage of the weather instead of being cooped up inside.

"I felt the changes that happened in Meat Cove while I was gone," Jeremy said smiling at Andy. "I saw how you were changing; the changes went beyond just you and your body."

Andy squinted his eyes and looked towards the horizon where the Three Tombs lay, feeling like he had a more in-depth sense of what the world was made of and how it worked. He replied, "If you had told me that a few months ago, I would have called you crazy. But now I understand.

"I feel nuts for saying this, but the other day I was able to see the energy of the trees. I could see parts of its matter moving. Every tiny piece of the tree was connected to every other part, not only physically but also energetically.

"I saw the energy of one tree connecting to another and moving into the earth, disappearing into a mixture of energy below me. It then connected to something else, I think," Andy paused for a moment, having

---

1. Discussed in: Green, *Love Without End: Jesus Speaks* (2002), pgs. 24-25.

second thoughts about revealing what he had seen. Jeremy smiled from the corner of his mouth, impressed by Andy's new perception of the world.

"I was thinking, maybe, the energy of these trees is connected to their parent trees. That the energy was traveling to the place where it had been when the trees were growing as seeds. Not physically connected any longer but still linked in some way." Andy crinkled his face, as he spontaneously said his ideas aloud. "So it makes sense that you knew what was happening here. Just like the trees are connected, you must be connected in someway to your home," Andy was slowly putting together what he had experienced and looked towards Jeremy for approval.

The wind was blowing steadily from the east carrying warm air from the tropical waters of the Three Tombs. Thinking about the wind the same way he had thought about the trees, Andy closed his eyes and felt the wind not only go around him but also course through him. It entered through his lower abdomen like a solid piece of matter. The color of the wind energy mirrored the sky: light blue shading into darker blue toward the periphery. The texture was that of a smooth, solid rock as it continued to track through his body but then changed into that of a powder, soft and light feeling, flowing up from his intestines and stomach into his lungs. The light blue powder sought out every square inch of his lungs, ebbed for a moment, and then rushed out of his mouth back into the surroundings where it raced to catch up with the rest of the wind.

Jeremy began speaking, as he did to Andy before, "There is another part of our being that lies deeper than our brain, Andy. I believe you are starting to find it. This other part exists in a world where the wave function is not collapsed."

Andy eagerly listened, as Jeremy's voice did not seem to speak these words, despite the fact they were coming out of his mouth. His voice sounded unusual, now with a deeper, more powerful force behind it, as if he was imitating a wise old man. Intuitively, Andy had a sense the words came from the Three Tombs, carried within the wind over miles of ocean.

The wind entered Jeremy's stomach too and came out of his lungs, vibrating his vocal cords as his breath normally does.

"In this extra-cerebral state of the self," Jeremy said, "the brain is not present to sort through all possibilities of reality. It, however, must not be blamed for collapsing the wave function in physical reality since that is its purpose, just as the heart's function is to pump blood. Without our heart, our physical body would not survive. The same is true for the brain. Yet, even though we need our heart, disease can develop from its function. If blood is pumped with too high of a pressure, damage is done to blood vessels. Similarly, the brain's job of collapsing the wave function can have unwanted consequences as well. The brain determines the way the world is perceived and creates subjectivity. Everything we see is created by the brain, hence, all is subjective. This can lead to disease depending upon how the brain wants the world to be."[2, 3]

Andy reflected on this statement for a minute. He was beginning to escape his disease and looking back upon it, he did not understand how he had created his illness. The Conscious Whole had told him that his body, his DNA, created disease, not Andy himself.

As if he were reading Andy's thoughts, Jeremy continued, "Take your body as an example. What you draped around your core being is what you think is your true self. After the initial conception of your body, the forces that control creation stay stagnant to sustain the image of your body. The forces believe in and hold onto the initial structure of your body and do not want to destroy their creation. They keep your body as they made you. Forbidding change. Only altering their course under extreme circumstances.

---

2. There is extensive literature regarding the "mind-body" connection (i.e. how the mind controls the body). One such example: Taylor et al. "Top-Down and Bottom-Up Mechanisms in Mind-Body Medicine: Development of an Integrative Framework for Psychophysiological Research." *Explore: The Journal of Science and Healing* (2010).

3. How the mind creates disease discussed in: Bach and Wheeler, *The Bach Flower Remedies* (1979).

"Your core being is a driving force in creating the body you were born with.[4] When you choose to come into this world, your core being brings what it has learned from previous experiences, both useful and harmful. This energy is not only something the core carries around, but it is also written into the framework of the reality surrounding the body it makes.[5]

"In terms of collectiveness, the whole seizes onto concepts the core beings contribute. You are intertwined with this whole and cannot completely escape it, just like you cannot truly escape subjectivity. Your body becomes an image of what your core and the collective whole think it should become based on instructions they receive.

"In the physical world, as a life begins, DNA is created from the light signatures of the core being and the whole within a one-celled creature. This entity grows and grows and eventually turns into a person, who still carries the same lessons the core being brought into the physical world. The individual will embrace and cherish their physical body, their DNA, as if it is *all* they are. They are being fooled, Andy! DNA is only a temporary state of existence and can change. It can change from disease to health or vice versa.

"DNA is created, from moment to moment, and lives in a temporary existence.[6] The created world is a part, a fraction, of infinite reality. After the core provides a blueprint for the initial form of the body,[7] the brain takes over, reproducing the light code from its neurons to maintain the body as it thinks it should be. Stable. Diseased or healthy until it is convinced otherwise.

"The brain holds onto a stable image of the self for fear of losing its identity. The core being, however, lives in fluidity, where the wave function

---

4. "The soul...chooses the sperm and egg...overseeing the biomolecular construction of a new body..." from the oil painting "Pregnancy" by Alex Grey (1988). Additional work in: Grey, *Sacred Mirrors: The Visionary Art of Alex Grey* (1990).

5. Similar notion in: Green, *The Keys of Jeshua* (2004), pg. 131.

6. When DNA is sampled and prepared in a lab, its sequence is frozen in time and studied. However, DNA may mutate while inside the individual. So, why do we believe a disease discovered in our genes is static in our body?

7. Similar concepts with references therein: Oschman, *Energy Medicine: The Scientific Basis* (2000), pgs. 92-93.

is not collapsed. It is not the brain and does not follow the rules the brain lives by. The core can recreate the self and has the capability to alter the outcome of reality by choosing any quantum state of molecules; drafting new blueprints; rearranging the code. New bases of DNA can make the body healthy again, as you are experiencing, Andy. The brain is a masterfully complex tool that when used to its fullest extent and when its limitations are understood, can accomplish greatness. However, its power and insecurities, when manifested by exponential growth in numbers, can be dangerous."

So, I chose this disease and kept myself ill!? Andy reflected. *Why did I make myself suffer?*

Andy attempted to quiet his brain and listen to the subtle energies surrounding him. Buried emotions raced through his body, ones he had shut away for years and expressed in other ways.

It was Leah and her death.

I didn't even get to say goodbye, Andy thought. *I didn't go to the hospital the day she died because I couldn't accept what was happening.*

After her death, Andy had wanted to die, too. He **wanted** to suffer. He thought somehow it would make up for her pain if he felt it too. Andy wanted to go where Leah had gone.

The moment Andy decided he wanted pain, the instant his core wanted to escape its physical body, a DNA mutation was born.[8] His disease began. It started slowly, producing faulty proteins deep within his organs before he finally noticed the physical effects. A gentle man by nature, Andy would have never consciously taken his own life. Yet, his intentions were broadcasted and presented to the Conscious Whole. It accepted them as part of who Andy would become. He wanted to die, and more than that, he wanted to suffer. The Conscious Whole obeyed his commands and physically changed his DNA, producing the path for an eventual, painful death.

Andy's new genetic fate became a different, created genetic destiny than he was born with.

---

8. "DNA already is programmed to find a rationalization to fail." Null, "The Gary Null Show," *Progressive Radio Network*, August 8, 2013, 30:25.

22

As it entered the world and opened its eyes, everything around was moving so slowly; how bizarre, such a slow speed of life, it thought; the being, having entered from a high spatial and high frequency dimension, required an abrupt transition to secure the requisite biological parameters to continue functioning; as it was, the heart rate and neuronal activity would not be supported by its material dwelling for much longer; it could feel urgency surrounding its form by some, while others peered into its portals with amazement and relief; suddenly, it became aware of a gentle input; it was taught about the transition but the frequency of its father being was much lower than expected; yet, it yearned for this connection that would aid in habitation; a gradual slowing of its substantially higher operational frequency ensued, and the biological parameters followed; the being rested and prepared for the journey as its purpose was specific; it had volunteered for the service, and a mass of others followed closely behind

"Remember the piece of the puzzle that was missing with Schrodinger's cat in the box?"

"Kind of," Andy said, not really recalling what Jeremy was talking about.

"We talked about nonlocality and how two quarks can know what the other is doing. Like the brother and sister," Jeremy said.

Andy nodded, as the dusty hamster wheel in his mind began turning once again.

Jeremy began again in his wise, mellow voice. "The conscious mediator is the effect of our consciousness on the world; it can be one person or a group, creating a collection of conscious mediators, a collective consciousness that has joint power over reality.

"As a collective force grows and matures, individuals forget about their own power leading them to assume the role of an unconscious mediator: a being who unknowingly and unconsciously creates. Individuality is seemingly lost. The beings believe they no longer have power and what's worse, they no longer *know* they contribute.

"Well," Jeremy continued, "the consciousnesses that come together to form one whole, a united consciousness controlling everything, is what creates the nonlocal effect,[1, 2] the connection, the Mother Connection, between particles and people. The oneness of the united consciousness is a network of energy from all of the consciousnesses and if a change occurs at one end of the unit, it will be experienced throughout. Since there is oneness of consciousness, there is no longer an infinite number of observers but only one, the collective group, who creates a subjective reality. A collective subjective framework of the world is called 'objective' because no other reality is known! Objectivity is an illusion of collective subjectivity!"

Shaking his head, many thoughts ran through Andy's mind. He asked, "So, don't the people each control the collective conscious mediator?"

"Yes! They do! That's the whole point! Unfortunately, when individual conscious mediators coalesce, they often become unconscious and lose awareness of their contributions, a herd-like mentality. The power of creation is always present, however, it simply dwells in an alternate layer hid-

---

1. Analogous concept, including references, of a nonlocal, unitive consciousness discussed in: Goswami, *Quantum Doctor* (2004), pgs. 66-67.

2. Also discussed in: Gribbin, *Schrodinger's Kittens and the Search for Reality* (1995), pgs. 15-16, 142-143.

den away from daily wakefulness, ostensibly out of reach but functioning as strong as ever, building a reality the individual feels helpless within. Lack of awareness leads to delusion and disease.

"In Meat Cove, there are only conscious mediators. We started as such and have worked very hard to maintain our independence. You see, when you stay conscious in a group without falling prey to mob mentality, individuality and its power can be preserved. In contrast, the unconscious mediator becomes its **own** life force. Apparently separate from the people who are blinded to its workings, yet built from their power and intentions."

"Well, then can anything be done about the unconscious mediator?" Andy asked.

"You see, the unconscious mediator depends upon the people who form it, who sustain it. It feeds from them to form a world where insecurities are protected and validated. But, when people become more conscious of their lives and the way they affect the world, their mediator awakens.

"The unconscious mediator is dependent on the brain's ability to collapse the wave function. After the cerebellum calculates probabilities and the reticular formation filters them, the person then unconsciously chooses.

"The brain's world, which we mistake for absolute reality, is only one such reality. Importantly, don't put down this beautiful world we live in, for this is where we make a difference. This is the theater where we change lives and create a better future. It is where our ideas manifest and where our actions take place! You must not resent the physical realm because it is part of reality but understand where it comes from! It manifests from infinity!

"Bound and contracted to the biological and physical world, the brain is obligated to create a definitive reality that on the surface appears to exist indefinitely but is actually newly formed every second. Our core being accepts this contract upon entrance into the physical self and as a result of the necessity of our brain to make things appear permanent, our brain also makes our bodies and DNA appear 'permanent'. Diseases are born and aging takes place.[3, 4]

"On the contrary, the human body continually regenerates itself with cell turnover ranging from days in the intestines and up to years in the brain.[5] Meaning, over the course of our lives we walk around in a number of new physical bodies![6] Even our body that seems so constant is not but instead is continually being turned over, making new bones, muscles, nerve tissue, and even DNA[7] from what we eat.[8]

"So, why are we fooled into thinking we are stable structures?"

Andy blankly stared at Jeremy.

"The brain, Andy! It's our brain! This is why many people don't like change. It's hard-wired into our brains to deny change and to love permanence. But, change occurs on all levels of life, from daily alterations in our schedules to molecules in our DNA. Our brain doesn't want to allow change because it requires a stable environment to function. And rightfully so! Yet, this limitation must be realized in order to leap towards health and happiness!"

Jeremy's voice and facial expressions became more serious as he continued, "Please don't misunderstand me, Andy. It's not right to be vengeful towards the mind for thinking that it maliciously takes away possibilities, because the mind makes possibilities real! It picks a reality out of only po-

---

3. Aging is not necessarily an inevitable process. Psychological stress physically shortens a part of the genome called the telomere, resulting in aging, age-related diseases, and mortality. Reviewed in: Kiecolt-Glaser and Glaser. "Psychological Stress, Telomeres, and Telomerase." *Brain, Behavior, and Immunity* (2010).

4. Also see: Chopra, *The Essential Ageless Body, Timeless Mind: The Essence of the Quantum Alternative to Growing Old* (2007).

5. Spalding et al. "Retrospective Birth Dating of Cells in Humans." *Cell* (2005).

6. For a related discussion see: Dossey, *Space, Time, & Medicine* Boston (1982), pgs. 72-81.

7. Bridges. "DNA Turnover and Mutation in Resting Cells." *Bioessays* (1997).

8. Neese et al. "Measurement in Vivo of Proliferation Rates of Slow Turnover Cells by 2H2O Labeling of the Deoxyribose Moiety of DNA." *Proceedings of the National Academy of Sciences* (2002).

tential and gives us life! Without the brain, we would have nothing in the physical world. But, in doing its job, confusion and misinterpretation of reality can ensue. It is important to know that without our biological world we could not exist on this planet and in this universe the way we do now."

When Andy lived in the Conscious Whole, he had felt disconnected from his surroundings. The bubble he lived in was all he knew. There was nothing outside of what was known, and he never thought about what was "beyond" like he did while living in Meat Cove. Thinking about the vastness of the universe and what the Three Tombs were like gave Andy hope, which kept him moving forward, stirring his stagnation, and connecting him to a world beyond his sight.

Andy only realized, while sitting with Jeremy, how he used to think his body was not his responsibility, it was someone else's; he was partly right because it was the Conscious Whole's.

Jeremy continued speaking, "There used to be a group of people in Meat Cove who went to the extreme. They misunderstood the ideas we are talking about and completely denounced the physical realm. They cut off everything coming into their consciousness that had to do with material life. They stopped working, they stopped going on walks, and they stopped having conversations. Rather, they would communicate only through the metaphysical. They stopped being part of our tangible community and drifted away from the town, slowly fading into nothingness. Long before their bodies died, their consciousness fizzled out, leaving shells of what they had decided to become."

Jeremy appeared disheartened. One of these people had been a close friend who he had tried to help enjoy the physical world more. Jeremy stopped speaking for a few moments as sadness quickly overcame their space.

Shaking his head, he quietly continued, "Moderation is important on both ends, Andy. We mustn't ignore either or become obsessive of one."

"As such, the core can not easily cope with the rigors of everyday life without also satisfying its own needs. It must not be neglected, for it's visiting the earth as a companion to our bodies to evolve to a higher state. This world can be toxic to the core if not treated correctly, for the core needs to be reminded of what it truly is: infinity.[9] Before the core paired with a body through birth, it preexisted, and must not be misled into believing it is limited. This makes the core ill, and the body follows suit.

"The immortal mind, the core's mind, can understand infinity for it is infinity. A mind everyone possesses equally in order to see what is beyond what we think is real. The brain is like a calculator and as such, if given a function beyond its programming, it cannot perform. The brain can think of numbers really close to infinity, really big numbers with a lot of zeros after them, but to tangibly hold infinity is not possible with just our brain.

"Look into space, at the stars. They are so far away, but our brain still tries to compute a measurable value so it can limit infinity! What a crazy thing for our brain to do! Limit something that by definition has no boundaries! This is what it can do with our lives too, Andy."

Darkness was falling, and the sun had set behind Andy and Jeremy. Strong wind had kept clouds far inland making the night sky to the east extremely clear. Countless stars were shining through the atmosphere.

Jeremy continued, "Look between the stars and see the stars that are in the blackness. These have already been born and died, their light shining for eons but yet to reach our eyes. The earliest light from this star's birth is still so far away that its beginning has yet to be witnessed by us, yet its death had occurred before our earth was born.

"Our brain tries to grasp this computation and make it finite. We can try to imagine the finite numbers associated with this concept, yet we truly fall short. We need the infinite mind, the mind that is buried deep inside our biological casing, sitting back, awaiting its awakening."

Andy stared off towards the sky. Looking between the stars, he saw nothing but darkness. He thought about how there are stars in the field

---

9. The following statements of the core in relation to the mind are also discussed in: Green, *Love Without End: Jesus Speaks* (2002), pgs. 24-29.

of blackness, unperceivable to him. *What else in the world do our eyes not see?* he asked himself.

Jeremy carried on, "Infinity is everywhere. Do you care to fathom a guess as to how many atoms make up your hand?"

Andy sat quietly, looking at his hand. He muttered some words but just ended up saying he had no idea.

"When you think of it, there are really an infinite number of particles, not only the ones in your hand right now but also the ones that are still possibilities, awaiting their turn to become real.

"Try to imagine an immortal life, one that lasts forever. We attempt to put this in the context of the finite; in the framework of our supposedly fixed and predetermined biology. If you wish to believe your life ends with the death of your body, then so be it, but how can our body be finite when it is surrounded by an infinite world?

"Paradigms, temporary explanations for the current worldview, are too often afflicted by the unconscious collectiveness and not treated as temporary but instead as permanent views of the world, falsely providing security to unwary minds. Constant. Fixed. Reliable.

"We close a cage around ourselves and force temporary reality to become absolute reality. If we were to maintain a fluid worldview, then we would be on a path towards elevating our understanding of nature.

"I know your ideas have been turned upside down, Andy. It's a lot to take in, and I can see how your life and body have changed since you've moved here. I know the place you're from is different," he paused for a moment as Andy sat in silence.

"It's getting late and I need to get some rest. It's been great talking with you, Andy." Jeremy got up from his chair and started to make his way into the house. As he was walking away, he turned around and said, "I almost forgot to tell you. There's a man in town who wants to meet you. He's a friend of mine."

"Oh, ok," Andy said, surprised. "Where can I find him?"

"He said he would be at his home. He'll call for you. Goodnight, Andy." Jeremy left Andy alone to reflect.

Andy's thoughts moved like the wind: fast and with purpose. *The brain and the other*, he thought. *My constant struggle. The brain is like my paralyzed hand, and the healthy hand is my infinity. Both hands connected and dependent upon the other, yet separate and polar opposites.*

Like the dominance of one hand over the other, the brain can be dominant over infinity and vice versa. The brain produces analytical and functional components of life, whereas the infinite connects to the intangible and is free to explore all possibilities in the universe. A balanced partnership is necessary.

The savant who innately knows how to play a piano with no training does not use the brain-centered hand but instead uses the infinite hand. Alternatively, the rigorous process of learning an instrument can be obtained by using the analytical brain. While the savant may be lacking "normal" brain function, he or she is using their more than functional infinite self, like Andy's healthy hand. The infinite hand does not know boundaries, does not know disease. The analytically-bound hand only knows limits and is therefore limited to disease.

Part IV

"We see what we believe, and not just the contrary; and to change what we see, it is sometimes necessary to change what we believe."

JEREMY NARBY, PH.D.[1]

---

1. Narby, *The Cosmic Serpent* (1999), pg 140.

23

As the being woke, its solitude diminished and others became of aware of its presence; it could no longer hide or expect that its actions would go unnoticed

Dark shadows lured Andy into an empty room of his house. He peered through the doorway, fearing what he would encounter. He could not help but go into this sinister room, as an even more menacing presence lurked close behind. *I can hide in the shadows,* he thought, misled by his terrified mind, not knowing that what was chasing him was born from darkness.

Andy pressed his back against the wall and held his breath. He felt his heart pounding and quickly snuck a glimpse towards the lighted hallway. A shadow was moving near him.

It stopped.

Getting out of the house was his only chance. Thin branches bounced in the wind outside of the tall multi-paned window on the other side of the room. The presence was moving again, slowly forcing Andy deeper into the dark room.

Now, with his back against the window, Andy trembled, fearing what would enter. He looked outside and noticed he was at least two stories above the ground. He was trapped! He tried not to look at what was approaching, but his head and neck were stuck facing the door! The thin branches dancing on the window reached through the glass and restrained Andy's body, forcing him to encounter the pursuing figure.

It walked through the doorway, its shadow cast across the room to Andy's feet. He feared the worst and could do nothing about it! Adrenaline rushed through his body as he squirmed, trying to escape, but the branches constricted him tighter, shearing his skin.

He woke up screaming, clenching the bed, covered in sweat.

This recurring nightmare began the first night he came to Meat Cove and had been escalating in intensity. The figure in the dream always got closer and closer; Andy knew the Conscious Whole was not through with him.

As he recovered from his terrifying night, Andy looked out of his bedroom window and was surprised to see a beacon of light shining from a house, which was gently resting on the slope of the northern hills behind the storefronts in town. No different from other homes around it with the glaring exception of light beaming from its source. The light was pure white in the center with all of the colors of the rainbow on the perimeter; a circular rainbow that radiated outward in every direction, a signal of hope after a difficult night. While everything around it seemed in flux, the light held firm and did not dim, flicker, or move. A very low-pitched noise emanated from the light, like a low note played on a xylophone, slowly going up and down in volume, oscillating.

Andy began the increasingly painful and tedious process of getting ready for the day. Life was much easier with his new healthy hand, but the rest of his body was continuing to deteriorate. He became so short of breath dressing he almost passed out and was forced to lie back down in bed until he recovered.

I'm not going to die like this, Andy thought. *I must get better.*

If there was nothing else he would do today, he had to see the source of the light. After eating breakfast, Andy slowly made his way to the beacon of light, and as he drew closer he was surprised the light did not hurt his eyes as it towered into the sky above. Through a front window of the house, Andy saw a human silhouette sitting in the center of the light.

He approached the front door, which was made from dark wood and had a brass lion's head holding a metal knocker in its mouth placed squarely in the middle. He was trying to figure out how to reach the knocker from his wheelchair when an etheric voice welcomed him to enter. He maneuvered into the home and eagerly peered around the corner, trying to find the source of this mysterious voice.

The figure in the light was sitting in a chair, slouched down. A very tall man with long skinny arms and legs and a head seemingly too large to be held up by his neck, which kept him bent forward, as if perpetually reading a book on his lap. Andy's judging mind tried not to make any assumptions.

The man had thick, dark brown hair and an equally bushy mustache to match. White light radiating from him contrasted with the dark color of his skin. The light filled the sparsely decorated room that had a bed in one corner and a simple kitchen with a wood-burning stove in the other. A cane leaning against the wall was so tall it seemed more like a coat hanger. The wallpaper design looked centuries old and its repetitive intricate pattern seemed holographic.

The man struggled to lift his head enough to see Andy as he peered out of the corner of his eyes, leaning his head to one side. A boundless depth in his eyes seemed to reach to the farthest expanse of the universe, giving Andy a fleeting glimpse of infinity.

He smiled at Andy, welcoming conversation. Andy wanted to ask about this man's condition: his illness. Obviously, something was not "right" about the physical qualities he possessed. His head cocked halfway to the right, he looked at Andy struggling to keep it in one place.

"My name is Norman. My disease does not allow me to speak for long periods of time." He struggled to push every rasping word across his vocal cords and it reminded Andy of his own failing voice. Norman held out his hand, which had very little muscle remaining; his fingers were long, skinny, and dangled loosely without any intrinsic movement.

Andy could hear Norman's thoughts through the Mother Connection. He wanted Andy to take hold of his hand. Cautiously, Andy extended his own, still amazed by the ability to move his once diseased hand.

He first noticed how warm Norman's hand was, even though it appeared to be just bones covered by a delicate layer of skin. The hand looked translucent, making it seem like it hardly existed at all. However, Andy felt it vibrate at a very high frequency, like the buzzing of a honeybee's wings.

"I want you to experience, not just know, what the composition of my hand is. Do you know what makes up a hand?" Norman asked.

Andy did not know exactly what Norman meant, but reflexively falling back onto his old ways he responded, "Well, in your hand there are bones, muscles, nerves, blood vessels..." he paused for a minute.

"Yes, but is that all?"

"There are cells and proteins and molecules making up all of the components of your hand," Andy hoped this would satisfy Norman's question.

"Sure, all of what you said is correct. However, do not be afraid of what you *now* know. Can any of what you said completely explain my current state?"

The room became unstable. Nothing seemed to be in place anymore. There was no solidity to the surroundings. All was impermanent. Not just the furniture or the walls but also both of their bodies.

"We are led to believe the world around us is permanent. But now look. Nothing has a definite place. This is the quantum world," Norman confidently stated.

Losing himself in the experience, Andy focused on a single tulip in a vase across the room. It rested on top of an antique desk used as a side table next to the bed. The flower was a brilliant noble red with yellow vertical streaks. Its stem floated centrally in the water. Andy glanced away for a moment, and the following events would change the way he perceived reality forever.

As he was looking outside the window, he **experienced** the tulip. It became part of the beingness around him. It was part of him, and he was part of it; like being able to feel your feet even though you are not looking at them. Even stranger, the tulip was not only red and yellow but also every other color in the light spectrum. There was even a state where the tulip was not present; instead, there was a void where it was supposed to exist. It acted dead and alive, like the cat Jeremy had taught Andy about. Every possible configuration of its DNA was simultaneously expressed. Every possible arrangement of molecules all existing at once.

Suddenly, Andy could hear his frantic calculating brain becoming overwhelmed with the situation. Unpleased with the uncertainty, it yearned to make life permanent. He had an unrelenting urge to look back at the flower and **make** it exist in one state to console his confused brain. The calculating brain tried as hard as it could to peek its uninvited head back into the world, demanding the world exist in one form. This brain would surely destroy the beautiful quantum flower. This time though, just before the brain collapsed the wave function, Andy had the strength to quell his thoughts and judgments about reality and simply allow the present existence to be.

Andy was able to temporarily set aside his calculating brain, just as a blacksmith sets aside his hammer after a long day of shaping iron, not to get rid of it or to expel it from his life but to save it for when its functions are needed.

With his brain temporarily placed aside and pacified, Andy came back into the strange state of perpetual existence, now realizing it was the same world Russell had shown him. Norman and Russell were close friends, and Norman also spent a great deal of time in the quantum world of infinity. He, too, could access it at will, but unlike Russell, Norman was not able to gain health or strength.

The wave function would collapse every time Russell tried to bring back potential for Norman. He tried as hard as he could to help him, to heal Norman like he healed himself but was never successful. Nothing worked. The people in Meat Cove knew all about the quantum world and how it was intertwined with their world, yet they were not able to bridge the worlds like Russell had.

Andy, however, did something special when he met Russell. He too brought back potential for the development of the health in his hand. A feat not accomplished by anyone else, except Russell. Russell was perplexed when he realized what Andy had done, so he immediately told Norman.

Now, with Norman, Andy was experiencing the world of infinity but on a more profound level than before. He dug deeper than he had with Russell, which was only a training session for what was about to unfold. Andy was seeing all dimensions of reality: the infinite as part of the four-dimensional realm, one in the same. The outer layers, the higher-order dimensions Jeremy spoke about, are nothing more than an arbitrary separation of all the layers of reality. The four, six, and ten dimensional worlds are not separate, they are all here, right in front of us. The illusion created by our brains only allows us to experience four dimensions, yet there is nothing separate or external about the infinite world.

That's their problem! Andy thought. *I can see it now. Clearer than ever! We think the infinite world is separate; like a place to go to. That's what Russell taught me! But it's not detached from us! It's right here in front of us! Russell didn't have to go to or come from the infinite world. We are living in it!* Andy's thoughts raced as truths hidden behind the veil on the world were becoming revealed. He looked intently at Norman, wanting to tell him everything he was thinking.

Andy slowly turned his head and looked back at the flower without the filter of his brain. There it was, the most beautiful thing he had ever seen: all of the colors of the light spectrum coming out of a prism, all of the realities right in front of him, a spectrum of tulips. There were at least twelve he could count, but many more faintly appeared.

He heard Norman begin to speak, weak at first, but his voice became louder and more forceful as his condition was no longer holding him back. Norman had the same illness as Andy; an identical defect in his DNA; the same pathology except the course in Norman's body was different compared to Andy's. Norman was born with the disease and was a product of a different environment; a different amalgamation of collective consciousnesses. Like Andy, Norman too was once a child of the Conscious Whole. He came to Meat Cove when he was eleven years old as part of the missionary trip sent from the Conscious Whole. His parents brought him with them as they tried to incorporate the people of Meat Cove into their reality. The invaders were driven out of town, but Norman was left behind in the battle and was eventually adopted by Sandra. His conscious cloud then contributed to the collective consciousness of Meat Cove; he learned their ways and was valued as an equal. At eleven years old, Norman's disease had already started to affect his body. His bones, muscles, and connective tissue were already wasting away at his young age, exaggerating his naturally lean proportions. The plan for Norman was to continue down the ordained path of illness his body was taught to follow by the Conscious Whole, yet being left behind changed his fate. It changed the way his DNA would manifest in his body.

The energetic fields of Meat Cove were different than those within the Conscious Whole and shaped Norman's DNA accordingly, pausing his disease progression. As such, Norman would not die from his illness as Andy would; he was nourished by the energetic fields of Meat Cove and his DNA, the quantum molecule, changed upon his arrival. The nucleotide became what Meat Cove believed should be there. The collective cloud of consciousness in Meat Cove energetically resonated at a frequency Norman had not experienced within the Conscious Whole. This novel frequency brought strings of energy to life, out from dark matter that was previously only a potential for Norman. New strings replaced old ones and built the correct nucleotide in his DNA, which could manufacture the proper proteins his cells required for life, keeping his vital organs alive.

However, because of Norman's past, he was rooted deeply in his prior existence, and like a scar, the wasted parts of Norman's body stayed as they were. He wrote the emaciated, weak image of his body into the collective consciousness of Meat Cove when he was a child. This form was followed by the whole, since it did not impose on others' thoughts or ideals.

The honest force of creational reality.

Andy and Norman were Schrodinger's cats in their own box. Each permutation of reality was real to them at the same time. If an outside observer were to enter the room at that moment, their wave functions would collapse, and illness would become a reality for both. Now, disease was just a potential along with health, acting side by side.

Andy looked down at his hand, which was now encasing Norman's. The blue, soft energetic blanket of potential covering it before had completely transformed into a perfectly healthy physical hand: the hand he had used at work writing on the chalkboard teaching his students, the hand he had used to throw a baseball from center field, the hand he had used to pull weeds from his garden.

Andy's palm faced upward while Norman's hand rested inside of it. Norman's very large hand, which was clenched shut, fit within Andy's and now was surrounded by the same indigo blue light. For Norman, spikes of light came out in every direction and appeared fuzzy, like thin, soft hair. Layered on top of the lightly colored indigo energy, were darker blue colors emanating further away from the skin, oscillating in every direction, as if being blown in the wind. The fresh blue light of potential was transferred from Andy and even though the energy from Andy was nothing new to Norman's vital organs, as they were already bathed in it from Meat Cove's collective cloud, Norman's scarred muscles and skeleton did not know infinity. They only remembered what the Conscious Whole had ordered.

24

Torch bearers symbolize advancement; traveling through time they show others it can be done and provide inspiration; yet, their deeds are not novel for they are only a mirror, reflecting the past and future in their light; firestarters on the other hand, take pride in their tasks as pioneering but must realize they use a spark from the torch bearers; the firestarters must learn to pass on sparks to others who require help for it is not enough to simply mend yourself and shut out those who need help; no one does it on their own

The dying cells in Andy's brain resulted in an unexpected consequence; his neuronal connections were unlike any other and something happened unforeseen from all of the knowledge known to exist.

Death of Andy's unconscious mediator from the Conscious Whole.

Death of the repetitive, intrusive, and persistent thoughts that once created his self. True and complete release from the Conscious Whole. The pattern of electromagnetic energy representing the connections in his brain now held a code for release. Rewiring the circuitry the Conscious Whole embedded from conception. Andy no longer collapsed the wave function as before, as now he represented all possibilities simultaneously, free to explore and tap into the endless world.

With the death of his unconscious mediator, Andy was able to see, consciously, the collective cloud of Meat Cove. It hung high in the atmosphere, translucent, with light blue, satin pink, and finch yellow highlights. Thin streaks of fluorescent green energy raced through the cloud, like needle fish that swim around rocks on the coast, coursing rapidly through the sky from the north and west areas of Meat Cove. Andy could see this energy travel out towards the sea over the fishing grounds. Beyond his vision, the energy coalesced at the Three Tombs, where similar bands of energy journeyed back towards the village.

Above the semi-transparent energetic cover of Meat Cove, Andy saw plumes of clear clouds rising beyond the upper layers of earth's boundaries. Intuitively, he thought of a similar framework where he came from: the force of the Conscious Whole, which was hidden behind a veil of secrecy and deceit. Only now was he completely aware of his former surroundings.

Andy was able to do what Russell could not; give Norman's scarred body the potential it needed, the potential it denied. Not even Norman could believe what was happening; such a feat was thought not possible, even within the paradigm of Meat Cove. But, Andy was not a man of Meat Cove, nor was he any longer a man of the Conscious Whole. He was everything. Potential in every form.

Just as the Conscious Whole set limits to the paradigm, the collective consciousness of Meat Cove established limits as well, limits set by each individual, including Norman, for there was knowledge even the wise people of Meat Cove did not know existed. Andy was elevated by the collective consciousness of Meat Cove but was never bound by what they believed. He now obtained perspective to see limits set within Meat Cove, which made the confines of the Conscious Whole even more apparent.

Physically, Norman's hands looked thin and malnourished as before, but there was also a layer of muscle and healthy skin appearing just beneath the worn, pale skin. Andy saw both the ill and healthy, famished and nourished, tired and energetic, weak and strong.

"Knowing without a doubt in the core of your existence these possibilities exist is crucial for giving the impossible an opportunity," Andy said, amazed he even spoke those words. They rolled off his tongue without an ounce of thought being processed in his brain.

He was now the teacher, "Seeing these possibilities and knowing they exist is where you find health. But, beyond just knowing about infinity, you must see the finite within you. What preconceived notions about yourself do you believe in? What do you tell the world around you so it will accommodate who you think you are!?" The authority and confidence in his voice, which seemed to come from a distant source, focused Norman's mind.

Norman emitted an off-white shadow on top of the pure white light. It silhouetted his lofty frame but then began to crouch, hiding behind what was becoming a healed body. Shaped like the dying figure of a man suffering from a terminal disease, it did not want to change. Concealing itself from sight, the scar wanted to live in the shadows and subsist on a rudimentary level of wants and needs. It wanted to only be illness, and it needed to feed from the pureness resonating within Norman. It crawled further away from Andy as his energetic body approached Norman's scar. Andy reached out with the indigo blue light from his hand, stretching towards the old self Norman thought he had to believe in, and pulled it from Norman's thoughts. The scar writhed in pain, screamed in agony, as it held tightly onto reality; its fingernails scraping the ground, it hissed between its rotten teeth. Norman physically felt the scar's pain as it was being released from its existence in Meat Cove.

Norman looked up at Andy, now able to hold his head high while concurrently having his head slouched down as if asleep in his chair. He spoke in both his usual hoarse voice and a melodious baritone octave like that of a professional singer. Andy could see the sound waves traveling towards him; all different wavelengths and oscillations, the healthy frequencies and the ill ones. The way he saw the sound was not through his mind's eye but through his actual vision, as if seeing ripples on a still lake after a stone strikes the surface. Unlike smooth waves, the waves Andy saw streaming towards him had small spikes within them. Spikes of energy. Like a confused sea with choppy waves and large rollers, the ill voice hitched a ride on the smooth healthy tones, doing its best not to be left behind.

"I thought I would never feel like this. I have strength and health! But it is strange, because I also feel weak and ill. It is difficult for me to accept this change."

"Why!?" Andy asked, pushing Norman to find his way.

"I...think I must stay as I am or...I'll lose part of my self..."

Andy replied, "But this change is real, and it's there. It's your **choice**. Why are you still holding back?"

"Because I feel like I'd be letting go of who I am!" Norman fired back.

"This is who you are. You can choose at any time to change the framework of your existence. You are strong and weak, healthy and ill. Don't you see the quantum state of reality permits the possibility to be who you have the potential to be!? To be whom you want to be? Don't you see the choice you're making!? Holding onto your old self does not allow the wave function to be open. It collapses into one state. The one you keep making real! Your diseased body!" Andy's words seemed to precede his thoughts. After he spoke, he was surprised by the implications of what he had just said, thinking of his own health.

A torch of light was passed from Russell to Andy to Norman.

Andy was an open channel for the infinite realm and, unlike Russell who could only live in and show people this world, Andy was learning he could actually bring potential into material existence for others. Without the unconscious mediator, he could hold the wave function open in a **conscious** state and walk across a bridge of light connecting the physical realm to the infinite, breaking down a perceived, created barrier.

Sitting with Norman, he could see this bridge as it hung over an immeasurably deep ravine. On either side of the bridge were the two worlds: the material and the infinite. Strings naturally cross the bridge, mediated by the gatekeeper, the unconscious mediator within the conscious clouds. Andy was going to be the first to cross and choose which strings to bring back, usurping the gatekeeper's post. From the physical side of the bridge, he looked down into the gorge; neon green foliage covered the vertical wall below him, its brightness contrasted by dark black rock beneath. The vegetation was fluid and in no time had crawled right next to Andy! The vine-like plants meandered onto his feet and began to grow up his legs, rooting into his skin, holding on as tightly as they could. Cementing his body into the physical, they did not want to release. They did not want him to make the journey to the infinite. The grip of material reality restrained Andy's being as best it could.

He picked up his foot, tugging the bright green vines, ripping them from their roots, and took a first step onto the pure white bridge, which caused the vines to disintegrate, becoming dust. Planks of light supported him as he held onto white ropes on either side of the bridge. Intense white light dripped from the bridge and looked like comet tails, as they streaked into the iron-black gorge. Andy continued walking across the bridge, which felt surprisingly solid beneath his feet. As the grip of reality weakened, the last of the vines clinging onto his body fell apart into nothingness. He approached the infinite side, and the cliff wall beamed with light; every color he had ever seen sparkled on the wall and as if soaking wet, the colors dripped into the gorge below. Every few seconds, however, one of the sparkles of light would shoot across the ravine towards the physical world. *Strings becoming real,* he thought.

Stepping onto the infinite plane, Andy felt unstable and impermanent, similar to his experience with Russell and Norman. It was difficult to think, and he felt confused, but concentrating on his task, he pressed on. The ground looked like the cliff wall, covered in sparkling light of every color. The colors fell through the ground like a waterfall, through the multi-dimensionality of the earth of light, which made Andy feel like he too was going to fall into the land beneath his feet. As he walked, his unique, inherent light resonated with certain strings, the sparkles of light, drawing them near him like magnets to metal.

Andy knelt down and reached into the ground, collecting units of light in his hands as if scooping sand on a beach. As strings clung onto him and he clung onto them, he circled back towards the bridge, focused on his goal. He found great difficulty in placing his feet on the ground and needed to be absolutely certain where he walked. Andy was sure he would fall through. Making his way across the bridge, he felt physical reality closing in around him; two handfuls of immaterial becoming permanence perceived as the only truth.

Vines stretched from the opposite side reaching out in anticipation of his return as Andy guarded the strings he brought back so they would not be destroyed. Sustaining them in his grasp, he imagined a metallic gold chest for the strings to reside in, protected from consumption by the wanting and needing vines.

Andy approached Norman as he stepped back onto the vine-covered ground of reality. It once again wrapped around his feet and grew up his legs, but he protected the container of light in his arms, embracing it closely against his body.

He opened the chest in front of Norman, who eagerly peered within.

The strings inside were in a tightly wound ball with swirls of apricot orange, oxblood red, crescent moon yellow, and organic turquoise erratically swimming across the surface. Deep purple dots dove into and out of the ball, like bees hurriedly darting around a hive.

Andy spoke to Norman from his intuition once again, "Your brain wants to hold onto your old self because that's where it's comfortable. But you're not your brain. You're a manifestation of the infinite potential in the universe, every moment given the opportunity to choose from all possibilities. Do not allow your finite brain to collapse the world around you into a framework of limits. There is infinity everywhere around you![1] Simply look to the horizon of the sea or calculate the unimaginable number of atoms in your body. You are part of the infinite state of nature. Infinity does not know limits, yet you are creating limits in your life! Your brain does this for survival, a necessary condition for living in this bio-

---

[1]. The presence of infinity in our world and beyond is extensively discussed throughout: Green, *Love Without End: Jesus Speaks* (2002).

logical world, but it is only conditional, not absolute! Give your brain the opportunity to select possible configurations of reality that correspond with who you want to become, not who you think you are destined to be!"

Andy lifted his arms upward and released the ball of light into their conscious clouds. His gift, the light, trickled into Norman's body resonating with strings he needed to release the scar and build his new body.

Norman was not the only one with scars from a prior existence; Andy too had issues he buried within his conscious cloud, masked from apparent sight. No longer bound by his unconscious mediator, Andy could see the process of his becoming; a self-inflicted agony and state of defeat with no possible outlet, a terminal path towards one endpoint.

He had attached himself to the pain of losing Leah and did not recognize the difference between holding onto the event and cherishing the love and connection he had with her. The latter was what he should have done.

Leah's presence was written onto the surface of the particles that once made up her body, and Andy's particles were connected to these, no matter how far away. The Mother Connection flowed while energy and information from her death was transferred from her particles to Andy. In addition, the loss and pain Andy felt was incorporated into his body from his conscious cloud, which precisely followed his instructions to suffer, outside of the conscious daily operation of his life. The Conscious Whole observed the interaction and was subsequently given a master code from Andy's conscious cloud on how to operate, resulting in a seemingly unstoppable source for his disease.

Similar to Norman, Andy's idea of his illness did not hurt others, so it was allowed to exist in Meat Cove. Andy though, was not nourished by the energetic field as Norman was when he entered Meat Cove; he told the collective consciousness of Meat Cove his disease was terminal and specified details of his illness according to how the doctors said it would progress. The collective whole followed his described destiny and his illness went along as he thought it would, as he told it to become.

Seeing how he was in fact responsible for his fate broke the bond of his predetermined future, and Andy was free. The ill identity did not need to exist any longer and no longer served its purpose of teaching him about perseverance and strength! His scar, too, was removed by shining the light of possibility onto the shadow it was living under. Just as he wrote his archetype into Meat Cove, he un-wrote the scar by changing the way his light was portrayed in the collective whole.

25

Stars are born to illuminate the path; the choice to walk determines the form

NORMAN WAS STARING OUT THE WINDOW, FEELING uneasy about change. Both he and Andy were still living with the wave function open, while hundreds of incarnations of Norman and the tulip hung in limbo, patiently waiting for a decision. Andy felt time was running out. As the physical world fought for permanence in the unstable quantum transition, its green vines pierced barbs into Norman and Andy's feet. The force of certainty would not wait long.

Action had to be taken; the present could not be delayed. Then suddenly, in the blink of an eye, the wave function collapsed, and Norman was standing, now with his head held high. He walked to the window, leaning halfway out, as if he had never seen the sky before. His long, wooden cane remained leaning against the wall, a relic from his past. He spoke to Andy, as he hung out the window, "I knew you could heal me. The knowledge of Meat Cove alone could not have healed me. We needed you. Your light is like nothing we have ever seen. What you have made of yourself will manifest too. Your infinity, your light, and the body you will become. It's your unwavering belief[1] that we needed, that I needed. Your belief is more

---

1. Related concepts discussed in: Braden, *The Spontaneous Healing of Belief: Shattering the Paradigm of False Limits* (2008).

powerful than anything you could have learned. No matter how hard I tried, I could not match it because deep down, in my unconscious mind, I didn't believe."

Andy's unique light code, created by the death of neurons from his disease, destroyed his unconscious mediator, removing the guardian, while an absolute, steadfast belief kept the wave function open, allowing the infinite bridge to be traversed.

Andy so passionately, even blindly, believed in the idea of infinite possibility that it became real. His beliefs were reflected in his conscious cloud as a characteristic, symmetric light code, which was beginning to expand beyond his own body. Light energy was drawn from the bridge at every new moment, channeled by Andy.

Andy walked out of Norman's home, no longer paralyzed by disease. Just as nothing is permanent, neither is the idea of illness. As simply as it had been put into the collective cloud of Meat Cove, Andy and Norman's illnesses were removed with an equal and opposite simplicity.

The light generated from their brains, from the electromagnetic radiation of the firing of their neurons, went from their conscious clouds into the collective cloud of Meat Cove. The light, their created light, then traveled back down from the collective cloud, into their individual clouds, and coursed through every particle of their being.[2,3] The energy resonated with specific strings bringing them from dark matter of the infinite world into Andy and Norman's physical bodies.

Novel strings created new particles, building the exact atoms needed by nucleotides in their DNA. Specific frequencies provided by the collective cloud surged through the double helix, instantly transforming the impermanent DNA into what the men told it to be. For Norman, where

---

2. An interstitial matrix interconnects cells in the body, providing channels for energy to flow. Reviewed in: Oschman, *Energy Medicine: The Scientific Basis* (2000), pgs. 41-68.

3. Is the matrix of microtubules in the brain an integral part of consciousness? Hameroff and Penrose. "Orchestrated Reduction of Quantum Coherence in Brain Microtubules: A Model for Consciousness." *Mathematics and Computers in Simulation* (1996).

Meat Cove had not already changed his DNA in childhood, new DNA in his muscles and connective tissues now made the correct protein his cells needed for health and rebuilt what once wasted away. In Andy's body, DNA was changed in every cell and no longer made the toxic protein that was killing his body.

Andy looked over his shoulder as he walked away and could see Norman standing at the window waving, his body a rainbow silhouette within the pure white light, with the red end of the spectrum towards the lower part of his body and the violet end of the spectrum towards his head.[4]

Light energy from Andy's body flowed into the ground, where it combined with all of the energy coursing through the land, just like the energy of the trees he saw diving deeply into the earth a few days ago. Andy's light was now a purple color mixed with thin strings of orange rippling vertically, spilling out over the top of his head and towards his feet. As the energy came in touch with the ground it quickly rushed in every direction, following the contour of the terrain and extending beyond the horizon, flooding the land. In discrete intervals, the energy went upward into the collective cloud of Meat Cove, affecting all of the beings in Meat Cove, consciously writing in his beliefs and hope.

Sandra and Coco were standing at the top of the northern cliff when a shockwave of explosive energy coursed at an infinite speed over every surface; they knew Andy's true intention; even Coco, who also created a conscious cloud, was given the opportunity to accept the new. The elders awakened to the new energy that asked to become part of the whole. Jeremy viscerally experienced it as he worked at the docks on his boat. Russell knew a change was coming as he sat next to his small wood stove tending to a fire. The beings of the Three Tombs knew what Andy was asking of Meat Cove.

Just as Andy gained the ability to see the collective cloud, he could now see individual clouds of each person in Meat Cove and the connections made between the individuals and the whole.

---

4. For a discussion of energy foci of the body see: Bek and Pullar, *Healing with Chakra Energy: Restoring the Natural Harmony of the Body* (1995).

The energy, moving at the speed of light where time does not exist, allowed an infinite amount of time for the decision to be made.

They all agreed. Andy's energy, from the electromagnetic activity in his brain corresponding to his hope and beliefs, was going to elevate the collective consciousness of Meat Cove to an improved state of being and keep the bridge of light open for new strings he brought to their world; a superior state of health, wellness, and understanding for all. Everyone would benefit from Andy's contribution, giving all in Meat Cove the ability to become channels for the deeper realms explored by Andy, Russell, and Norman. Andy realized the freedom associated with a collective creational reality that provides true sentience and choice. However, there also came great responsibility.

26

Forces were assembling; their small size made them an unappreciated opponent; however, numbers were their strength, a fact not accounted for by the opposition

Over the next few weeks, both Andy and Norman worked on strengthening their physical bodies. Given the potential to make a healthy body was only the start of rebuilding their lives; importantly, they also needed to physically nourish themselves by consuming nutrients required to build molecules to make healthy cells. In addition, they needed to be physically active, conditioning themselves to **become** the potential given to them. The physically active body keeps the conduit open for strings that support health and wellbeing; a flux of energy from the infinite world vibrating at the same frequency as strings within healthy molecules. The more the connection is tapped, the stronger it becomes. The physical needs the energetic, and the energetic needs the physical.

After his interaction with Norman, Andy no longer had a survival mentality. He no longer fought through the day, no longer struggled to breath, and no longer struggled to eat. He had been losing a battle and had wanted to surrender, but now he could walk like he had been able to before his symptoms started. His mind was sharper, and his thoughts were clearer and more directed. Andy looked towards the future with an optimism he had not felt in years.[1,2]

How do I change the world? Andy pondered in the days after his fateful interaction with Norman. The answer was obvious, but he did not want to admit it.

I have to go back home and show them what I have learned, show them how I have changed.

As the decision was made, the collective cloud of Meat Cove morphed and began to undulate at a steady pace, cloaking itself, blending into the surroundings, posing as physical clouds in the atmosphere.

They all knew the consequences of Andy's intention, and as a condition, they had to hide what they were about to pursue. If the Conscious Whole knew the plan, it would be on the attack.

Andy spoke to Jeremy about going back home, but Jeremy did not have a good feeling about him leaving. Jeremy had traveled far out to sea and faced many dangers, but in spite of his strength and fearlessness, even he felt apprehensive about going anywhere near Andy's old home, the Conscious Whole. The elders of Meat Cove had stories about how the Conscious Whole had tried to change Meat Cove and enslave them to its ways using physical and energetic forces; memories of this encounter were not forgiven or forgotten.

"Everything is going so well here," Jeremy said, trying to counsel Andy. "You have gotten your health back. You can live again!" He tried to hide his fear of the Conscious Whole and persuade Andy to stay.

I've heard all of this before, Andy thought. *My family and friends didn't want me to leave when I was sick. I knew then what I had to do, and now the next step is even clearer than it was before.*

---

1. An optimistic outlook on recovery after suffering from heart disease independently predicts better survival: Barefoot et al. "Recovery Expectations and Long-Term Prognosis of Patients with Coronary Heart Disease." *Archives of Internal Medicine* (2011).

2. A positive mood is correlated with a longer lifespan: Steptoe and Wardle. "Positive Affect Measured Using Ecological Momentary Assessment and Survival in Older Men and Women." *Proceedings of the National Academy of Sciences* (2011).

Andy was thinking more lucidly than ever. Having flashbacks to when the doctor said he was out of his mind pushed him even harder to go back home. Simply smiling at Jeremy, as he continued to list reasons to stay, Andy could not help but see the similarities of this conversation.

For Jeremy and the others in Meat Cove, it was perfectly logical for Andy not to travel to such an oppressive place. Just like the people of the Conscious Whole, the people of Meat Cove also had a comfort zone within their community, within what they knew to be true and real. However, Andy was not like either of them anymore. He now knew neither the Conscious Whole nor Meat Cove was all there was in the world; there was even more. They were both just two different places, with two different paradigms. He had gained so much knowledge and had such enlightening experiences that Andy knew he must pass it on and give it to the people of the Conscious Whole, who were still suffering as he had suffered and who needed the lessons he had learned.

Jeremy feared Andy would be turned back into his previous state, but his concerns fell on deaf ears. Andy had more strength than ever, physically and mentally. He knew he had the ability to stay strong and remain true and clear to the path he envisioned.

Sensing Andy's determination, Jeremy reluctantly agreed to help with his journey but made it clear he, himself, would not make the journey. It would be a solo voyage. Planning the trip back would not be simple as there was not enough gas in the car Andy arrived in to bring him home.

"What about hiking back?" Andy asked.

"It will take you months!" Jeremy exclaimed

"Well…can you teach me how to sail?"

"Have you ever been in a boat before?"

Andy shrugged.

"Guess not…I don't think I have a choice," Jeremy replied half smiling and half worrying about Andy's plan.

"There's a small, old, wooden sailboat in the harbor nobody's using. It needs some work, but we can have it seaworthy in a week or so."

The next day, Andy and Jeremy dragged the boat out of the water and onto a sandy beach on the north side of the harbor, protected from the wind. A steady leak in the hull required repair so they spent the better part of a week sealing the hole and fixing the wooden mast. Andy had never worked on a boat before, so Jeremy gave him much needed guidance. Jeremy obtained a sail from another fisherman who owed him a favor; it was beat up and battered, but with some sewing it would work like new.

Planning his voyage, Andy discussed the best route with Jeremy, but Jeremy's nervousness could not be hidden as it had been ingrained within him to never venture south. Nonetheless, Jeremy apprehensively described the plan. "You see, the winds are predominately from the west when you are near the coast, particularly this time of year. The most efficient way to travel south would be to sail southeast to eventually catch the strong and consistent northern winds, which you can pick up when further out at sea. These will carry you south much faster than hugging the coast and fighting the wind."

"Seems simple enough," Andy naively replied.

"Well, you'll have to be far offshore to catch the northern winds, and the ocean out there is a different world."

Andy got a sick feeling in his stomach. It would not be easy. In fact, it was going to be dangerous. Nonetheless, he was determined and pushed doubts out of his mind.

In time, the boat was seaworthy and ready for a test ride. A confused sea sloshed around in the harbor. Andy hoped to postpone the test until the conditions were calmer, but Jeremy convinced him it would be better to learn to sail in difficult conditions. Timidly, Andy placed one foot aboard and fell the rest of the way in, after which Jeremy quickly pushed the boat away from the dock.

"Hey! Aren't you coming with me!?" Andy cried.

Jeremy replied with a smile, preferring the 'getting thrown in the deep end' technique, "You can do it. The worst that will happen is you flip the boat!" Jeremy laughed on shore as Andy struggled to put up the sail in the gusty wind as it flapped around like an unruly bed sheet. Finally, it caught the wind, and Andy shot off like a bullet towards the shore, getting thrown into the back of the boat with his feet in the air. It took him a few seconds to right himself and see where he was going, and he barely had enough time to get a hold of the rudder and steer away from the beach. Jeremy couldn't stop laughing, and Andy's bewildered face made him laugh even harder. Andy quickly came to learn that rudders worked backwards as he pitched one direction then the next. Over-adjusting to a gust of wind, he made a sudden movement with the rudder, the boat darted to the left, and Andy went overboard to the right. The boat capsized and a disgruntled Andy floated in the water.

Jeremy started to feel badly for Andy, so he waded in and helped his friend flip the boat upright.

Andy squawked incessantly, not too pleased with getting pushed into the deep end. "How do you expect me to learn if I can't even get settled in the boat!?" Andy felt embarrassed as insecurities probed to the surface.

"Believe it or not, I did that for a reason," Jeremy explained as they both pulled the boat onto the beach next to the dock.

"Sure you did! I think you wanted a cheap laugh!" Andy fired back feeling angry. His mood was not aided by the fact they skipped breakfast and lunch to finish the boat.

"Well, you see, now you won't be afraid to tip the boat and fall in! The worst that can happen is over. Okay, seriously, now I'll teach you how to sail."

27

Parallel journeys of the same deed embarked, seeking advancement and providing support; those below called for help, as construction of the energetic form beneath was not near completion, but urgency raced above

ANDY SPENT THE NEXT MONTH HONING HIS sailing skills, getting constant advice from Jeremy, and began to develop confidence while on the water. Based on how long it took Andy to drive to Meat Cove, Jeremy calculated it would take approximately seven days by sea to travel to the Conscious Whole. As such, Andy and Jeremy built a small cabin in the bow of the vessel to get out of the sun and rain, only big enough to hold Andy's large frame if he sat cross-legged. He had to duck his head and wondered why they had not added six more inches of height. Nonetheless, according to Jeremy, the northern wind would be strong soon, so they had no time to change the cabin.

On the day before the planned departure, Andy was securing the rigging on his sail when Jeremy approached with an armful of supplies. "Here, Andy," Jeremy said handing him a map, warm clothes, rain gear, a knife, fishing line, and a hook, which he stowed on a small shelf in the cabin. Jeremy drew the map based on his knowledge of the local waters and the patterns of the wind. He also brought bread, dried fruit, and dried fish all sealed in a large watertight package. "It's best to be as prepared as possible out there. Things can change at any moment. I wish I could have done more to get you ready."

"You've already done enough," Andy said. "The rest is up to me."

As Andy was organizing his supplies, he noticed a compass on the dock, which sat on top of a wrinkled piece of paper. He picked it up and was initially surprised by how heavy the corroded bronze metal felt, which looked at least two hundred years old. Through the thick, foggy glass a large, red needle wobbled about and pointed towards a letter 'N' at the top. A simple design from a simple man.

The note read, "Andy, there are many different ways to see the world and many paths to follow. Let this guide you when your eyes no longer know the way. Your friend, Russell."

That night, Jeremy and Andy sat on the back porch where they had spent so much time. The sweet air of a warm early fall made it hard for Andy to think about departing. The men did not speak much, both nervously anticipating the journey, but exchanged some details involving the voyage and went to bed early. Andy lay awake in bed, his mind racing, anxious to set sail but feeling sad about leaving Meat Cove, the land where his body was healed, the home of people who accepted him as their own, and the place of friends whose company he truly enjoyed.

Nonetheless, the plan was set. His determination unwavering, he would travel back to his forsaken home, the Conscious Whole.

After a fitful night of sleep, Andy awoke early in the morning, tensely organizing and reorganizing the provisions. The warm air from the night before passed, and a cold breeze was steadily blowing. Andy noticed Jeremy standing on the dock, tucking his hands into his long black jacket, emitting sadness, for he was going to lose a close friend, and fear, for he was afraid of what Andy was going to encounter. Andy did not want to make eye contact with him, as the overly expressive frown on his face made him second-guess his decision to leave. Wind blew through the unsecured sail as it flapped in the wind, no one else in town was awake, the sun had yet to break the horizon, and the western stars still shone brightly.

Andy looked up at Jeremy from his boat, forced a smile and said, "You know, I can't ever thank you enough for what you've done for me."

Jeremy smiled from one corner of his mouth.

"I'll see you again," Andy said reassuringly, hoping what he said was actually true.

After a long pause, Jeremy replied, "Repay me by sharing what I taught you…and don't forget about us in Meat Cove!"

Andy pushed the boat off the dock, tightened up the sail, and his little vessel took off towards the pink sky forming to the east. He headed with the wind and did not want to look back. Driven by purpose, he had to look forward.

The sun did not take its time rising up to the horizon, and Andy finally looked over his shoulder as the early morning sun began lighting up the small town of Meat Cove. The houses were all but small dots tucked between the tall mountains that dove into the sea. From this perspective, Andy realized how isolated that small village was; fortified by treacherous cliffs and endless inhospitable coastline on either side, you had to be right in front of the village by sea to even know it was there. *It would be easy to sail right past it,* Andy thought.

High clouds littered the sky, reflecting beams of light from the orange sun that was making its presence known. Fine orange streaks teasing the outer atmosphere.

The wind blew stronger as Andy fought his way into open waters further away from the coast. Even though he had been sailing for a month, he had never been this far away from land, and suddenly fear swept through his body and boat, covering every surface. It was the same fear that taunted Jeremy.

*This is the **real** ocean,* Andy thought. Every eight seconds rolling swells from the northeast picked up his boat and gently placed it back down in a trough. As Andy traveled further, the height of the waves increased, seemingly plump and lazy but their anthropomorphic features belied their true power, which dictated the pulse of the sea. A thick wind filled the sail and pulled Andy further away from the safety of Meat Cove, drawing him into another world where he felt more like a passenger than a captain of his boat.

Any sense of sureness Andy had been feeling earlier in the morning seemed to be left behind on the dock. *Maybe the sea is not for me*, he thought, feeling unwelcome in an alien world with no protection and no safe haven to quickly sail back into if he suddenly encountered a problem. The sea was alive, and it sensed Andy's uneasiness. It was ready to jump on the slightest mistake and make him pay for being a weak sailor.

Yet, as time passed, Andy gained confidence, feeling more comfortable operating the sail and rudder and was even able to walk around the boat and into the cabin to grab breakfast from his rations. Letting the world carry him back to his home, he contemplated the vastness of the world and how minute he was in relation to it all. Nonetheless, the importance of one individual could not be understated and with his intent back in sight, Andy tightened up the sail and pressed on.

A long first day of learning the rhythm of the sea concluded with sun-etched clouds draped over the mountains that were now out of sight. The same mountains Andy had traversed on his way towards Meat Cove, now nonexistent in his new world.

28

Secrets were placed within cloud-covered mountains, hidden from view; shrouds of white mist concealed their information while custodians maintained silence, ensuring transients would not see the truth

WITH NIGHT RAPIDLY DRAWING AROUND HIM, AND having just gotten used to sailing during the day, Andy was not looking forward to a pitch-black night. Exhausted, he wanted to sleep but feared what would happen if he left the helm to catch some rest. A sliver of moon nestled itself low in the sky, as if it too was preparing for sleep. Andy pulled out the map Jeremy had made while he still had some light, which showed Meat Cove, the direction of the winds, and a group of islands, labeled 'Three Tombs'. Jeremy said it would take a full day and a half of sailing to reach the winds blowing from the north, but between Meat Cove and the northern winds are the Three Tombs. Jeremy had instructed him to stay as far south as he could, as the water around these islands is very dangerous.

"The currents around the Three Tombs," Jeremy had said, "draw vessels into their shallow waters. Razor sharp, poisonous coral reefs surround each of the three islands, and many great sailors have died trying to navigate and fish around these waters. You, especially as a novice sailor, should stay very far away from these islands!"

Jeremy's words echoed in Andy's mind as he tried to figure out if he was anywhere near the Three Tombs. According to Jeremy's map and instructions, he should have passed south of the islands by late afternoon, so he figured by this time any danger was in his wake.

Andy looked up from his map scowling. *Everything looks the same,* he thought. Straining his eyes over the bow, a pink light peeked over the horizon, very faint at first, but as he sailed forward waiting for the northern winds to take him south, the pink light became more and more dominant as the sky darkened.

Another boat? he pondered. *Jeremy said there was a crew of fishermen looking for big game fish way out here.* Andy sought for an explanation to sooth his increasingly apprehensive mind.

Wispy rays of the stationary light increasingly rose into the night sky like a cloud raining upward. Perplexed, Andy focused on the light and became more and more obsessed with its presence as he slowly made his way east. Fighting fatigue, his eyes became heavy, and soon he could not tell if he was dreaming when he noticed two very dim yellow lights on either side of the pink light. *It looks like a city! Am I going in the right direction?*

Andy dove into his tiny cabin, was fully awakened after hitting his head on the entrance, and grimaced in pain. He rifled through his supplies and pulled out the compass Russell had given him. The large red needle swayed with the movement of the sea, but sure enough, he was on course, headed east. *There's no known city this far east of Meat Cove,* Andy convinced himself, trusting the directions from Jeremy, fooling his anxiety-ridden mind, and continued on.

He spent the whole night sailing, not able to sleep as the lights covered more and more of the sky; he felt a sinking pit in his stomach, ironically feeling trapped by the endless, infinite water surrounding him; dread filled the never-ending empty space.

The sun finally broke the horizon after its journey around the earth, and Andy was beyond exhausted. His little wooden boat bounced up and down on a turquoise colored ocean; the choppy waves made him seasick, his head pounded, and his stomach moved like the sea. As the boat rose to the top of a wave, directly in front of him, no more than a half a mile away he could see the Three Tombs! All night obscured by darkness he had been heading right for the islands without even knowing it! Instead of passing them to the south hours before, his small boat could only manage a slow haul through the waves making his course much slower than expected.

The three islands rose vertically out of the sea, each coming to a point at the summit. Huge waves crashed against jagged, midnight-black, volcanic rocks lining the coast and sinister toothed reefs poked their heads through the surface, barely submerged, only seen in the troughs of the waves. The shallow sea floor picked up swells and smashed them against the islands, the slopes of which were covered in bright green glowing foliage that appeared to be constantly moving right before Andy's eyes. Waterfalls spilled over the sides of the steepest areas creating rainbows all over the radiant islands, contrasting the menacing sea; an intersection of opposing forces.

It looks exactly like the vines I encountered when crossing back from the infinite, he thought. A fleeting idea about the significance of these islands crossed his mind, *maybe these are a gateway between the material and infinite worlds?*

The sea quickly interrupted his thoughts, and he was again overcome by a sinking feeling induced by the morphing danger surrounding his craft and Jeremy's warnings about these islands. A large wave lifted up his minuscule vessel and threw him to the back of the boat, nearly tossing him overboard. As the wave crashed down on a razor sharp reef in only a couple of feet of water, Andy hung on for dear life. The hull scraped against the bottom, and he cringed, fearing the worst. A quick peek down surprisingly revealed an intact boat, and Andy clumsily grabbed the rudder and adjusted the sail trying to control his vessel. He was thankful for the metal they by chance used to repair the previously leaking bottom.

The convincing currents of the shallow waters around the Three Tombs carried Andy's vessel whichever way they pleased. Despite his best efforts, he was being funneled between the monstrous cliff walls of two of the islands. The green plants covering the islands masked the sharp dangerous rock they clung onto, softening the underlying nature of these islands. Andy grasped the rail of his boat with one hand while the other helplessly held onto the rudder. He anxiously anticipated the real possibility that he would have to jump overboard if he were to hit one of the countless reefs a few feet below the surface.

The boat managed to slip through the treacherous pass, as the third island rose into the sky over the bow, gaining height with every moment as if growing out from the sea. It was twice as tall as the other two, and the deeper water surrounding this island calmed the seas and Andy's nerves, giving him time to more closely observe the islands. Complex vertical spines and ridges gave the islands a skeletal appearance, concealing deep hollows. Laced on the spines were what looked like red-dirt trails that disappeared and reappeared from the recesses of the islands. As Andy was resetting the twisted sail, he was shocked to see a person about halfway up the third island!

Jeremy never mentioned anything about people living on these islands, he thought.

The man was briskly walking up a narrow trail that hugged the side of a cliff. Andy directed his boat to the southern side of the island, trying to go where the water looked deeper and where he could hopefully pick up some wind to carry him away from the Three Tombs.

He kept a close eye on the figure traversing the mountainside, ever cautious about the danger Jeremy warned of. *Is it the hazardous sea or does this person have anything to do with the name of these islands?* he thought, wanting to quickly leave his nearly disastrous encounter behind him. Keeping one eye on the man and the other on his course, he pressed on. Looking over his shoulder, the man was now running trying to keep Andy in his sights, his white clothing sharply contrasted against the bright green island.

As Andy panned the landscapes, he saw a person on each of the other islands as well! They were all intently staring at him, as they knelt down on outcroppings near the top of the islands. The other two people, also dressed in white clothing, gave off rays of light, illuminating the surrounding plants, producing an incandescent halo around their bodies. Andy was not close enough to see their faces, but he felt them intently focusing on him.

If he was not nervous enough having to deal with the hazardous sea, the sight of three bizarre people eyeing him down made Andy feel very uneasy. The ominous name "The Three Tombs" echoed in his head but then, without warning, a warm air unexpectedly draped over his vessel like a secure-feeling blanket. He looked up and pink light covered the sky accompanied by an instantaneous release of his anxiety. The sea settled. The water lapping on his vessel now caressed it, instead of attacking it.

Tranquility.

Peacefulness.

Support.

Andy was sensing the collective consciousness of the Three Tombs, previously composed of three individuals it was now four strong, including Andy. They were isolated in space and free to create as they pleased. With the entry of a new consciousness, these sensitive beings viscerally felt what he was experiencing when sailing through the rough waters, far from the safety and shelter of Meat Cove. They felt his fear, uneasiness, and anxiety. This temporarily put them into the same state, as his conscious cloud became part of their collective cloud. The overwhelming urge to escape the surrounding water compelled them to run to the top of the island, however, being intimately aware of their collective consciousness and the fragility of its health, all three knew they could achieve balance once again.

Centering themselves, knowing without a doubt what they wanted, the beings of the Three Tombs used the strength of their intentions to calm themselves, and Andy too, creating a state of peace. The people of the Three Tombs were able to reestablish the condition they chose to live in, and Andy reciprocally sensed the new state of consciousness. The pink light he saw overhead, and from afar the night before, was the conscious cloud of the Three Tombs. Upon entering, he shifted the cloud by putting in his feelings, beliefs, and preconceived notions about the sea and the Three Tombs into their cloud, stirring the waters, yet, Andy's anxiety without a firm foundation, could not match the peace the individuals of the Three Tombs reflected into their world.

Gentle waves splashed against the bow, spraying seawater into his face. The salt tasted good, and he felt like he was becoming part of the sea, one with it. The boat effortlessly glided through the calm water as the winds changed direction once he rounded the southern point of the third island, blowing strongly from the north.

"This is my wind!" Andy exclaimed, relieved to have found the invisible force that would carry him to his old home.

The sail grabbed hold of the wind, redirecting the vessel towards the Conscious Whole; Andy leaned against the rail of the boat, one hand on the rudder and the other dragging in the water. He looked over his shoulder as the tombs sunk back into the sea.

Peculiar place, he thought. *I wonder what it will be like going back home. How will it affect me?* Feeling both eager and unsure about his next rendezvous, thoughts about the upcoming journey raced through his mind as fast as he sailed towards the Conscious Whole.

29

Rounds of thunder woke the builders beneath; their job was not finished but there was no time to continue on the same course; the resistance was awoken by a single arrow; no longer insensate, it began to materialize in the sky above

DAYS BLENDED TOGETHER. *It's easy to forget about land when all you see is water,* Andy thought. His mind drifted, and he spent hours thinking of his family and friends he had so hastily left, wondering what they were doing, and what they would think when they saw him. *Will they remember me?*

The landscape did not provide much distraction for his mind, a lattice of sea and sky holding a small boat. *Sometimes it's hard to tell where one ends and the other begins.* Andy unfocused his eyes, dissecting the layers of reality, tuning his body and mind into the surroundings as he did in Meat Cove, and could see the ocean's energy moving him towards his destination. There were four-foot tall brisk rollers picking up the boat to the crest and then slowly bringing it back down into the trough, as well as another aspect of the sea, intertwined with the physical.

Just ahead of the waves were parallel arrows of dark blue light, which seemed to pull the waves, one arrow for each. Andy looked down into the deep blue sea, and fifty feet below long streaks of the dark blue energy coursed below the shallower ones, all moving in the same direction.

The pull of the Conscious Whole, a vortex sucking in energy on the outskirts coursed into its center. However, this force was gentle where Andy was, just a small tug, barely convincing enough to bring a bubble to the ground, simply suggesting where he should go. As he crossed into the periphery of his old home, a less aware mind would follow the Conscious Whole's evocation, not aware of the external influence.

Believing he was guiding his vessel, Andy would have been brought in the right direction no matter what. Energies flowing through the entangled web of life, previously in a blissful unawareness, now, in his little boat alone at sea, more vulnerable than he had ever been; he felt the wicked hand of the Conscious Whole at his back shaping reality around him, pushing him deeper and faster into a realm where he would have less control. No longer protected in the sanctuary of Meat Cove, fear crept into the vessel like small, shiny black spiders crawling up the gunnels. There was no escape.

It transforms it.

It creates it.

Andy was now entering another world, controlled by a force larger than he could have ever imagined.

The energy flowed into his body, trying to grab hold as it rapidly went through his back and out his front, riding the wind. Its fingers reached inside and picked at his atoms, and he soon felt a familiarity, a comfort, like coming home after a long vacation, the feeling of security. Yet, there was a sense of deceit, the force that manipulated him in the past was taking up residence.

Off in the distance, clouds were beginning to form in the southwest sky. *A storm? I can do without that!* Andy was troubled by the isolation and exposure of the vessel. The sunny, bright blue skies were just a fond memory from the morning as escalating clouds fiercely assembled in the distance. Puffy, pure white, and appearing innocent at the top, the clouds touched the dangling feet of outer space and rose with an intensity he had never seen before, yet, their angelic appearance did not mislead him long as the blue sky was now almost covered. Spirals of energy rising from the ocean fed the clouds, twisting upward to the top of the now mountainous formation. *It's like they are building an army,* he fearfully thought.

The sky changed at a violent pace, and Andy noticed one colossal black cloud in particular, which was racing towards him from the epicenter of the vast meteorological phenomena unfolding before his eyes. Looking like an enormous coal-colored barrel, it catapulted towards him, ferociously growing larger and larger, skimming the surface of the sea. Andy's tiny vessel helplessly bounced up and down in the building seas. Waves and wind were now coming from every direction, which made his sail dither in the wind.

Within the rolling cloud were spools of the Conscious Whole's potential, wound up and ready to be released. The reels of energy looked like pieces of black metallic string wrapped around the barrel extending from one end to the other. Suddenly, from one of the spools shot a bolt of shiny, opaque lightening straight into the water. Then another. And another!

I guess those wouldn't be called "light"ening, Andy thought, surprised he could find irony and humor while feeling terrified.

Shrieks of thunder sounded like sickening screams as the spools of energy began to move towards the center of the barrel that was now right in front of Andy! He was sitting in the back corner of the boat, one hand on the rudder, afraid to let go, the other holding the hood of his jacket, sheltering him from the now falling rain.

He was terrified; an inexperienced sailor at the mercy of the sea in a storm like nothing he had ever seen before. *It came out of nowhere and only in the matter of minutes!* Andy had no idea what to do, and his boat was no better than a floating piece of wood. *I wish Jeremy were here! He would know what to do.* As the wind and waves grew, he thought he was going to either get tossed into the sea or get struck by lightning!

The spools of energy within this black rolling cloud were now almost on top of him, spinning faster and connected to each other by smaller pieces of energy. Metallic black bolts of lightning continued to shoot out from the spools into the sea and traveled through the water under his boat. Suddenly, a piece of the spools' energy started to track outward in front of the rolling cloud, snaking its way through the sky, eerily moving up and down, left and right.

It's coming right for me!

The tip of this serpent-like energy contained one hundred smaller strings of energy, fingers, which had the same characteristic movements as the larger piece. All the while, the base of the cloud became larger and larger as more potential poured into the arm that was reaching out for Andy.

He was shocked and could barely move. He pressed his body harder against the stern of the boat, his jacket now draped over his head, seeking what little protection he had. Rain poured down as he peered from beneath his shield, the fearless self from Meat Cove only a distant memory as the shiny black arm of energy with all of its fingers crept closer.

Before he knew it, it had grabbed hold of the bow! Strangely, the energy steadied the boat in the turbulent sea with a few of its lithe fingers. As the rest of the creature slyly moved along the top of the small cabin, some of the fingers crept up the mast and onto the sail, while the rest made their way towards the stern, sliding back and forth from port to starboard. The energetic venom of the snake-like being paralyzed Andy, and his thoughts were frozen by the snake's planned future it willed into truth.

The fingers stared into Andy's eyes, his reflection mirrored off of the shiny black surface. He was shocked to see himself as he was before with sunken eyes, coarse and brittle hair, and paleness like a ghost. The shiny fingers acted like a web of mirrors showing him his thin and malnourished body with arms hanging limply by his side and legs as skinny as twigs.

"Thissss is who you should be. Dead!!" the Conscious Whole hissed as one of the fingers crawled into Andy's ear, piercing his eardrum, reverberating a sharp pain throughout his skull and body.

When Andy left, the Conscious Whole's immune system did not recognize his dissent, but now, changed into a healed being, he was a foreign invader, particularly considering that he carried unknown knowledge from Meat Cove.

No matter how hard he tried, he could not look away from his reflection, personified by the Conscious Whole. By this point, if he had stayed in the Conscious Whole, his muscles, lungs, heart, liver, intestines, and brain would have stopped working long ago, but now there was unfinished business. Andy's script written long ago must be played out, and his difference could not exist.

The snake of energy moved its attention to Andy's hand, disgusted by what it saw: a form of matter created by a force other than its own. Instead, a reflection of a thin, skeletal appendage with long, thick, dark nails, lying limp and useless was shown to him as a surge of regret washed through his space. *Why did I leave Meat Cove? What have I gotten myself into?* The energy of the Conscious Whole was suffocating.

Jeremy was right. There is no reason to go back home! The Conscious Whole was draping every feeling of sorrow, remorse, and fear over his body. It was overwhelming.

The arm of energy, with its long, filthy fingers, reached out for his hand, and its grip stung, like hundreds of opaque needles driven into his skin, each one traveling into his nerves, electrifying currents of energy coursing through networks of nervous tissue, including his brain. An intense stinging and burning sensation radiated through every square inch of his body, transforming the matter it touched, beginning the process of turning him back into who he was, who he should have become. Just as Andy had changed his own matter in Meat Cove, the Conscious Whole was reversing the process, making him into what it thought he should be: a diseased body.

The energy of the black cloud contained codes used to create physical forms, blueprints of what Andy had been, memories of previous structures allowed to persist by those who knew him as an ill, dying man, etched into the collective memory.

The arrangement of atoms in his healthy body and new thoughts of himself as a healed being were readily recognized by the immune system of the Conscious Whole as different from what it knew, and it would not compromise as it orchestrated a metamorphosis to bring life back into harmony.

The black arm's vibrational frequency correlated with particular strings of energy, which built specific configurations of subatomic particles, creating the former state of Andy's DNA that made malevolent proteins. The strings of his old particles manifested back into the reality of the Conscious Whole, given life to become real again. One by one, the strings of his healthy body went dormant, now just potential hidden away in the endless land of Meat Cove.

The immune system of the Conscious Whole was doing its job, cleaning up difference for its survival. Beginning in Andy's hand, structures morphed into the diseased state; the same part of his body where he first experienced health in Meat Cove was where the turbid energy began spreading, affecting every corner of his being. His whole body was now suffering from the illness he had so desperately overcome, and he could only observe what was happening, his muscles no longer of any use. Pain tracked throughout his body as a serpentine trail of black energy left its mark, removing the energy from Meat Cove, resulting in the old Andy, the diseased Andy, the Conscious Whole's Andy.

Death of cells was overcoming him as the polished black energy now completely surrounded him. Sitting inside an impenetrable shiny metal sphere, he could see himself, the reflection he had seen before, but now his whole body was visible at once.

The few neurons left in his dying brain asked, *Does it hate me? Why is it killing me?*

Yet, it did not hate him. It actually did not have anything against him. The Conscious Whole simply had to change him to conform to its memory, which was originally built by Andy's intention of who he should become.

This is me, Andy conceded. *Me of the past and me of the present. Strangely, I'm comfortable in this diseased body. It's familiar,* he thought. *It's so easy to just let go and allow the forces around me to take over.* **Mindlessly** *easy, just like before. I don't even have to be conscious of anything. I can just let it happen,* he reflected, put at ease during his last moments by the comforting support of the Conscious Whole.

He began to think about Jeremy, his dear friend back at Meat Cove. He thought about the great times they spent admiring the ocean, the magnificent sunsets and clouds, the mind-bending conversations, the warmth of the summer sun on their faces, the thick ocean breeze.

He then thought about Russell, a man he barely knew, but who literally showed him the world.

Norman, a man as ill as Andy but who blossomed into health and happiness.

He thought about how he was going to miss everyone. About how they would never hear from him again. About how they would wonder what had happened to him. He was sure they could not imagine the fate he was succumbing to as the last breaths of air moved in and out of his necrotic lungs.

30

Barreling in, they hung off the vessel like vagrant cowboys off of a freight car; masters of the fleeting life, as tightly bound to the physical as pollen in the wind to earth, they were called and arose to the moment; quickly enveloping the environment, they shadowed light and created a tornado of spinning energy; as unpredictably as they came, they left, steaming down the tracks for their next duty called

IN MEAT COVE, JEREMY WAS SITTING WHERE he and Andy had spent most of their time, on the backside of the house, facing the ocean. Waves crashed below, and the wind blew strongly. Jeremy had an uneasy feeling deep in his stomach; he knew something was wrong. Looking down the southern coastline, the direction where Andy was dying at sea, Jeremy peered between matter. The Mother Connection was strong.

The winds began speaking to Jeremy, as a message was being carried upstream in a delicate vessel. He looked more closely. Most of the energetic movement was the same as the physical, towards the west, however, within the background of this energy was something different, which at first was very difficult to discern, but he saw it tacking against the flow of the wind, coded and disguised, recognizable by only a few as thin, nervous waves of energy, all out of sync, colored deep orange.

Deep within Andy's body there was one spot the black energy had yet to reach, an ember that had yet to extinguish, hidden beneath ashes of his healed self. The seemingly tranquil core held unwavering orange light and dispatched packets of energy that ran through the battleground like individual fighters leaving the pack.

Many, many miles to the north, Jeremy sensed Andy's distress signal and the information within;[1] the form of a healthy Andy and information about the old Andy the black energy had recreated. One black wave hitchhiked on the orange energy, trying to eliminate it before it reached Jeremy.

Jeremy knew Andy was in trouble; the Conscious Whole's intent to destroy was tenacious and it wielded power that could not be matched. Andy was nearly dead in his boat, and Jeremy acted quickly, concentrating on the waves of energy coming from him. The composition of Andy was constructed from particles that existed in a lattice of reality everywhere in space, once made real, and Jeremy knew the particles could be brought back to the forefront of reality. In his mind's eye, he thought of Andy's physical healthy form and of all of the small particles that made up his body, intently focusing on this image, burning it into reality.

Coursing through his skull as electrical activity, neurons fired and connected with others around them, from one circuit to another, each neuron giving off a different frequency of electrical energy. The summation of electrical activity in Jeremy's brain, while thinking of a healthy Andy, manifested as a complex, frequency-dependent electrical code that numbered in the trillions of different frequencies, each corresponding to a different inherent vibrational resonant frequency of a string that made a subatomic particle that made a particle that made a molecule that made a cell, eventually building a human body.

---

[1]. Look no further than nonlocality (as previously cited) for a mechanism of nonlocal communication.

The electrical activity of the neurons in Jeremy's brain also induced a magnetic field of energy surrounding each of the neurons,[2, 3, 4, 5] which was the vehicle that moved the coded frequency of Andy's healthy body through space, traveling from particle to particle, from the particles that made up Jeremy's body to the particles that made up the air and wind, all the way to the particles that made up Andy's body. The magnetic code physically traveled through space to reach Andy miles away at sea, piggy-backing on the existing magnetic framework of the universe. Within the magnetic energy was the imprint of the electrical energy; like the negative of a photograph, only the magnetic energy traveled the distance leaving the electrical energy behind.

Circular loops of very thin and extraordinarily delicate vibrations navigated the magnetic scaffold of the world, like soap bubbles floating through the wind, containing lifesaving keys for Andy's survival. They moved unhurriedly, gingerly at their own pace, but distance and time were not relevant to these pieces of energy for they operated at the speed of light, at which time does not move, so it took no time to go everywhere. The small rings of magnetic energy jovially made their way to Andy, sliding right through the opaque circular sphere of the Conscious Whole's energy.

Attracted magnetically to Andy's orange smoldering core, the opalescent rainbow exterior of the magnetic ring poured into the core and then throughout Andy. Momentarily, Andy lit up, mirroring the loops of energy as its colors resonated with strings he required for health.

From Jeremy's thoughts, matter was created, and Andy was reborn.

---

2. Electrical current induces a local magnetic field as a fundamental law of physics.

3. Electricity and magnetism of the body are discussed in: Oschman, *Energy Medicine: The Scientific Basis* (2000), pgs. 27-39.

4. See the prior reference regarding the Superconducting Quantum Interference Device (SQUID), which detects the magnetic field of the brain.

5. Transcranial magnetic stimulation uses magnetic energy to influence brain function: O'Shea and Walsh. "Transcranial Magnetic Stimulation." *Current Biology* (2007).

The pearly magnetic loops overflowed out of Andy's body, now attacking the black sphere, fracturing the once solid enclosure. Cracking sounds pierced his ears, as the Conscious Whole shrieked in pain. Suddenly, the prison broke apart into millions of pieces, shattering like glass, crystals of its existence flew in every direction, going back into the cloud.

Andy was exhausted. His body had almost died, and he had believed what the Conscious Whole showed him; he had succumbed to its wants. The thought of seeing his own dying body was catching up to him.

How could I have been so content? he thought. *I was at ease and unconscious of what was happening. I believed I wanted to be in that dying, sickly body!* He felt ashamed he had so easily given up on what he had fought for. *I thought I was stronger than that. I can't believe what I looked like.*

A reflection. A portrayal of what the seer sees. The Conscious Whole was in Andy's mind.

Andy barely had enough strength to pull himself to the side of his vessel, where he kneeled and hung his head over the gunwale. His lungs felt heavy and his breathing was sluggish. Only moments ago cells in his lungs were dying and releasing toxic fumes. He expelled this air and took a full deep breath as his whole body once again began vibrating with life. The storm was backing off, the air was settling, and calm water splashed against the side of his vessel. Andy could see himself in the water.

Once again a reflection of the self; how different this was from what the Conscious Whole had shown him. His red hair was blowing in the wind, his blue eyes captured the iridescent ocean swells, and his arms and hands were strong and full of life.

Life only needs a moment to change. The power of that storm was like nothing I have experienced before, he ironically thought, never before consciously aware of how reality was manipulated by the rules of the Conscious Whole.

Back in Meat Cove, Jeremy saw the energetic echo within the wind of what had happened, as Andy's revitalized energy coursed rapidly through space; yet, it was different than before, transformed by his near death experience, now reverberating with thick, weighted, fiery orange energy, altering space as it drove through matter. Strong enough to move the physical world and push through the challenges he would soon encounter.

Andy looked towards the southern sky, which was bright blue and filled with puffy white clouds. The Conscious Whole had recoiled back to the southwest, over the land where its core dwelled.

He toiled with uncertainty. *It would not be hard to find Meat Cove, it's just right up the coast.* The wind steadily gained strength from the north as Andy's beat-up sail flopped in the wind. The sea was convincing him to carry on.

Quelling his perseveration about the future, Andy tightened up the sail, filled it with wind, and the little boat took off towards the southern seas. A sense of worldly importance and urgency filled his space. *It is worth risking my life,* he thought.

Part V

"...societies are immensely complex systems involving a potentially enormous number of bifurcations...highly sensitive to fluctuations. This leads both to hope and a threat: hope since even small fluctuations may grow and change the overall structure. As a result, individual activity is not doomed to insignificance...threat, since in our universe the security of stable, permanent rules seems gone forever."

ILYA PRIGOGINE, PH.D. AND ISABELLE STENGERS, PH.D.[1]

---

1. Prigogine and Stengers, *Order Out of Chaos: Man's New Dialogue with Nature* (1984), pgs. 312-313.

31

The portal was nearing completion, but as they gained access to the outer layers, their work would be revealed; a tunnel was assembled, covered in mirrored forms, obscuring the remaining work to be done

THREE DAYS PASSED AFTER HIS ENCOUNTER WITH the black cloud, and Andy's provisions were getting low. Nonetheless, the strong winds continued to pull the battered vessel towards the center, like a vortex sucking in the surroundings. The seas rose high and sank low. It was getting more difficult for Andy's boat to handle the heavier conditions, and he was hoping for landfall soon as he approached a world many knew, but none had truly seen.

Feeling clarity about his next task, his mind was surprisingly at ease. He did not over-think or worry about future decisions or situations, much different than how he used to be, and was absolutely sure he was on the correct path, no matter what the outcome. As such, he allowed the energetic flow of the earth to carry him to his next destination.

As he sat aft in his boat, with the winds blowing steadily at his back, Andy reflected on what had happened to his life since moving away from the Conscious Whole. Before leaving, he was entrapped in his old life and old ideas, living by what he was told. He strictly followed the rules surrounding his being, the laws his mind drew from the paradigm of the Conscious Whole creating his existence and found comfort in his daily routine, the daily pattern of nature around him, and the schedule broadcasted by the Conscious Whole.

At the time, the true reason to leave was not conscious, but something deep within lifted him up and took him away, changing everything, morphing a death sentence into a new beginning.

Once again, Andy took a leap and followed the direction he was magnetized towards, taking a chance and relying on a feeling deep inside his core. He figured he would go because he was healed and to show everyone they could do the same. However, sitting alone in the boat heading towards the Conscious Whole, Andy could see the larger picture echoing in the vastness of the open water. It was suddenly so clear what he needed to do: advance the whole of all consciousness.

The boat moved briskly through the sea, and Andy was beginning to feel like an expert sailor; the prevailing wind was helping him look like one, too. The repeating landscape of the ocean played tricks on Andy's mind and he often imagined seeing land in the distance. The high sun made the midday air humid and tropical, so he was surprised to see what he believed were enormous snow-covered mountains in the distance.

How weird, he thought. *It has to be about eighty degrees but it looks like there's snow! Another illusion?* The dissonance of senses made Andy even more unsure of his surroundings.

The snow got closer and closer, and before long, Andy was completely enveloped in whiteness; it was fog. So much for being an expert on the seas.

The wind died down, and the air temperature dropped almost twenty degrees in just a few minutes. The fog was so dense Andy could not see the front of his vessel or the top of his mast! The moisture in the air was soaking him, as if it was a downpour, and he quickly realized he had lost all sense of direction.

Andy promptly remembered the compass Russell had given him and specifically the message it came with, "…there are many different ways to see the world…let this guide you when your eyes no longer know the way."

He found his way to the front of the boat, which was out of sight from the back, and like going into a different dimension, he crawled into the cabin and rifled through the once organized supplies, finding the heavy compass beneath a pile of charts Jeremy had given him. He sat back at his helm with the compass now in hand, and it showed he was facing north, the opposite of where he had been heading just a few minutes ago! Similar to the way Russell saw the world, Andy used the compass to see without using his eyes, righted the direction, and slowly began trudging through the fog, deeper into white nothingness.

Slipping between the molecules of mist, using them as cover, a wolf hid in sheep's clothing. White energy dotted the surface of the Conscious Whole's smooth black appendages, as if hastily spray-painted by a teenager. Distracted, closely following the magnetic dipole of his compass, Andy did not notice this subtle energy in the fog. Meanwhile, the lithe fingers discreetly grabbed the stern of his boat, the nails scraping against the wood, and slowly turned it towards the north; it would get rid of Andy.

The Conscious Whole had not forgotten his presence, it would not give up, and it would certainly not be discouraged by the battle it had already lost. The Conscious Whole would survive, **no matter what.**

Andy had stared right in its face and experienced first hand the creational force of the powerful being the **people** of the Conscious Whole **created**, which then became an entity of its own, crafting a false impression of separation between it and its people. The people, in turn, thought they were in no way tied to the external force of nature, but in truth there was no separation; the Mother Connection linked everything.

Yet, the weakness of the Conscious Whole paradoxically existed in the strength of its creators, the people, for only they, as a whole, could overcome what they had formed. Andy had to show them their power and upon revealing the Conscious Whole to them, the illusion of the limited and finite structure it built would become apparent and fall to pieces.

Andy forged deeper through the fog, deeper into the heart of the Conscious Whole, fighting the persuasive rotation of his stern. Guided by

Russell's eyes, he could find the way towards its center along the magnetic path that the blanket in front of his eyes tried to obscure.

Before long, he was surprised to hear the cry of seagulls. Soon after, the crashing of waves along a shore filled the air. The fog was still very thick, and he was frightened because he could not see anything in front of him even though he knew land must be nearby. He slackened the sail, slowing the boat down as much as possible and then, a gentle rubbing sound on the bottom of the hull caught his attention.

The boat came to a gradual stop on the sandy bottom as small waves splashed against the side of the vessel. He had made it! After days at sea, land finally! Andy quickly hopped out of the boat and was up to his knees in water. He walked forward, holding onto the side of the boat guiding his way to the front and soon was standing on dry ground. The seagulls overhead were going crazy, making all sorts of sounds. *Maybe they're lost in the fog, too,* Andy thought. Or maybe they were signaling the Conscious Whole of his arrival.

Andy could have been standing on a sandbar in the middle of the ocean for all he knew, as he still could not see any solid land around him. Nonetheless, he packed the small amount of remaining supplies into his backpack, strapped it over his shoulders, and started walking along the shoreline hoping to find civilization. He looked back at the boat as it disappeared into the fog and strangely, he was going to miss it. Just before it completely went out of sight, he ran back to the boat and pulled it further on shore.

It needs to stay safe, he thought, hoping it would be there for a sail back to Meat Cove, if needed. Anxiety started to creep into his mind as escape plans and second thoughts were becoming more welcoming actions.

Refocusing on his goal and pushing the uneasiness aside, Andy used the compass to get his bearings once again. It was a great feeling to be back on land even though he felt like his body was still swaying to and fro from life on the ocean. As he walked along the soft, warm sand on the beach, he tried to formulate a plan. He knew he needed to educate the people of the Conscious Whole, but he had no idea where to start.

I'll try making it home first, to see my family and spend time with them. Then I'll start teaching in school again, get my job back. I can even travel around giving lectures! Andy felt energized as a plan was seemingly coming together.

Perfect! he thought. *I just have to get back home and get my old job back! I'll save up money, and I'm sure my family and friends will help me get started at first.* Andy had hundreds of ideas running through his mind and before he knew it, he had been hiking down the sandy shoreline for a few hours but was still enveloped in thick fog. He was enjoying the walk as his revolutionary ideas radiated outward from his conscious cloud, spearheading his creational movement, but he did not foresee the consequence of his thoughts.

32

Haste resulted in incompletion; pieces of the world were missing like an unfinished puzzle; yet, there was no time and the present form would have to do

H<small>E FELT IT BEFORE HE SAW IT</small>. His bare feet on the warm wet sand sensed change. Andy looked down and was surprised to see each individual piece of sand; every one separate from every other grain, individually vibrating, as if held apart by static charge, oscillating in different directions with unique frequencies, some fast while others slow.

As Andy's eyes tracked further down the shore, the fog eased revealing more of the landscape, and a more consistent and uniform vibrational pattern emerged. All pieces of sand, on the whole, were working together, pulsating with a common intention. Waves of the vibrating sand traveled in unison towards him like swells on the ocean, coming from a source somewhere in front of him. Andy thought his eyes were fooling him; he was just getting used to solid ground, but then he felt a wave of sand splash onto his feet producing a tingling sensation.

The sandy waves of energy rippled up his legs causing the particles of his feet and lower legs to simultaneously vibrate at the same frequency, forming physical waves just like in the sand on the surface of his skin, which dissipated as they reached his knees. The energy entered deep into his body and made him feel wobbly like he was standing on a gelatinous surface. Andy felt sick to his stomach and tasted metallic, polluted toxins in his mouth; he spat, trying to get rid of the foulness.

Andy trekked forward towards the source of the bizarre energy, mostly because he had no other choice; behind him was the boat, to his right were steep dunes where the going looked tough, and to the left, an endless ocean. He would have to continue on his course, no matter how sick he felt. As he progressed forward, fighting the urge to vomit, the thick fog thinned out further revealing long stretches of beach and the dunes, which morphed into red rock cliffs to the west. It was not long before a strange sound started to seep out of the air, as if precipitating from the fog like rain; a mechanical churning, over and over, in tune with the waves of sand.

Tall smokestacks appeared first, rising out of the fog, as the body of a factory sat vaguely in the distance, unnaturally cast against the sublime coast. Gray smoke poured from the stacks, blending into the fog, feeding it waste, and staining the pure fog an off-white color. Foul smelling fluid emptied out of a dozen pipes onto the sand as waves innocently lapped up the pollution, titrating it into the sea.

Andy had felt this being long before he could see it, and the filth it produced was viscerally sickening. He scanned the enormous factory, noting all of the different compartments and tubular connections. The entrance sat at the top of the sand dunes, at least two hundred feet above the sea while the smoke stacks rose far into the sky above. The rest of the factory rooted itself into the beach, where it emptied into the water. Andy was astonished by such an unnatural structure, especially compared to what he was used to seeing in Meat Cove.

At least I found some "civilization" before walking too far, he thought, somewhat relieved to have stumbled upon this human-built structure. Uneasiness lurched behind him as he cautiously stepped closer, hoping to make contact with someone who could help him get to a nearby town.

Andy looked up and saw dump trucks unloading garbage at the top of the dunes while bulldozers pushed the piles towards the factory; loose trash spilled over the sides of the dunes. A gnarly crane picked up the large piles and dumped the garbage into a chute funneling into the factory.

Looks like they're feeding an animal.

Andy had not seen people for days and instinctually felt the strong urge to approach the workers operating the machines. He made his way up the sandy dune, crawling on his hands and knees before finally reaching a steep set of metal stairs that led to the top. When he was halfway up, and almost completely out of breath, a person peered their head out of a window and yelled, "Hey! What do you think you're doing!?"

"Oh, hello! Maybe you can help me...I'm trying to find the nearest town," Andy innocently replied between gasps for air.

The mysterious figure from inside the building popped back inside. Andy shrugged his shoulders and resumed his hike up the stairs. Moments later, three security guards came running down the stairs towards him; the manner in which they approached suggested they were not running to his aid. Andy froze, not knowing what to do, surprised by the guards' apparent hostility. He looked back down the stairs, and two more guards were on their way up towards him yelling.

"Don't move! Stay right there or we'll shoot!" they shouted in fury.

Before Andy knew it he was restrained, his face pressed down by one of the guard's knees on the cold, rough metal stairs. It hurt, and he let them know about it.

The guards pushed him down harder and relentlessly asked questions, "Who are you!? Do you have permission to be here!? What's your name!? How did you get here!" they all demanded.

Andy was flabbergasted, he did not do anything wrong! "I'm just trying to get to the closest town," he fired back at them.

A generously proportioned guard slowly made his way up the stairs, out of breath he huffed, "Who...are...you?"

"Already asked him that, boss," a young guard promptly replied, trying to impress his supervisor.

"Oh…whatever…put…him…in…" he coughed, hacking up dark green phlegm and spat on Andy. Clearing his throat he continued, "…the car."

They tied his hands behind his back and dragged him up the stairs, scraping his legs along the way. Andy yelled back at them demanding to be released, but the more he spoke the rougher they were. A small, white vehicle was parked by the front entrance, its blue lights flashing. A cage separated the front from the back seats, as if they used it to transport tigers and wolves. He was forced into the back seat; his bloodied legs and face throbbed in pain. Two of the guards squeezed their tall frames into the front seats looking like adults in a toy car, did not acknowledge Andy, and began driving.

It turns out Andy illegally, albeit accidentally, trespassed. What he initially thought was a factory was actually a garbage disposal plant where all of the waste from the city of the Conscious Whole was transported, burned, and dumped into the sea. The plant was located at the far edge of the Conscious Whole to keep people from seeing its less than environmentally friendly waste disposal methods.

All trespassers were treated the same: locked up in jail to keep them quiet, masking the truth.

"I'm sorry, I didn't mean to do anything wrong," Andy kindly pleaded, even after being mistreated by the guards, as he was being driven away from his crime.

The men in the front seat paid him no attention. He was a criminal, and it did not matter what he said. Besides, he had already seen too much, and they could not just let him go.

The road leading away from the disposal plant went up and down the dunes like the waves on the ocean, as the sandy landscape eventually transformed into grassy fields. They drove for at least two hours, and Andy's dry mouth soon became more agonizing than his cuts and bruises. He tried to distract himself by looking out the window, but there was nothing in sight except for rolling fields and tall grass.

However, within the shoulder-high grass that blew uniformly in the wind, Andy caught a glimpse of a rectangular red sign with white borders. It barely cleared the top of the grass and looked like it floated on the surface. In bold white letters the word **North** was written, the name of the farthest known town north of the Conscious Whole.

Just as unnatural as the garbage disposal plant looked on the beach, the police station appeared alien on the side of the road among the pure green grass. The car pulled up to the small, gray, square building, and Andy was hurried into a corner office in the back of the building.

A burly woman sat behind an undersized metal desk in the back office. Her hair was pulled back so tightly it drew her eyebrows up giving an expression of constant surprise. She had a big nose, penetrating glare, and olive complexion.

The two guards who transported Andy sat him down in a chair in front of the woman and quickly left the room leaving him handcuffed. The woman gave him a disgusted glance, looked down at her desk, and began writing. Andy felt very uncomfortable as he was still barefoot, had sand all over his body, and dried blood covered his legs. His shorts were dirty from getting dragged by the guards, and his shirt hung loosely around his body, only buttoned halfway up, the way he liked to keep it while sailing on the warm ocean. An ocean-combed hairstyle and long beard that was normally neatly trimmed completed Andy's current appearance.

No wonder they arrested me, I look like a vagabond, he thought to himself. *All I have to do is to explain my situation, and I'll be on my way. At the very worst, I'll have a fine to pay for trespassing, but my family can loan me money considering the circumstances. I'll be on my way in no time,* he continued to convince himself.

The woman was absorbed in her paper work, and Andy sat patiently in front of her, smiling, waiting to clarify his situation. His eyes were drawn to a plaque on the desk that read "Inspector Goulrich". Then, without looking up, the woman said pedantically, "What is your full name?"

"Andrew Fergus," Andy briskly replied, trying his best to get on her good side.

"Where are you from?" her monotonous voice continued.

Andy enthusiastically replied, "Well, I came here by boat from a place called Meat Cove. It's north of here, a small town where I lived while I was ill. Before that I lived in Franklin, I don't think it's too far from…"

"Wait. What did you say!?" the woman said in disbelief, interrupting, suddenly interested in what Andy had to say. "North of here? There's nothing north of here. No towns or people. This is the farthest point North. I know of every place on this coast and all of the towns around here. Did you say by boat!? There was no mention of a boat in the report I received…" she stopped speaking and shuffled through some papers on her desk.

Andy looked around the room. There was not much on the walls besides a detailed map of the area showing the coastline. Andy followed it north, but it did not extend to where Meat Cove was located. *Huh, of course she doesn't know about Meat Cove, it's not on her map.*

He looked back at the woman and noticed something unique about the field of energy surrounding her body; a swirling disc-like cloud was hovering about four inches from the top of her head and connected to the crown of her head by a thin wobbling string of energy. The disc rotated slowly, completing one revolution every ten seconds and was about four feet in diameter with a ceramic texture and crisp edges. Very bright apple red streaks with lava orange highlighted the surface of the otherwise gray energy field.

Andy noticed every so often, the cloud would shake violently, as if startled by an invader, which corresponded to a quizzical expression on the Inspector's face as she examined the paperwork. The cloud of energy gave off pulsations from equal increments on the circumference of the disc, beams of light representing the colors in the cloud, paralleling the ground going outward every time the disc made a complete rotation like a lighthouse transmitting its signal, traveling far off into the distance. There was also a reciprocal connection with incoming energy that came in at the same increments as the outgoing signals; however, the incoming light was mostly gray and blended into the woman's cloud, changing it ever so slightly.

Some type of connection to the rest of the world, Andy thought.

The Inspector was unconsciously sharing her information with the rest of the Conscious Whole,[1, 2] and in turn it was telling the Inspector exactly what to think.

"Meat Cove? I've never heard of that place before. Are you sure that's the name of the town..." she trailed off with a puzzled look on her face. Looking back up at Andy, glaring for a few moments, and then squinting her eyes seeming to say, "Ah ha!" to herself.

"It's called Meat Cove. It's north, well beyond the edges of your map. I just came from there. Really is a great place, with nice people," Andy said, trying more and more to convince this woman he was not crazy. *Of course Meat Cove exists, as does everyone who lives there,* he thought. *I'm not mad. This woman is!*

"It's OK. Just stay calm and we'll get you some help." She pressed a button on her desk phone, and the two guards who brought Andy came rushing in, almost tripping on each other, frantically looking for somebody to save. The woman nervously looked at the guards, and they both put a hand on Andy's shoulder, pressing him down into the chair, as if to prevent him from helplessly drifting away in zero gravity. Disc-like clouds were above their heads too, each composed of different colors: one was pale yellow with flakes of orange, like one of the many beautiful sunsets Andy had seen in Meat Cove, and the other was deep, rich green like that

---

1. Groupthink describes social influences leading to poor decision-making: Esser. "Alive and Well After 25 years: A Review of Groupthink Research." *Organizational Behavior and Human Decision Processes* (1998).

2. Crowdsourcing uses the collective power of a group, particularly on the internet, to solve problems or complete projects: Brabham. "Crowdsourcing as a Model for Problem Solving: An Introduction and Cases." *Convergence* (2008).

of a pine forest. However, there was a predominance of gray overshadowing the uniqueness each cloud possessed.

Andy felt the restraint: by the handcuffs around his wrists, by the two men holding him down, by the building he was trapped in, and by the oppressive gray force of the clouds surrounding him. The situation was never in his favor; the Inspector was told what to do, and the Conscious Whole orchestrated every last detail.

Corpuscles of energy from the woman's cloud snaked towards Andy and the guards along hair-thin wires that linked the guards' and Inspector's clouds; her red and orange blended into their colors, changing the palette ever so faintly.

Her view of reality tainting theirs.

The Conscious Whole's terms and conditions spread amongst all.

The energetic foundation of creation by the stipulations of collective, subjective reality was occurring right before Andy's eyes.

As they sat in the small, cramped room, the sight of Andy confirmed their inherited beliefs: a scraggly looking man who appeared, and smelled, like he had not taken a shower in days with an unkempt, long beard, dirty clothes, and a wild, elaborate story. It all made sense, and their experience would confirm what they were told.

The Inspector and guards unconsciously added their subjective perceptions of Andy back into the collective experience, building and reinforcing ideas subtly told to them by the Conscious Whole; a feedback loop of reinforcement of what the Conscious Whole wanted to hear, echoed from its own voice.

Andy tried to speak, but one of the men told him to be quiet, and he was forced to sit in silence. *What are they going to do to me? I didn't do anything wrong. When will they let me go?*

Inspector Goulrich motioned to have him escorted into the main room of the building, and he was handcuffed to a bracket on the wall, forcing him to stand.

They're treating me like a criminal! I guess I broke a serious law, but there must be a way to work it out. Looks like I'll need to get a lawyer. Surely a judge will see the situation from my perspective. He was still confident his detention was temporary, but the Conscious Whole had other plans, which were already set in motion; Andy was right, judgment would soon be upon him.

33

Lurking through the bellowing tunnels, they hoped to gain access; all the while, the cavernous way station stirred with activity, and rumors spread of an unknown force that was awakened

B ACK IN THE SMALL ROOM, THE INSPECTOR explained to the guards that Andy was psychotic.

"He has a mental illness," she told them with confidence. "He made up some place that doesn't exist, called Meat something or other…"

They all laughed, trying to ease the tension and fear of what Andy would do next.

"He lives in an imaginary world that's not real." They all nodded and agreed, the guards fully accepting the Inspector's assessment. "Besides, you can tell just by looking at him; all disheveled and clearly not able to take care of himself. That's how these people look," she continued, educating the guards, not knowing she was really parroting what the Conscious Whole wanted them to believe.

"Of course, a professional will give an official opinion, but it's quite obvious what his problem is. What's his name again?"

"Andy," said the sinewy guard. "But that might not even be his real name!" an orchestral laugh rumbled out of the man's lungs as he proliferated the insanity of Andy.

"Well, he was trespassing anyway and shouldn't have be probing around the 'factory,'" the Inspector said, giving further justification for detaining Andy. "I'm not sure how dangerous he is, so keep him handcuffed and be careful as you transport him to the city." She handed the guards her report for the transfer and gave instructions to take Andy to Brave, a metropolis at the heart of the Conscious Whole.

A city of three million people, Brave was energetically the strongest part of the Conscious Whole due to the shear number of conscious clouds resonating as one; there was physically no room for uniqueness. Andy's difference would be diluted, washed out, and destroyed by the power of many.

The Kay Institute, a place for the mentally ill, kind-heartedly considered a hospital, but functioning as a storage place for people whom others did not want living in society.

The Inspector phoned ahead after the guards and Andy departed on the six-hour drive to Brave, the energetic footprint of her thoughts piggybacking on the electromagnetic message within the phone call; a predetermined image of him for others to base their judgments upon; who he was, how he looked, and his mental state. Andy's creation would be dependent upon those waiting for his arrival.

"He's crazy," the Conscious Whole whispered into the Inspector's ear, the message sent energetically through the network of connected clouds of consciousnesses, vibrating at a frequency only allowing certain particles in nature to manifest to create the reality in which Andy was perceived as mentally ill. The neuroanatomic structure of the Inspector's brain was changed, Andy's image was perpetuated by the guards, and he was soon to be detained in the Kay for his perceived status. A positive feedback loop built into the structure of the Conscious Whole to strengthen ideas and connections ensuring its longevity.

Held more tightly in their grips than ever before, Andy's self-identity would be impossible to maintain. The city of Brave and the Kay Institute were now primed for his arrival.

Andy's physical being was being forced into a metamorphosis as the Conscious Whole defined mentally ill neurotransmitters and then created a mentally ill brain structure observable with their imaging devices; a mentally ill brain the science of the Conscious Whole had **discovered**.

It was a long drive, and Andy became very tired as darkness fell. The last time he had a good night's sleep was in Meat Cove, since he only slept for short periods of time while sailing on the ocean.

Five giant beasts lurked with long teeth hanging out of their mouths. Dark maroon eyes were bound deeply in sockets and light brown, matted hair covered their bodies; ape-like in form but walking like humans and at least one hundred feet tall. They did not seem to notice Andy, so he just hid behind a tree near the top of a field. In the valley below children were playing on a playground next to a baseball field. Andy snuck closer to get a better look, hiding behind another tree. A happy rush of emotions overcame him when he realized it was the school where he used to work! He scanned the crowd of people and could see himself! He was different, the old version of Andy who used to live within the Conscious Whole. *I look disconnected and uncomfortable,* he thought. *I look constrained.*

The beasts marched around the perimeter of the schoolyard, but no one seemed to notice their presence. Andy wanted to yell and warn everyone but feared the beasts would hear him. He impatiently continued to observe as the tall, brown animals stayed on patrol.

Suddenly, one of the beasts grabbed a chunk of the sky, and the energy swirled in its hand, trying to escape. The gray and white colors dripped out of the animal's grasp, running down its arm as it held the separated piece of sky above its head. Then, with all of its strength, the animal threw the piece of sky down at the people! Racing towards the earth, the gray sky separated into one hundred little pieces, each like a drop of rain but gaining speed and becoming long, straight, and very thin, like arrows going straight to the children! The arrows of sky all lined up exactly with each person, spearing into everyone's head. Andy ran forward trying to stop this terrible assault but fell forward tripping on his own feet, which he then realized were atrophic and diseased. He was not able to do anything. The energy coursed through each person's body causing a fast vibration, as if each were a tuning fork.

Time stopped.

Everyone on the playground was frozen as the gray energy coursed through their bodies, resonating every physical piece of matter at the same frequency as the gray color of the sky, physically changing their bodies. Andy was horrified, but all of a sudden, the children and adults started moving again, as if nothing had happened at all. They all looked oblivious to what had just occurred; the children ran around and the adults monitored them. He could see his old self; he too penetrated by the sky arrow. On the surface, no one seemed harmed. The four other beasts joined in the assault as Andy lay quietly on the top of the hill, forced to be an observer. The Conscious Whole was at work.

"Your disease is controlled by your biology, a force outside of your power," Andy was confidently told. A false separation invented by people, relinquishing responsibility from their own self-destructive ways.

The people of the Conscious Whole, however, tricked themselves, deceived into believing potential is **only** potential, and there is only **one** potential. In truth, potential becomes real and potential is infinite. The infinity available to every single being was crushed by the beasts who injected predetermined forms of energy.

Every second, arrows encompassing code for one reality were flung at the people, and they had no idea, impacting in between moments of time, each one representing a single functional unit of the sum of potentials for the subsequent reality. The wave function for the next moment in time. Continuously repeated, determining the outcome of the next piece of time.

In a semi-dream state, lucidity permeated and Andy saw how his illness was created: the joint reality of the whole, perpetuated by the beasts, stemming from his original self-harming intentions forced into his body. Seeing the beasts allowed him to understand how his reality was truly shaped while he lived in the Conscious Whole, giving him understanding of who he was, his degree of influence, how he had changed, and the breadth of his undertaking to help the people of the Conscious Whole.

"Get the hell up!" the wiry guard shouted as he jabbed Andy with a nightstick.

Andy was startled and recoiled to the other side of the back seat. Bitter cold air rushed into the car through the open door; they were a long way from the warm waters of the coast and had arrived at The Kay Institute.

The guards had driven through the night, had gotten lost twice, but had finally made it. They exchanged paperwork with people from the institute and complained about the directions given to them. Daunting buildings towered above as Andy stood on the sidewalk in front of the "hospital."

At least I made it to the city, he thought.

He was still barefoot, and the freezing sidewalk sent sharp pains through his feet. He felt uncomfortable, still in a ragged shirt and shorts, and his legs remained covered in dried blood and sand.

This place doesn't feel very friendly, Andy thought, as cold wind snaked between buildings, piercing his skin, going directly into his bones. *Everything looks the same. All the buildings are brown and gray. I don't see any trees or plants.* Gray and monotonous, Brave was far from the vibrant diversity of Meat Cove.

"The Kay Institute" was clearly written above two old, heavy, windowless, brass doors. The granite face of the building blended into low hanging clouds and looked like a sheer rock face. As Andy and his new guardians approached the entrance, a strong gust of wind pushed him from behind, nudging him inside.

34

Tucked away in a barren vacuum beyond the known solitude, it lay in wait; placed before time tracked forward, it was saved by a weary being known to have endless foresight; loose chains hung from the creature's neck, its remoteness shaping the form; having inhabited this desolate space for all known time, it knew no other way; it was not attached but could not see any destination from its land, as such it never traveled and carried the burden of being a myth; yet, alterations in the geometry of space changed its perspective, now able to see beyond the seemingly impenetrable desert

ANDY WAS OFFICIALLY INSTITUTED AS A PATIENT of The Kay; not a voluntary admission. Patient number 1287739 was printed clearly on his olive pants and matching button-down shirt. He was given his new outfit in exchange for the tired old clothes that had been seasoned on the sea. They allowed him to shower and clean up, and he was spoken to as if a violent prisoner.

"Wear this. Don't move. Don't try anything stupid."

"Excuse me, why am I here? Can I talk to someone in charge? I didn't do anything wrong," Andy pleaded.

"A doctor will be with you shortly," a skinny man with a short mustache told him.

A doctor? Guess they want to make sure I'm okay first.

After showering and changing, which made him feel much better, he was put in a small white room with a metal table and two chairs. He heard people outside the room talking.

"This is a real crazy one. Apparently, he thinks he's from some land up north. He called it Meat Cove..." their laughs echoed in the hallway.

Andy was getting more anxious and tense. He had been held captive since the day before, and no one had explained anything to him! *When am I going to get out of this place? Why aren't they talking to me like I'm a normal human being?* Increasingly agitated thoughts raced through his mind as he sat handcuffed to a chair in his new olive-colored outfit.

He yelled towards the door, "Excuse me! Excuse me!! I don't belong here! There's been a mistake!"

"Hey! Stop the yelling! Don't make us sedate you!" the man with the short mustache shouted through a slot in the door. "We can't have these people out on the streets you know..." he said under his breath to a timid looking woman drawing up medications.

Andy was getting more upset. *Why aren't they acknowledging my questions?* He felt a surge of anger go through his body and screamed as loud as he could, "Get me out of here!!"

Suddenly, five people came running in, and before he knew it there was a sharp poke in his arm. He thought he got stung by something and turned to see what had gotten him but then everything became blurry, and he felt clouded, like the fog he sailed through on the sea.

Andy awoke in a tiny bed with olive sheets matching his uniform. A small square window nearly at the ceiling revealed night had come. *Where am I? What happened?* He felt groggy and tried to get up, but a voice from across the room gently rolled towards him, "Mr. Fergus?"

He rubbed his eyes to get a better look, but it took him a minute to focus. "Yes, I'm Andy. Call me Andy. What happened?" he innocently asked.

"You're at The Kay Institute. It's a hospital to help you get better", the voice kindly replied.

Looking at the floor, still not feeling great, Andy quickly said, "I'm fine. I don't need help. I need to leave."

"Well, how about we try to talk for a bit," the now nervous voice said, seeming to steer further away.

Andy was now able to see the voice, a new doctor at The Kay Institute fresh out of training, petite and very attractive. She had soft skin with a slight hint of bronze, like she had just gotten back from a vacation on a tropical island. Her red hair with bronze highlights glamorously fell over her shoulders. Dark eyes peered out at him from behind a lock of hair, and her thin lips gave an unsure smile towards him. She was dressed professionally with a long white coat and a dark suit on underneath and was the only person who looked him in the eyes since he arrived onshore, which helped him calm down.

"My name is Dr. Rubin. Why don't you tell me a little about yourself?"

Andy felt confident that the doctor was his way out and went on to explain everything, from his previous illness, to traveling to Meat Cove, to becoming a healed body and mind, to sailing down the coast, and to becoming a prisoner. Dr. Rubin wrote down all of the details as fast as she could, trying to keep up with Andy's story. He spoke with such haste and emotion that Dr. Rubin had to ask him to repeat a few parts of the story, particularly about him and Norman, the Three Tombs, and his encounter with the black sphere. Andy did not stop talking for over an hour. She was the first person he was able to have a conversation with since leaving Meat Cove, and he had so much to say! Dr. Rubin was actually listening to him, and he felt like she understood his situation and that his imprisonment would soon be a long lost memory.

"Acute mania with a delusional disorder. Treat with sedative and neural altering medications," was written at the bottom of Dr. Rubin's admission paperwork after she left Andy's room.

Dr. Rubin specialized in science developed by the Conscious Whole about mental illness, neurons, neurotransmitters, and medications that treat the brain. She also studied human behavior, which stemmed from examining how humans interact and carry themselves allowing her to categorize people. Every behavior, action, thought, and emotion was defined.

People were definable. However, within the Conscious Whole to be defined was to be created, an existence maintained by an assigned definition, collapsing infinite possibilities naturally within every person into the one finite category, leaving very little chance of breaking the mold. The categorical system assumed control of creation from the individual.

Seeing beyond the weak latticework of categories built around people was difficult as the categories were steeped in the mire of reality and to realize the created categories were merely invented would be to look into the eyes of the creator.

Free thoughts were well contained in the Conscious Whole's categorical system, reigning in consciousnesses that went beyond established limits while coaxing others to stay, preventing new paradigms from forming, forcing everyone to place ideas, inventions, and thought processes into the already established categories. Even those that seemed to escape definition were categorized, giving others perspective to judge and persecute. No room for the sublime.

The Conscious Whole was defining Andy too, wrapping its arms around him, and preventing escape. The diagnosis of mania with a delusional disorder should have been enough to contain him but Andy, no longer a person of the Conscious Whole, was like a star in the black sky, a contrast the Conscious Whole tried to devour yet still bright enough for everyone to see.

The assessment by Dr. Rubin determined the course of Andy's treatment at The Kay Institute. Part of the workup included a brain scan to see if there was a so-called "organic or anatomic" cause for his behavior and delusions; a physical problem they could blame for his mental illness.

The Conscious Whole

Of course, the scan showed the problem. In the eyes of the observers, Andy's brain was active in areas normally considered silent. Well, of course they would find this, as he was unique! His body and brain transformed while in Meat Cove, he was not like the people of the Conscious Whole, and the brain scan demonstrated this difference.

Yet, the doctors would interpret the data differently for they believed in sameness and Andy was unusual. "His **difference** is the pathology," they proclaimed, an outlier who did not fit into the average of a statistical bell curve.

For Andy, the doctors only cared that he was beyond one end of the curve, which is what the Conscious Whole saw as being the problem, for their curve was paramount. Deviation from **their** mean, **their** calculated mean, made Andy unusual enough to warrant treatment. The goal was to bring him back towards their average to be more like the others; more like the way the Conscious Whole wanted him to be.

"You see," a neuroradiologist said to Dr. Rubin, "his brain is much more active in this area called the reticular formation than it **should** be," he said pointing to a spot on a computer screen.

"Ah yes," Dr. Rubin replied, also convinced she was seeing where Andy's mental illness existed. "That helps a lot, thank you! Now we know how to treat him."

Andy would be given a predetermined dose of medication specifically designed for overactivity in the brain. Brain-Ex was found to calm down the mind in scientific studies, chemically altering the operation of the neurons making transmission of signals less likely. The medicine was designed to sedate him for a few days, resetting his brain; the excessive activity on the brain scan must be stopped.

Presenting at a weekly conference to discuss new patients, Dr. Rubin pointed to a picture of Andy's brain and assertively stated, "The overactivity is right here." Her green laser-pointer outlined a bright red area, which contrasted with the uniform grayness of the rest of the brain. "**This** is the **cause** of his mania." [1,2,3,4,]

"What a great example of this disease," the chief physician of the Kay remarked. "You should publish this result for everyone else to see!" The Conscious Whole salivated at the opportunity to perpetuate this fallacy.

"We will give him Brain-Ex, the standard drug for this condition. It has been shown in many studies to reduce mania, particularly when delusions are present."

"It's amazing we can now see where mental illness *begins*," an old rusty doctor affirmed from the back of the room, proud of the accomplishments of the trusted system. The doctors had found the answer! There was no arguing against what they saw with their own eyes.

Andy's journey through the layers of reality in Meat Cove had changed his physical body. Learning to view the world differently built new brain connections, which the brain scanner detected but were interpreted by the doctors as pathology instead of uniqueness. The Conscious Whole would quiet the dangerous intruder.

The room full of perpetually educated physicians relied on much more than their knowledge when assessing Andy's condition. It was not just their comprehension of the human body or neural networks of the brain that was used to establish the final diagnosis. A much more powerful force was at the root of their deductions.

Judgment.[5]

---

1. The paradigm of neuroscience relies heavily on imaging of the brain. There is extensive research correlating behaviors with differences in brain structure and function (several examples are subsequently listed). Correlation is not causation! The brain scans may show a problem, but do not necessarily show the *cause* of the problem!

2. Guedj et al. "Clinical Correlate of Brain SPECT Perfusion Abnormalities in Fibromyalgia." *Journal of Nuclear Medicine* (2008).

3. Sun et al. "Progressive Brain Structural Changes Mapped as Psychosis Develops in 'At Risk' Individuals." *Schizophrenia Research* (2009).

4. Just et al. "Identifying Autism from Neural Representations of Social Interactions: Neurocognitive Markers of Autism." *PloS One* (2014).

5. Patients' perception (i.e. judgment) of their illness has a measureable effect on health outcomes: Petrie and Weinman. "Patients' Perceptions of Their Illness: The Dynamo of Volition in Health Care." *Current Directions in Psychological Science* (2012).

Before even presented with the data the doctors knew the answer they were looking for: mental illness, by any means and by any cause. A man found wandering, disheveled, and with a fanciful story was where judgment began. The doctors needed nothing further and all other evidence, no matter what the result, would only be used to support their prejudice. However, the fatal crime was the subsequent management of Andy; the doctors treated their own judgment and not the patient. They quelled their own needs, not the patient's. The physicians of the Conscious Whole were no more than servants to the egocentric, half-witted, malevolent ways of the collective whole.

From the perspective of the Conscious Whole, Andy was mentally ill. But was he truly mentally ill? Was that the only way to explain his behavior? The altered brain activity is not the *cause* of Andy's difference but instead the *result* of a deeper force. The doctors' use of reductionism led them to believe they could diminish the overactivity and make his brain more like theirs, fixing the problem; they treated the overactivity as the *source* of Andy's behavior, disregarding the deeper foundation of quantum particles and energetic forces shaping matter.

The brain is dynamic and changes in response to the environment[6, 7, 8, 9, 10, 11] and in response to the energetic fields. Particles making pieces of

---

6. The following literature is to dispute the inherited/genetic basis of psychiatric disease that is centered upon neurochemicals, and instead argues for environmental influences creating disease states.

7. Neurochemical levels in primates depend upon their social standing in the group and will increase or decrease with changes in hierarchy and community environment: Raleigh et al. "Social and Environmental Influences on Blood Serotonin Concentrations in Monkeys." *Archives of General Psychiatry* (1984).

8. The brain physically changes its structure depending upon body use: Langer et al. "Effects of Limb Immobilization on Brain Plasticity." *Neurology* (2012).

9. Stress can alter the cellular composition and physical structure of the brain: Chetty et al. "Stress and Glucocorticoids Promote Oligodendrogenesis in the Adult Hippocampus." *Molecular Psychiatry* (2014).

10. Pearce, *Evolution's End: Claiming the Potential of Our Intelligence* (1992).

11. Horwitz and Wakefield, *The Loss of Sadness: How Psychiatry Transformed Normal Sorrow into Depressive Disorder* (2007), pgs. 39-40.

the brain are susceptible to minute forces from vibrational frequencies of energy in the environment, which change the strings that manifest as new particles, creating new atoms, forming new molecules, structuring new DNA that builds new cells, making new neurons that build new connections. Connections that did not exist in the brains of the people of the Conscious Whole. Andy's rewired brain was the result of his life in Meat Cove and the physical manifestation of his uniqueness, not his pathology.

The difference in Andy was deeper than what the brain scan showed, deeper than the physical materialization of neuronal activity, and instead came from the energetic and observer-based powers acting on quantum particles in his body *resulting* in transformation of his brain! A simple medicine would not fix the "problem" or even get close to changing Andy into someone he was not.

35

Ushered through the vastness by a lone signal of hope, the being's original purpose was awoken; a source code of infinity to be used when the existence of infinity was no longer seen; its intent was only to show, not to preach; to display what inherently existed in every morsel of space but had been forgotten

I F AN OBSERVER SPENT TIME IN THE woods but knew nothing about plants of any kind and if he or she came into contact with the poison ivy plant, they would itch their skin and not know why. However, upon close inspection the observer would see blisters.

"Ah ha! The source of the problem," the observer would say. "The skin itches **because** of blisters!"

The observer may note this same type of skin condition at seemingly random points throughout their lifetime, not knowing that contact with the poison ivy plant caused the blisters to form, and may wish to tell others about this phenomenon by reporting it in a scientific journal. The paper would be accepted for its brilliant observation and would be titled: "The correlation between malformations of the dermis and the sensation to scratch." Logically, blisters cause scratching. The eruption of blisters seemed so random that the observer did not know there was a connection between poison ivy and blisters.

The original scientific paper even postulated reasons why blisters appeared: stress, emotional instability, skin color, parent's traits, but it did not foresee the seemingly unrelated contact with the poison ivy plant. Treatments were focused on removing the blisters with hot iron rods, acidic solutions, and surgical excision.[1,2]

Years later a different observer made a new discovery, "when an individual comes into contact with the poison ivy plant, oils on the leaves cause a delayed skin reaction resulting in the release of very small, invisible molecules from white blood cells in the skin. The molecules produce blisters as well as the sensation to scratch." A deeper understanding. The true source of the scratching behavior that connects walking in the woods, invisible molecules, and blisters.

The Conscious Whole did not understand Andy. They feared him. With fear came force to protect the Conscious Whole.

Andy got a shot of Brain-Ex in his arm right after he finished breakfast. The nurse trainee came to pick up his empty tray and distracted him as the senior nurse quickly delivered the loading dose. The medicine worked quickly as Dr. Rubin watched from the window of his door. Andy uncontrollably slumped over, and the two nurses helped him into a comfortable position on his bed. Watching this unfold, an innocent fleeting thought raced through Dr. Rubin's mind. *Is this right?*

---

1. This tale of poison ivy is fictional, but a search of prior medical literature will reveal similar false research based upon logical deduction (one example below). How amusing will our current research sound someday?

2. The thymus gland is a normal anatomic structure in the chest but can be very large in children, which is usually completely normal. Yet, physicians in the late 1800s through the mid 1900s inappropriately attributed a "large" thymus to sudden death in children because of airway compromise. It logically made sense: a large thymus, which is around the airway, can cause breathing problems or death. As such, many patients received prophylactic surgical removal or radiation treatment of "enlarged" thymus glands with mortality rates approaching 33% for surgery and for acute radiation injury; radiation induced cancer was another result. Deductive science at its best, which was described in the scientific literature at the time, but turned out to be completely wrong. Reviewed in: Jacobs, Frush, and Donnelly. "The Right Place at the Wrong Time: Historical Perspective of the Relation of the Thymus Gland and Pediatric Radiology." *Radiology* (1999).

"Don't worry, it may look bad now, but it's for his own good," the senior staff physician said to Dr. Rubin, reading her facial expressions.

"Have you ever traveled to the north?" Dr. Rubin freely asked, leaving her typically composed and professional façade.

A hearty laugh roared from the staff physician's barrel-shaped chest, "It's not uncommon to have those thoughts...you will see as you gain more experience, the patient's mind can concoct an amazingly far-fetched reality. Sometimes it seems so real, but there's only one reality."

The omnipotent surveillance of the Conscious Whole sensed distrust in its ways and promptly rushed into Dr. Rubin's brain in an effort to eliminate opposition to its plan. The energetic fingers worked rapidly, probing through every inch of her mind like a surgeon, the long, sharp, shiny black fingernails sounding like knives against metal as they worked. The skeletal appendages of the whole projected from the background of matter, from the so-called empty space[3] within atoms, and continued working, as if shuffling through papers straining to find one line of information to destroy from her consciousness.

Suddenly, the fingers stopped and could not go any further, shocked by what they had found. *Her brain has been changed,* the Conscious Whole's seared voice whispered to itself as the limbs reluctantly retreated.

The Conscious Whole's frustration seeped into the physical, and Dr. Rubin suddenly felt mad and annoyed. She hustled off to her office sure there was some meeting she was late for and being forced to attend.

Dr. Rubin was unaware the ember orange, maroon red, and light violet energy radiating from the periphery of Andy's cloud had cautiously slipped between matter when they first met, a step ahead of the Conscious Whole's surveillance. The orange led first, darting behind atoms every time the fingers snaked past, which preyed on random pieces of energy

---

3. The Casimir effect, originally described by Hendrick Casimir in 1948, predicts that virtual particles in the vacuum of empty space can exert a real force on material objects. First experimentally proven in 1997: Lamoreaux. "Demonstration of the Casimir Force in the 0.6 to 6 μm range." *Physical Review Letters* (1997).

counteracting its force. Breaking into the grayness surrounding Dr. Rubin, the brilliant orange lit up her featureless energies while the deep maroon and graceful violet followed the blazed trail towards the doctor, gently incorporating into her monochromatic gray cloud.

She yearned for the color Andy emitted, and her wave function produced new solutions as Andy shared his convictions in flagrant contrast to the Conscious Whole's penchant for sameness and conformity.

The new vibrational frequency of Dr. Rubin's cloud percolated throughout her body, bringing strings of matter, that were only potential as dark matter, into her reality. New particles, new atoms, new pieces of DNA, new compositions of the cell membrane of her neurons all coalesced to change her neuroanatomy ever so slightly, just enough to create a brain able to repel the Conscious Whole. It could see her subversion but born from energy Andy channeled from Meat Cove, the flow of energy was not strong but rather persistent, like a tack stuck in the bottom of a bear's paw. Dr. Rubin was able to slip away through the tight grasp of the now frustrated and distracted Conscious Whole.

Andy's presence was affecting others; the Conscious Whole failed to suppress him and his energy had spread; now there were two; the collective influence was one less.

He woke up in a daze. The high walls seemed endless, distorted by the overmedicated coma he had awoken from. The single window close to the ceiling let in early morning light, but it was too high to see out of. He tried to sit up, but the room spun in circles.

Andy was unsure what had happened, and it took him several minutes to recall his last memory: a sharp poke in the arm, again. The metal door leading out of his room had a square window with thick, scratched, translucent glass and shadows moving past on the other side. A wet sensation on his chest helped to rouse him out of his semi-conscious state.

Drool? What did they give me? he thought as his grappled with the local structure of space and time.

The Conscious Whole

Brain-Ex had an incomplete effect on Andy, only resulting in severe sedation. The medication should have reduced the firing rate of neurons in his brain's reticular formation, decreasing the amount of incoming sensory stimuli processed, calming him down, allowing him to ignore his "delusions" about Meat Cove. However, the scientists had never tested the medication on someone like Andy whose neuroanatomy was unique. His conscious cloud resonated at his own unique frequency[4] he had picked up while in Meat Cove, which correlated to vibrational frequencies of strings producing molecules that made different receptors on the neuron cell membrane, where Brain-Ex normally functioned to disable neurons. The medication was not effective. Andy's "delusions" and "mania" remained.

It took a moment for him to notice a barely audible knock at the door. He could only make out red hair through the creamy glass and figured it must be Dr. Rubin, who came to conduct the first post-treatment interview to assess the efficacy of the medicine. According to the clinical trials, the effect of the medicine was strongest right after awakening from the loading dose, then over time the delusions would return and require smaller but equally censoring doses.

"Feeling alright today, Andy?" Dr. Rubin asked in a gentle, hesitant voice peering around the corner of the half open door.

Grunting, Andy responded, "Uh...yeah. I'm feeling okay. Just a little cloudy..."

"The medicine will help your thoughts become more clear. They won't be as wild as they were," Dr. Rubin said attempting to convince Andy of the treatment plan, blissfully unaware of the neurochemistry sparking away in his brain.

Andy knew he came from Meat Cove by boat, and that he was a healed being. He never felt his thoughts were "wild" but tried to relax his body and regain composure after processing Dr. Rubin's remarks.

What they think of me is all in their minds too, he thought.

---

4. As previously cited, similar concept in: Green, *The Keys of Jeshua* (2004), pg. 289.

Dr. Rubin took a seat next to Andy's bed with her notebook in hand, peeled it open, and placed her pen on the page where she left off last time. "So, are you feeling more calm than when you arrived?" she eagerly asked.

"Well, yes," Andy stated, changing his tone to reflect someone who was well-grounded and lucid but really thinking the same since he had been admitted.

"And having any thoughts about hurting yourself or anyone else?" she asked uneasily, glancing out of the corner of her eye to see if the security guard was still waiting by the door like she had asked. Despite Dr. Rubin's newly found separation, the Conscious Whole maintained a tight grip on what it could and continually reminded Dr. Rubin of the dangerous nature of Andy.

Andy gave her a puzzled look, "No…no. Not at all."

They spoke for thirty minutes more, Dr. Rubin analyzing Andy's behavior and responses while he tried to focus and deliver clear and concise answers. Andy centered himself trying to bring his intentions back into focus.

What is important? What should I be spending my energy and time on? What should I leave behind that is no longer useful? How will I get out of here and help the people of my home?

Andy sat up straight, took his time replying, and as the interview continued his thoughts became more and more coherent. *Once she understands my side of the story I'll surely be let go.* He figured his best option for release was being straightforward and again spoke about Meat Cove and his journey as calmly as he could.

"Since landing on shore, everything has happened so quickly," Andy said, recounting the events, but he was ill-prepared for the Conscious Whole, which would not fail as it did at sea. It wasted no time voraciously tunneling him down a one-way path, submerging him inside its core, forbidding escape; if it could not change him, it would imprison him. One moment Andy was tacking into the wind, in control of his path, and in no time he was locked up, medicated, and at the absolute mercy of the Kay.

The Conscious Whole

At the conclusion of the first post-treatment session, Dr. Rubin methodically wrote in her notebook:

Brain-Ex seems to have calmed his mind.

He is acting intelligibly.

It did not get rid of the delusions?

Supposed to have a 100% anti-delusion rate according to the research.

His story seems so real.

She stopped writing and thought, *He even looks like he spent a long time traveling out at sea*, not daring to write or speak those words. Conflicted between the old paradigm endorsed by the Conscious Whole and the new energy acquired from Andy, unknown was on the horizon.

With a perplexed and introspective facial expression Dr. Rubin said, "Well…everything is going great," doing little to cover up her emotions. She blindly walked out of the room consumed by internal confusion and confliction.

"Wait! What happens next?" Andy pleaded.

"Lunch is in 2 hours," the skinny guard wearing an oversized uniform replied and slammed the door behind the doctor.

Feeling distraught, Andy focused his mind and maintained his axis of vision around his body. He allowed himself to forget the madness and unfair treatment occurring at the Kay, mentally leaving the world he had so eagerly sailed into.

His eyes swept back and forth, looking in between the pieces of physical matter he was contained within, and he could see the Conscious Whole, seeping between the framework of the physical, seamlessly woven into the material. His eyes unfocused the physical matter, and he saw what was less obvious. What Dr. Rubin and the security guards could not see. What the people at the garbage disposal plant could not see. What they all **chose** not to see.

A foggy gray mist interlaced with metallic gray and black spider webs hanging between pieces of matter, inside of each atom, in the so-called empty space unoccupied by electrons, protons, and neutrons. The web was attached to each subatomic particle and held them in position, maintained constancy, and kept matter where it wished. The framework upon which the world was built lay in front of Andy's eyes, as the gray mist slowly pushed its way through the stationary webs, like the subtle tide of a bay.

Andy looked more closely, unfocusing his mind even more and saw long projections of shiny black energy, like pieces of fishing wire, quickly snaking through the framework, darting around webs, easily overpowering the ebb of the mist. Sensing matter out of tune, not resonating with the framework it rested upon, the deep force either drew away from or provided energy to these aberrant physical forms. To do so, the long strings of energy would stop, reach out with one finger and touch the dissonant piece of matter. With this simple motion, the matter would resonate at the same vibrational frequency as the wire's energy, bringing it back in line, changing its form. Andy watched this process occurring all around him and saw at least fifteen wires of energy swarming in the hallway with more appearing as people walked by, stalking them down the corridor.

Alone in his room, within the stillness of solitude, the world danced before his eyes while the subtleties driving nature became apparent. The wires of energy flowed past him in the mist, like water snakes in search of prey, not taking long to change direction to alter his matter, rework his body, but he was impermeable as his conscious cloud resonated with energy unlike anything the Conscious Whole had ever experienced. Reaching out, like a child unsure of whether or not his surface was safe to touch, the fingers immediately encountered equal and opposite energetic forces incapacitating any attempt to inflict change. The colors of light that made up his body broadcasted an absolute unbreakable belief in who he was. Nothing could destroy this.

The absence of doubt kept him safe.

The presence of hope pushed him forward.

Dr. Rubin walked out of the inpatient unit to her office still carrying a piece of Andy's energy, which remained shielded from forces sustaining her; the catalyst of change was spreading, but at what cost?

36

Rarely formed over the precipice, the energy assembled, like a cyclone forming over land; the rarity of the event would draw attention but the beings were prepared to show their hand; the one from the land of solitude was manifesting

Andy began adapting to the routine at the Kay. Wake up, take medicine, eat breakfast, talk to the doctor, get lunch, talk to the doctor some more if you needed adjustments to the medicine, then dinner, and sleep shortly afterwards. All of the patients were given so much medicine, many spent the entire day sleeping, and Andy wondered how long they could live on only small amounts of food.

There was one patient whom Andy felt badly for; he was tall and skinny with oversized round glasses and a uniform that hung loosely off his body. This man would devour half of his breakfast and promptly pass out on the table when the medicine set in. Like clockwork, the same draconian nurse who administered medicine to everyone would snap her fingers, and two men in white clothes would drag him to his room, which was close to the dining hall, so they would not have to drag him far. Andy never saw him during lunch or dinner and one time curiously peeked into the man's room before dinner, and he was still asleep!

What a dreadful place, Andy thought as he surveyed the common room where many patients would gather and bring their lunch, at least those not in a pharmacologically-induced coma. *We don't even get to wear normal clothes! It's all the same color: the walls, the floor, the tables, everything!* Ironically, the Kay was beginning to make Andy crazy and misery was creeping into his life.

As Andy forced down his pre-packaged, inadequately heated meal that tasted like a mixture of carpet and cheap sardines and looked no different than his olive-colored socks, he noticed something staring at him from the corner of his eye. It blended into the fading drab paint with only its oversized royal blue eyes contrasted against the sameness of the wall. The small cups on its toes kept the tiny gecko propped upside down. It cocked its head earnestly from side to side, analyzing Andy. A security guard walked by, and its big eyelids rolled over its eyes concealing the only visible trace of its existence.

Andy looked away, not wanting the guard to notice and then quickly looked back. The small reptile stared more intently at him and through the translucence of its skin two minute, pale purple and shiny turquoise vibrating packets of color floated weightlessly in its body. Andy was amazed by this creature, transfixed by its presence, and wondered where it came from, as it was far too exotic for the monotonous, cold city of Brave. They both stared at each other, and Andy had an overwhelming feeling the meeting with the small lizard was more than just a random occurrence.

Miles away, in Meat Cove, Jeremy intensely focused on Andy; he knew he had made it past the storm and landed safely on shore, but Jeremy worried what had happened once he entered the Conscious Whole. Jeremy stood on his deck leaning over the railing of his balcony and tapped into the Mother Connection. Arctic air blew strongly from the north and he sensed the biting wind was telling him about Andy's journey; the crystal clear skies of Meat Cove belied the happenings in Brave.

Concealed to the Conscious Whole, Jeremy tapped into the underworkers' network of beings, who molded ancient energy buried deep below Meat Cove and sent out two bundles of energy that hugged the rugged coastline, coursing in unison, one outpacing the other and vice versa. They cut through the cold air and turned inland speeding across the rolling hills of the northern plains, paralleling the top of the tall grass as it blew to and fro in the wind. In literally no time, two camouflaged containers arrived in Brave, penetrated the dense granite walls of the Kay and seeped out of the pores, manifesting as the gecko on the wall; a pair of cloaked eyes sent by allies of Meat Cove.

Jeremy could see despair on Andy's face through his long and wild beard as a frown was buried within. The two packets of energy danced through the gecko's body, mesmerizing Andy, and then localized to the back of its eyes, like a night sky full of fireworks. Andy's eyes perked up and a smile worked its way to the corner of his mouth.

Suddenly, the gecko turned its attention to the corner of the room as if being hunted; its disguise did not last long, and the Conscious Whole would not allow its presence. Matte black metallic fingers raced from the far side of the room towards the gecko, their sharp nails screeching across the metal tabletops. Suddenly, the gecko leaped at Andy, its arms and legs spread wide as the heinous black fingers shot out like spears, but the Conscious Whole was too late. The gecko's body disintegrated in mid-air and only the energy of its eyes persisted, de-forming into their original embodiment, becoming one with Andy's conscious cloud. Now protected by the still intact fortress of Andy's body, the capsules of energy sent from Meat Cove provided a dash of hope and helped to revitalize his diminishing morale. The Conscious Whole retreated, hardly content with the increasing violation of its boundaries.

Feeling energized, Andy was motivated to do something about his imprisonment instead of getting dragged into the mindless demoralizing routine. With few resources available to aid in escaping, he decided to tap into all he had: the other patients at the Kay.

The Conscious Whole deemed their inability to function unacceptable and separated them from the rest of society. Forced by family, friends, their own bodies and minds, and ultimately by the Conscious Whole to be institutionalized, their thoughts, beliefs, perceptions, and feelings were not compatible with others. They were categorized as mentally ill. Disabled. Sick. It was how the Conscious Whole made them.

37

The most coveted trait was carried by a few; its delicateness easily crushed by those seeking its virtue; yet, those bearing its fruit walked the path, which too often led to judgment

PERCEPTION. AN INCREDIBLY SUBJECTIVE EXPERIENCE. The collective perception. The Conscious Whole. A collective subjective experience.

The problem Andy faced was that the collective experience was misinterpreted as being objective and defined as "objective reality." In truth, however, it was simply a set of conditions and parameters many subjective observers agreed upon. Does individual subjectivity multiplied by everyone in the population equal objectivity? If all of the subjective observers were to leave, would the world, based on their subjective experiences, still continue to exist in precisely the same way as when they left it? With no one else to verify it, why would the people of the Conscious Whole think otherwise? Subjectivity is **all** there is in the world of the Conscious Whole.

The people in the Kay were not in tune with the perceptions of those outside of the strong granite walls. Yet, the immune system did not try to change them since they were not only built into the paradigm of the Conscious Whole but also contributed to it themselves. If the Conscious Whole were to destroy their differentness, their so-called illnesses, it would be destroying itself and, in part, the foundation everyone relied upon. It needed them so they could define normalcy. The people of society used the predominant collective thought, which was believed to be objective, for guidance, and those living on the fringe of accepted subjective reality were destined for the Kay.

"Their brains do not work properly!" physicians and scientists exalted with confidence. "They do not see the world in the same way *we* do, so *they* are sick!"

Separating you from me encouraged people to love and hate, and supported a dichotomous paradigm.

The paradigm defined mental illness by assessing structural connections or chemicals within the brain based upon evidence finding either different brain activity on brain scanners or alterations of neurotransmitters, chemicals, in the brains of those deemed mentally ill[1] when compared to those *defined* as normal.

"There is the problem!" they exclaimed. "Our patient does not see the world as we do because they are different in the brain!" the scientists said, reciting subjective collective agreed upon theories.

True. The people in the Kay are different in the brain but not necessarily because they have a pathological problem. ***They are simply different***. A conflict occurs in the Conscious Whole when someone's subjective view is not the same as the agreed upon collective, subjective experience, in which case, "pathology" manifests. However, they simply view the "objective" world differently.

Imagine a spectrum of truths where all are equally true but a choice of one over all others must be made, resulting in ***the one*** Truth, manifesting as the one reality the Conscious Whole follows. However, a problem occurs when someone believes in a different truth; this individual exists under the one physical reality of the collective group but is continually in conflict with what they believe and what they perceive, in spite of the

---

1. Medical imaging is becoming increasingly used for diagnosing mental illness (as cited above); the literature is consumed by the neurochemical and structural paradigm of mental illness; we must look deeper.

"objective" reality. He or she is different and perceived as such by the majority; combined with the individual's belief in **their** one Truth and the collective thought defining separation of "them from us" creates a unique material manifestation in the people who do not believe in the one Truth. The conscious clouds change matter, including the structural connections and neurotransmitters in the brain, based upon their own perceptions and the collective groups perception of their pathology.

Everyone sees the world through a subjective lens but declares it as objective. The tendency to call life objective becomes more and more powerful with increasing numbers of people declaring their world as the only "real" one. Thus, those who believe in a different worldview are outcast and told they have a pathological problem with their brain.

The issue is not a pathological medical problem. It is non-conformity.

38

Passed on from one to the next, the leader of light had a purpose; to see and to show what was beyond the unseeable; a gift to be used with prudence but too often shunned by those unable to see

WITHOUT HESITATING, ANDY WALKED TOWARDS A PATIENT sitting alone at a table in the common room, pushing aside fear and uncertainty. He noticed something particular about Jorge's hands that drew his attention. The rest of his large, disproportionate body was seemingly not connected: his sight was not connected to his eyes, his voice was not connected to his vocal cords, his thoughts were not connected to his brain, and his movements were not connected to his muscles. Jorge's hands however, appeared interwoven, inseparable from the rest of his body and looked physically overstuffed, as if someone with very large hands squeezed into a child's size pair of winter gloves. His hands revealed the true being of Jorge, surprisingly so close to the surface; whereas the rest was shrouded deep beneath his flesh, hidden in a cave, his hands were out in the light for the world to see.

"Hi, my name is Andy," he said in a cheerful voice, eager to speak to someone who would not either inject him with medicine or lock him up in a room. Jorge looked up at Andy, muttered something incomprehensible, and continued to write on a piece of paper, his hands communicating his true thoughts.

Jorge's hair was an equal mix of brown and gray and covered his head like an oversized helmet. He had a big bright red nose and closely spaced eyes set back into his head. Andy wondered how he could see out of those eyes, which were tucked away from reality. Jorge's hands moved quickly, scribbling down numbers, letters, and strange shapes creating bizarre patterns on the paper.

Jorge looked back up at Andy and said in a monotonous voice, "They're going through the houses and into the attic, which is the skin on my arm. All of the soldiers are escaping through it and out of the bottom of the ocean..." he paused, grunting some unintelligible words and continued, "...they come up to the roots and through the beast, eventually becoming clouds. They are all telling me to come, and I know the soldiers want me to come back into the ether from where we all came. They want me to put them back and make them clean again. I can hear them tell me this, and I see their feet walking on the ground like footprints in sand over to the emptying waters...he is coming to help us now, and they don't want him to. They know he is bad for them..." he trailed off at the end and whispered some more words. Jorge inquisitively looked at Andy, raising one of his bushy eyebrows waiting for a response. Andy did not know what to say and just stared back at Jorge, who eventually went back to his work and continued writing.

I used to be in a dead end too, Andy thought, seeing no plan, direction, or goal for the healing process this man required. *They all thought I was going to die. Not because they didn't try or didn't want to help me, they simply couldn't while living within the paradigm we created. We didn't know any better.*

"This man is like the old me," Andy whispered to himself. "He needs my help."

Peering more closely into Jorge's being, he looked beyond the veil cloaked over the truth Jorge believed in. Andy asked the world to show him what could be seen and importantly asked for permission to see the most intimate aspects of this person's beingness for the pure purpose of healing. *This is where I will start,* Andy thought.

Andy saw openness like an endless sea and suddenly felt hyperaware of his surroundings. Before coming to the Kay, Jorge created unique and extravagant drawings of the world and had become famous for his paintings with galleries all over Brave, admired by many. However, people became less interested over time as his expression of the world reached to areas others could not see and was criticized as "obscure and peculiar", falling out of favor. He could no longer sell his art and galleries no longer carried his pieces. Jorge isolated himself in his house, a lonely home on the outskirts of the Conscious Whole in a sea of tall grass on the top of a hill. In time, a friend brought Jorge to a doctor for help.

"It's call schizophrenia," the veteran doctor explained to Jorge's friend.

Defined by them he remained as such.

Since that time, over ten years ago, Jorge had not left the Kay Institute. "His illness is a problem with his brain. The chemicals are not balanced correctly. There's too much of a neurotransmitter we call dopamine[1] in certain parts of the brain," the doctor regrettably explained to Jorge's friend who was in tears as they dragged Jorge behind the cold walls of the Kay.

"Because of his illness, his artwork is very unique. As his illness worsened, his artwork became more abstract and disconnected from reality," the doctor continued to explain, hoping science would placate the friend's sorrow, stretching reductionism as far as it could go. "His perceptions are different from ours. He sees the world in a way that is not real. It is fictional," the expert of the Conscious Whole dictated.

They defined him based on ***their*** perceptions of the world, and he was labeled as they willed. Mentally ill. However, unknown to the doctors of the Conscious Whole, Jorge's uniqueness came from a deeper source than his biology or brain. Andy could see how Jorge's energy spoke of past experiences creating his current state, a condition the Conscious Whole kept him in, invisible to the doctors because of the narrow paradigm they

---

1. Howes and Kapur. "The Dopamine Hypothesis of Schizophrenia: Version III—The Final Common Pathway." *Schizophrenia Bulletin* (2009).

believed in, blindly and recklessly excluding any information not fit for their world. Jorge could not change for the better because of the status quo he was forced into; the wave function for him was continually collapsed into only one possible result. Mental illness.

Jorge's heavy hands scribbled away, and Andy sat at the edge of his chair, hunched over the table leaning forward, wrinkling his brow, curiously and innocently perceiving.[2]

Resonating deep inside of his abdomen, towards the back by his spinal column, Jorge's core churned with heavy energies stuck like a gummy paste, their movements labored, slowly growing in size over time.

As a child, both of Jorge's parents abandoned him, going in separate directions. Left to fend for himself, Jorge passed through many homes containing so-called parents, but even a child who has never seen his or her parents still knows it must receive unconditional love and care.

An imprint on his beingness.

Abandonment and loneliness combined with an inherent gift that went out of control resulted in Jorge's illness. His brain was slightly outside of the norm for the Conscious Whole allowing him to see and hear what those around him could not.[3, 4, 5, 6] Yet, living with others who did

---

2. For a discussion of innocent perception see: Green, *Love Without End: Jesus Speaks* (2002), pgs. 26-27.

3. The brain inhibits or suppresses a portion of incoming sensory input through a process called sensory gating; we are only consciously aware of a fraction of the stimuli surrounding us. Reviewed in: Cromwell et al. "Sensory Gating: A Translational Effort from Basic to Clinical Science." *Clinical EEG and Neuroscience* (2008).

4. Experimental evidence supports the presence of abnormal sensory gating in schizophrenia, allowing more sensory input to reach conscious awareness: Adler et al. "Schizophrenia, Sensory Gating, and Nicotinic Receptors." *Schizophrenia Bulletin* (1998).

5. As previously cited, sensory perception and filtering discussed in: Buhner, *Plant Intelligence and the Imaginal Realm: Beyond the Doors of Perception into the Dreaming of Earth* (2014), pgs. 26-67.

6. Fernyhough, T*he Voices Within: The History and Science of How We Talk to Ourselves* (2016).

not share his insight resulted in this gift being mismanaged,[7] plus his miserable childhood drove Jorge to seek a different truth, alternate planes of existence, and other dimensions of reality.

Andy saw remnants of his pain deep within, as a fixed, difficult-to-move energy containing a nearly infinite spectrum of all the shades of yellow. The color of a sunflower's petals, sun setting over the mountains, star fruit, midnight moon, mustard, comet dust, cadmium, daffodils, and shades of yellow the human eye is unable to discern all wound together in a ball of twisting, churning energy.

Leaving loneliness behind, Jorge transferred the pain of childhood into his body to escape the emotional anguish of abandonment, diving deeper into the other world as his childhood failed to improve. Beginning with the neuronal sparks in his brain, his worldview became incorporated into his conscious cloud and permeated throughout his body.

Jorge grew, and the yellow energy, his gift, which in the appropriate proportion could be used to healthily perceive beyond the collective reality, spread within him, moving other energy aside as his reality became even more separated from the collective belief. Eventually most of his body vibrated in tune with the now virulent yellow energy altering the structural makeup of molecules that created the framework of his physical matter. The strings of subatomic matter were susceptible, sensing the vibrations as strings appeared out of the dark matter, bringing to life physical forms that were asked to manifest. The old strings from Jorge's birth body disappeared back into dark matter, no longer having life-energy to maintain their existence while new strings built molecules, which built DNA, which created proteins. The specific proteins created were expressed in the brain, where they acted on neurons that produced dopamine in certain neuronal tracts, resulting in the excessive, above normal neurotransmitter production the doctors measured.

---

7. Auditory "hallucinations" that are well-received by others and are well-controlled have a positive impact on a person's ability to functionally live with "hallucinations". Powers, Kelley, and Corlett. "Varieties of Voice-Hearing: Psychics and the Psychosis Continuum." *Schizophrenia Bulletin* (2016).

The extremely unique range of energy Jorge created resulted in very specific physical changes and did not have an equal impact in all areas of his body; in some places, the strings already present had an equal and opposite force disabling the effects of the yellow energy, while in other areas the altered structural makeup of the DNA did not have significant effects because it was never expressed, therefore not resulting in any physiological consequences. For Jorge, the parts of DNA changed by the yellow energy were not expressed in the tissues of his heart, lungs, or muscles but instead were expressed in his brain, producing more and more dopamine as the intensity of the yellow energy grew. The naturally high concentration of dopamine allowing Jorge to controllably see other dimensions as a young child, his gift, went out of control as he sought deep realms of an alternate reality to escape his emotional sorrows.

By the time a doctor admitted Jorge to the Kay, his ability to see beyond the Conscious Whole's world had turned into a condition not allowing him to function in society, perpetuated by his childhood issues. Now producing too much dopamine, the doctors mistakenly identified the alteration of neurotransmitters in Jorge's brain as the *source* of his illness, instead of energetic perturbations in his field that intensified a gift into an illness.

From Jorge's cloud, his energy spread to other clouds and was eventually written into the collective conscious cloud, his childhood becoming a defining feature of how the Conscious Whole identified and labeled him. For the purpose of maintaining its integrity, keeping reality stable, and a selfish committal for maintaining the status quo, the Conscious Whole held onto what Jorge wrote into the collective consciousness and ensured his problem would last indefinitely. Once defined and established as being schizophrenic, the Conscious Whole reinforced his state and kept Jorge ill; a perpetual feedback nourishing and sustaining the yellow energy, keeping it alive in a continuous loop, maintaining a false sense of permanence, only allowing one possibility of the wave function: mental illness.

The physicians at the Kay unknowingly contributed to Jorge's illness because of a definition, their energy also written into the collectiveness, reinforcing the strength of ideas broadcasted by the Conscious Whole. The doctors did not consciously want Jorge to be ill, but by holding onto the diagnosis of schizophrenia, which in their paradigm was irreversible, their thoughts and actions had unforeseen consequences, literally helping to maintain physical matter in one state of existence.

Connecting to a different part of reality enhanced Jorge's artwork and brought success, however, a hole was created that he was unable to escape from when he used his gift for the wrong purpose. Jorge's problems, which he still grasped so tightly, were written into his energy and like traveling through time, Andy journeyed into the past to see what this man had dealt with, the true illness, not just the physical manifestation of such.

39

They anxiously watched in anticipation to see if his light would fulfill its purpose; the plan's first test was upon them

Andy looked at Jorge, concentrating on his abdomen, defocusing his eyes ever so slightly, just enough to allow his brain to unwind the permanence it tried to hold onto. Jorge continued to sit on the cold metal bench attached to the blank metal table, writing away, every once in a while saying something nonsensical to Andy.

Andy concentrated mindfully, allowing his etheric self to explore the limitlessness of the world and pictured himself inside of this Jorge's body, like a small one-twentieth scale version of himself, probing around intestines, climbing on parts of his bowel, making his way to the yellow energy towards the back. As he approached, the ball of energy swirled methodically at its center with the edges seeping outward like slowly moving lava, holding tightly to the bony structures of the spine.

Andy lunged forward not giving the energy a chance to see him approaching, thrust his hands into its core, and tugged at its roots, but the energy stuck to him like a wad of gum. The energy stood strong as Andy fell backwards, his hands free but covered in the yellow, sticky energy up to his elbows.

Like being covered in glue, he thought.

Andy was shocked to see and feel the yellow residue slowly crawling up his arms, trying to consume him! Not fearing the result of his actions, he stuck his hands deeper into the glob this time and worked them to the deepest root, but this made the situation worse. He pulled his arms out again, and the yellow energy had now attached itself to more of his body; it was beginning to make him feel nauseous and dizzy.

I need another line of attack, he thought, his mind dazed, feeling like he was running out of breath underwater.

Andy closed his eyes and calmly pictured ice blue light, slick as glass, flowing through each of his arms and out of his hands. The light felt cold as he coated the yellow sticky energy covering him and then extended it to Jorge's mass lesion, eventually completely covering the yellow energy like a big ice ball allowing easy extraction.

Jorge grimaced as Andy worked inside, dragging the heavy frozen ball of energy out of his body, which instantaneously dissipated into nothingness, now external to the framework it needed for survival. With the source removed, Jorge was able to see more clearly, and the Conscious Whole was losing its model to duplicate the reinforcing signal; the channel of malignant yellow energy from the collective conscious weakened as the feedback loop was breaking into pieces and in no time, Jorge's inherent birth energy that had been hiding in the corners of his conscious cloud willingly made itself apparent including a balanced portion of his gifted yellow energy.

Brilliant tropical ocean aqua blue and delicate yellow like high soaring clouds showered over Jorge from his conscious cloud and spread throughout his body. Surrounding dark matter vibrated more and more strongly in accordance with the new colors, no longer pushed out by the yellow, sticky energy; strings from his birth body came back to life as they resonated with the frequencies now spilling into each and every orifice of Jorge's being.

Jorge dissociated from the reality of the Conscious Whole as a child by using his gift to delve deeper and deeper into what others of the Conscious Whole could not sense; his artwork an expression of his perception of other dimensions of reality. Jorge's thoughts, speech, and visions included phrases that were seemingly disconnected, disorganized, and not real. Yet, they were organized for his world and true for the world he believed in and saw.

The yellow energy and the resultant changes in his brain led to Jorge's heightened awareness of reality, the extra dopamine the doctors measured, in actuality, tuned his brain into picking up signals out of earshot to others, which became stronger as he progressed. The apparently nonsensical words Jorge uttered to Andy were true visions he received in his mind, detecting energetic waveforms of information as they traveled throughout the latticework of the Conscious Whole, a code of what was occurring at all times.

Jorge saw Andy's arrival and the garbage disposal plant along the coast. The soldiers he spoke of were his interpretation of caustic chemicals released into the ocean and air that eventually deposited into peoples' bodies. Jorge's difference, what the Conscious Whole called an illness, gave him a unique ability to sense energies broadcasted by the universe.

The characteristics of Jorge's brain, as interpreted by the people of the Conscious Whole, were pathologic but in truth were only different when compared to what *they* defined as normal. The scientists found a biological source to blame for Jorge's talents, a scapegoat to avoid admitting possibilities the Conscious Whole did not allow. The true illness, though, was not the increased perceptive power or the excessive amount of dopamine in the brain but Jorge's inability to control his capacity to see beyond material existence, and his intentional escape from the physical world.

Sadly, Jorge had no guidance on how to properly use his gift or how to function in society as a hypersensing individual.[1,2] He did not develop

---

1. Creative individuals are more sensitive to incoming sensory stimuli: Zabelina et al. "Creativity and Sensory Gating Indexed by the P50: Selective Versus Leaky Sensory Gating in Divergent Thinkers and Creative Achievers." *Neuropsychologia* (2015).

2. Psychic mediums have been found to have less brain activity when perceiving extrasensory perceptions: Peres et al. "Neuroimaging During Trance State: A Contribution to the Study of Dissociation." *PloS One* (2012). In the narrative of The Conscious Whole, however, Andy displays increased brain activity; perhaps there is a wide range of brain activity in relation to "psychic" abilities; this field needs much more research.

The Conscious Whole

the capacity to make sense of the information in a meaningful or useful way and not surprisingly, as Jorge went deeper into the ether he was overwhelmed and could not manage the slew of data coming into his conscious experience. Being inherently unstable from his childhood abandonment, combined with the heightened perceptive ability, put him over the edge and then made his situation "pathologic." Unable to cope with all of the input his brain was receiving, Jorge isolated himself to escape, hoarding all of the information from the cosmos and allowing it to build up and overrun his life; the energy turned into a destructive force and became too extreme, pushing him towards insanity instead of letting him use his talent in a useful and effective manner to better society.

Even more disturbing than the lack of insight by the doctors was the Conscious Whole's hatred and aggressiveness toward the unknown. A person like Jorge, even if able to properly use his abilities, would be ruthlessly marked as outside of the norm. Because of their unbreakable belief in what was real and not, Jorge would be labeled as "crazy" if he claimed to see things occurring far away. As such, the society of the Conscious Whole most certainly would not nourish Jorge's gift, and the Conscious Whole would not allow an individual to peer into its inner working, revealing its inherent weakness within.

Jorge looked up at Andy and then back down at his work, seemingly confused by what he had just written. Sun shined through a window, a rare occurrence, and it caught Jorge's eyes. Slowly he raised his head, inquisitively looking out the window as if he had never seen light before, stood up and began walking towards the window. Halfway there, Jorge looked back at Andy and raised one eyebrow, his expression spoke of confusion but also of thanks. He smiled out of the corner of his mouth.

Andy got up and approached Jorge, "It's what you held onto that you have to release. It built up inside of you over time. Don't perpetuate the ill doings of your parents, for that serves no one. Be conscious of how to create yourself and work to keep your body and surroundings clear. Cherish your ability to see and use it to help others."

40

Having finally arrived, the beings above wandered about the periphery, amazed by what was created; having traveled from such a distance they had gained perspective and encountered many other clouds of belief; knowing its natural purpose allowed innocent acceptance; questioning why they were called, the keepers looked into the center for an answer

Her back was facing him, but he could already tell what was wrong: the body had become an expendable, finite resource, deteriorating from the inside out, all of its pieces used up faster than they were being produced, a self-inflicted loss of infinity.

As Andy passed her room he could see sorrow pouring outward, off-white with a shiny solid surface, flowing like a wave of thick paint out the doorway. Andy peeked through the door that was ajar; after his encounter with Jorge, he felt like he could be useful since people at the Kay seemed to need a different kind of healing.

"Are you ok?" Andy gently said, not sure how to approach her.

The woman stopped sobbing and turned towards him, "Mind your own business!" she angrily growled back.

Andy was silent, regretting he had asked and wanted to walk away. Yet, he stayed by the door knowing he should not leave, suppressing the awkwardness brewing inside him.

Upon her voluntary entrance into the Kay Institute, Violet had a psychological evaluation and physical exam. Afterwards, she met with one of the doctors who explained her problem, alcoholism, was caused by a behavior, a habit, resulting from a genetic source.[1,2]

"Since your father was an alcoholic, and his father was an alcoholic and your son and daughter are addicted to drugs, addiction runs in the family, you see. It was passed down from generation to generation. A genetic disorder. The mutation has even been found in DNA; there is nothing you can do about your DNA. It is who you are, permanently stored within your body," a young doctor confidently explained, having studied all there was to know, impressed by his Conscious Whole's aptitude at discovering scientific facts; discovering what it created.

Addiction. A trait built into her genetic code. The doctors explained they could take a sample of Violet's cells and isolate the DNA. From this, they could find a specific segment of DNA that created her addictive habits. Her family's addictive habits were in that same piece of DNA they all shared, something she had been given upon conception from her father.

"It's part of your being," the same doctor explained to Violet at a subsequent treatment session, shoveling more dirt onto the roots, "It's not anything you can escape or change because it's who you are."

Who they told her she was.

The contagious bacterial infection, tuberculosis, was once thought to be an inherited disorder passed down from one generation to another, from mother to child.[3] To the medical community at the time, this seemed so obvious. Their reasoning was *scientific*.

---

1. Tawa, Hall, and Lohoff. "Overview of the Genetics of Alcohol Use Disorder." *Alcohol and Alcoholism* (2016).

2. Abnormal brain structure has been found in siblings of drug dependent individuals, suggesting an inherited abnormality leading to addiction (Ersche et al. "Abnormal Brain Structure Implicated in Stimulant Drug Addiction." *Science* (2012)); yet, I argue this is not a permanent or fateful alteration but something that is fluid and can be changed.

3. Tomes, *The Gospel of Germs: Men, Women, and the Microbe in American Life* (1999), pg. 4.

Impoverished people lived with large extended families in small apartments and were in very close proximity to each other and to other large families in crowded cities. Not surprisingly many were infected with tuberculosis; the grandparents passed the disease to the parents who passed the disease to the children. Obviously, an inherited disorder.

"It's hereditary!" the doctors proclaimed. "You see! It goes from the mother to fetus. We have post mortem specimens to *prove* our point!"[4]

Logically, this story can make sense and it did for those doctors, but non-hereditary direct transmission of the bacteria, Mycobacterium tuberculosis, between individuals was not appreciated. Before germ theory, people did not believe hand washing, which supposedly eliminated *invisible* organisms, would prevent disease;[5] at the time it was incomprehensible. However, the microscope allowed identification of something previously invisible to become visible, and along with the acceptance of germ theory, transmission of the microscopic bacteria contained in sputum causing tuberculosis became a recognized principle.

There is good science and there is bad science.[6]

Years ago, there was a scientist who wanted to study brandy, vodka, tequila, and bourbon. He put brandy in a container with some water, vodka in a container with some water, tequila in a container with some water, and bourbon in a container with some water. He then administered each

---

4. Carslaw. "Abstracts from Current Medical Literature: Heredity of Tuberculosis." *Glasgow Medical Journal* (1892). Even though infectious transmission was beginning to be recognized at this point, it was thought "so infrequent" that it was not considered a common method of spreading; instead the spread of tuberculosis was "accomplished principally by transmission from generation to generation", i.e heredity (note that DNA was not discovered until the mid twentieth century).

5. Germ theory and hand washing are now massively central paradigms in preventing illness. Germ theory reviewed in: Tomes, *The Gospel of Germs: Men, Women, and the Microbe in American Life* (1999).

6. The following fictional example of bad versus good science came from my biochemistry professors at Pennsylvania State University, Dr. Sypes. He often quoted it during class but unfortunately I do not know if he created it or learned of it from someone else.

solution to volunteer subjects and observed their behavior. Believe it or not they all acted drunk after each solution was administered. The scientist's conclusion?

Water makes people drunk because water is the common variable among all the solutions. That is science. Logical deduction.

However, it is **bad** science.

41

Cracks appeared in the cloud mass, which were hurriedly sealed by binding energy; however, they could now catch glimpses of the action below; they poised for their opportunity

VIOLET'S LONG, CURLY, WHITE HAIR SYMMETRICALLY GREW out of her head, electrified, and her round face conveyed a wild look with skin too wrinkly for a fifty-six year old.

"I was in a bad marriage. He hit me all the time, and I could never do anything right. I drank as a kid, too," Violet said pushing the words past moments of sobbing. "My parents were always fighting. If it wasn't one thing, it was another. And if it wasn't that, it was me. My dad, if you could call him that, wasn't afraid to give me a good beating.[1] I guess he'd get tired of hitting mom." She paused for a minute.

Andy had not expected such a revealing conversation and was caught off guard, shocked by what Violet was saying. He had not come from a violent home; his parents always respected him.

She continued speaking in a harsh, tenor voice, now more composed, with anger echoing in its vibrations, "My poor kids suffered the most. They had to deal with everything happening in the house. They picked up

---

1. Exposure to violence as a child can change part of the chromosome: Shalev et al. "Exposure to Violence During Childhood is Associated with Telomere Erosion from 5 to 10 Years of Age: A Longitudinal Study." *Molecular Psychiatry* (2013).

my bad habits too. Both of them are either drunk or on drugs. I know I'm a bad mother, but I was too busy protecting myself. I had to be selfish. I would've died otherwise. Literally..." she trailed off looking into a corner of the room, shaking her head.

Andy studied Violet, observing not just her physical being sitting in that tiny room but also her as a whole throughout time. Hearing her story and seeing her body helped Andy to uncover the root of Violet's problems, which the Conscious Whole called genetics, but her tale spoke of a deeper truth. Violet's father, Clyde, did not only pass down his genetics, he passed down his life and problems too; the same problems that came from his father, Winston, ultimately resulting in Violet's lifestyle and the lifestyle of her children. Unfortunately, unless something was changed, Andy saw the same future spelled out in the lives of the unborn generations lying in wait in dark matter.

Andy looked with more detail into this woman's past, where every event was torched onto physical matter, a series of events set into motion many years ago by Winston, who continued to contribute to the surrounding coded message of where Violet came from and where she might go. Winston tried to maintain a life he could not afford; the frustration and anxiety overwhelmed him, never feeling like he was good enough, striving for a goal he believed was out of reach. To cope, he drowned himself in alcohol to escape self-inflicted shame; if he could not feel it, it did not exist, he thought. The consequences of this action rippled throughout the universe and through time,[2,3] born into the code of nature. Violet carried it with her, in her subconscious realm, in the energy surrounding her, and it manifested in her DNA.

Winston abused alcohol all the while his son, Clyde, lived with addiction as his reality. His life mirrored his father's, learning to live by what

---

2. Can future events influence the present? Nielsen and Ninomiya. "Test of Effect from Future in Large Hadron Collider: A Proposal." *International Journal of Modern Physics A* (2009).

3. For a discussion of signals traveling into the future and into the past, see: Gribbin, *Schrodinger's Kittens and the Search for Reality* (1995), pgs. 225 and 239.

he observed and by the way he was treated, intentions and actions, which were not omitted from the code of the universe. As an adult, Clyde predictably acted like his father and similarly Violet suffered, her life hell, and she learned only one way to escape it: addiction. The code of energy physically surrounding her body contained her behaviors and those of her father and her grandfather, all written into matter.

Intent[4] permeates space, resonating from the core being, acting like surrounding pressure at the bottom of the ocean; intent, the true observer in quantum theory, channels through the brain and operates in the background, often unseen and unnoticed by "conscious" experience, cloaked by energetic waveforms of the incessant mind, manifesting into reality.

Particular thoughts of intention occur before thoughts of action, both of which create a code of energetic activity in the brain. The electrical activity of neurons creates the conscious cloud, which then vibrates at a frequency specific to the intention and action.

Beginning with neurons in Winston's brain, the intention of drowning his misery in alcohol was born. From this, thoughts of action manifested and both became encoded as a waveform of electromagnetic energy in his conscious cloud, melding with the collective thoughts and energy of the Conscious Whole, then fed back as if it was extrinsic to Winston. Reassured by the permanence the Conscious Whole offered, Winston's thoughts became his belief, seemingly out of his control, albeit, originating from his brain; a belief he was living life the only way possible.

His electromagnetic code then brought strings to life from dark matter, changing molecules, and altering the structure of his DNA. The energy of his existence and physical form sustained throughout his life by his conscious cloud, the Conscious Whole providing the fate Winston cursed every time life did not go his way.

Clyde was born into Winston's life and immersed in Winston's conscious cloud, which broadcasted its signals to the dark energy plane where

---

4. According to Immanuel Kant our true intent determines morality: Kant, *Religion Within the Limits of Reason Alone* (1960), pgs. 149-150.

space and time are not dissociated but exist as one, not separating people or generations. The spreading electromagnetic energy from Winston sent encoded energetic waveforms to Clyde's strings in the dark matter bringing them to life.[5, 6] Molecules were born, creating base pairs in his DNA where addiction was written. Passed from one to another. Genetic inheritance by means of the energetic field, not driven by fate or some unstoppable force of biology but driven by intention and action!

Winston's behaviors were observed and imitated by Clyde, and as he grew, the strength of the strings existence in a state of addiction was reinforced. As time went on, the illusion of permanence became more concrete and weighed heavily on Clyde's belief in whom he was supposed to become.

The cycle continued as the energy was again passed forward but magnified, distilled among generations to Violet, her conscious cloud physically creating DNA, building her body from the bottom up. Addictive and self-destructive behaviors followed suit, kept alive in a life that was manufactured to be inescapable. Beginning with a choice a century ago and then written and manifested into material reality, the deception of an inevitable fate created a daunting reality for Violet, one from which she would hardly escape. It was not simply a matter of choice or free will for Violet to break away from her mental imprisonment, she had to redefine and recreate her physical existence.

---

5. Resonance in relation to biology: Oschman, *Energy Medicine: The Scientific Basis* (2000), pgs. 122-123.

6. DNA resonating with energy: Oschman, *Energy Medicine: The Scientific Basis* (2000), pgs. 239-241.

42

Hidden keys placed by the undead in the infrastructure of the world foretold impending events; their signal spanned time, confusing those who used time as a sequential marker for activity

Feeling helpless of her fate, Violet would say, "I can't help what I do, addiction is who I am. It was who my grandfather was, who my father was, who I am, and who my kids are becoming. It's in our biology. We can't help it!" unaware of her power to shape her future and control her life.

The downward causation of events that created Violet's "destined biology" was unseen to her, as the Conscious Whole successfully sold the illusion of permanence in biology, tricking not only Violet but also the scientists and doctors, who in turn reinforced a concrete house built on a foundation of fog. A guardian to the past, the Conscious Whole ensured the present stayed energetically and physically as it had been before. The transmission of energy and behavior from Winston to Clyde to Violet was the "genetics" scientists had indirectly measured in DNA; however, science defined heredity as **solely** the **physical** process of passing genetic material from mother and father to child; after conception there were no longer inherited exchanges. An inescapable fate of the human body gifted from generation to generation. Only so called "spontaneous" mutations could alter the inherent code.[1] The idea of DNA being born from actions and thoughts at every moment in time was never considered.

In the code of DNA, scientists had unknowingly discovered the physical manifestation of the energetic footprint of intentions, thoughts, and actions of all of society affecting all generations![2] Not fate! Just as the observer correlated poison ivy to blisters via nearly invisible molecules, to advance, the Conscious Whole needed to correlate material reality to the energetic dimension. When faced with this inevitability, a choice would have to be made by the Conscious Whole.

DNA was the bridge connecting the physical manifestation of Violet's body to her inseparable energetic being, where thoughts begin and have real effects, where her grandfather started his problem and where Violet's began; a bridge through space and time.

"You know that you have to forgive not only yourself but your family as well," Andy said compassionately. "It's not worth holding onto," he continued after a long pause.

Violet furiously glared at Andy.

"Start over," Andy bluntly said, realizing he would have to be even more straightforward and persistent. "Start from scratch, with everything! Do good things, one at a time. Do something good for yourself at first, or if you can't stand to help yourself, help someone else. Don't hold onto the past, it's not who you are. What you are right *now* is who you are," Andy felt frustrated with Violet's determination to hold onto her diseased state, and it was coming through in his voice.

Violet blankly stared at the floor, and Andy felt like he wanted to leave and give up. *Why is she holding on so tightly?* he thought, not knowing what to do next.

Suddenly, Violet angrily got up and slammed the door in Andy's face.

---

1. I propose energetic fields may be one cause of "spontaneous" DNA mutations.

2. The Native American idea of Seven Generations denotes being aware of the how our current actions and decisions will affect the next seven generations. Loew, *Seventh Generation Earth Ethics: Native Voices of Wisconsin* (2014), pg. xv.

He stood there for a moment, shocked, feeling like he failed and violated her space. Slowly, he turned down the hallway and walked back towards his room.

Yet, unbeknownst to Andy, a delicate wisp of energy, like a newly formed fragile cloud high in the sky at sunrise, fell off of his conscious cloud and lingered behind, circling, like a glider above the mountains, containing the rainbow of colors surrounding him. The energy easily soared through the door and covered the room, filling every space the Conscious Whole did not care to furnish, incorporating into Violet's space as she lay in bed, weeping, attempting to cope.

Feeling discouraged, Andy went back to his room, again with the heaviness of imprisonment on his mind. Yet, he was surprised to see a large, old book just under the door of his room with an attached note, "Andy, I thought you might like this. From, Jorge."

The cover of the book had a striking picture of the northern plains, which possessed movement, the tall grass seemingly blowing in the wind with parallel grass-like streaks of color producing depth that appeared endless. Andy closed his eyes and could feel the breeze on his face as he mentally escaped the drabness of the Kay, recalling the excitement of driving through the plains on his way to Meat Cove and how the boundless landscape allowed him to feel infinity.

He opened the book to a random page and was shocked by what he saw! It was Meat Cove! Andy could not believe his eyes! The painting had all of the details of the small village including Jeremy's house, which sat on the hillside and had the unmistakable blue siding, green roof, and balcony where he and Jeremy had spent so much of their time. Andy nearly fell over in shock as he looked more closely, squinting at the painting pulling it even closer to his face.

No way! he thought, *It can't be!!*

There were two figures painted on the balcony, one with black hair and the other in a wheelchair with bright red hair. Andy was baffled and quickly flipped through to see who the artist was. On the back cover was a picture of Jorge.

"He must be no older than twenty in this picture. That was at least thirty years ago!" Andy said aloud.

Andy turned back to the picture of Meat Cove, analyzing it further and found all of the other unique aspects of the town portrayed in the painting: Sandra's house on top of the cliff, Russell's home on the southern cliff wall with a little smoke stack coming out of the roof, and in the foreground was a red-headed figure in a small wooden boat like the one Andy left on!

Sitting in the blandness of the Kay, Andy could not help but miss Meat Cove. He missed the landscape, the serenity, and his friends. Daydreaming about being at Jeremy's house, looking out over the ocean, he longed for the cool breeze from the sea and the salty smell in the air.

This is such a terrible place, he thought. *So unnatural and unlike Jorge's wonderful paintings and Meat Cove, where I was healed. How do they expect to help anyone get better here?*

Part VI

Pacifist gorillas move undetected through concrete jungles
New forms are beginning to take shape
Once occupied minds are activating
People are waking up!
The insurgency is alive and well

We are building up a new world
Do not sit idly by
Do not remain neutral
Do not rely on this broadcast alone
We are only as strong as our signal
There is a war going on for your mind
If you are thinking, you are winning
Resistance is victory
Defeat is impossible
Your weapons are already in hand
Reach within you and find the means by which to gain your freedom

FLOBOTS[1]

---

1. Flobots, *"We are winning."* Fight with Tools, 1:47.

43

Only a spark was needed to start a wildfire; the energy lay within, potential waiting for activation; however, they wondered if containment would be broken

A NDY AWOKE TO A FLURRY OF COMMOTION outside of his room. Crashing, yelling, and general chaos. He jumped out of bed and cautiously stuck his head out of the door, fearing an unidentified flying object might hit him. In the common room, tables were getting turned over as staff members chased a patient who was not being cooperative, to say the least. It was a man named Sean whom Andy had only seen while getting food and medicine. Sean did not want to take his medication that day and was revolting against the staff, tossing tables and chairs behind him, blocking his pursuers.

"Code 3! Code 3!! Code 3!!!" A crackling, increasingly frantic voice said over the intercom. More security guards went running past Andy's room as he ducked back in, trying to stay out of the inevitable altercation. He peered out again and saw Sean taking refuge in his room down the hallway, stacking his furniture, blocking the door. He pushed his mattress against the pile as more and more staff and guards rushed to the scene. Andy caught a glimpse of Sean's face through the small window on his door as he was now throwing clothes on top of everything else.

The guards easily pushed through Sean's weak barrier, infiltrated his room, and now had the difficult task of restraining him. One guard grabbed a leg, then another, and another. It was not long before four guards were holding onto each of his extremities as Sean writhed, looking like a large spider. Despite being restrained, he had a huge smile on his narrow face revealing teeth firing out in every direction; his wild eyes shot a glance to Andy.

Without warning, Sean partially broke free with only his legs restrained, but the rest of his body unbound floated above the crowd. Andy stood in his doorway, worried about what they would do to Sean as he gradually got sucked into the sea of staff and guards, disappearing.

"Now is your chance!" a voice in the back of Andy's mind exalted.

He looked towards the main entrance, which had been mistakenly left ajar by someone racing to restrain Sean. Beyond this door was a room that separated the resident living space from the administrative side of the building, importantly where there were no locked doors. Andy glanced back, saw the crowd still preoccupied with Sean, and made a break for it!

Briskly and discretely Andy slipped through the doorway, grabbing a security guard's jacket hanging on the wall, trying as hard as he could to not look like a patient of the Kay, but the olive-colored jumpsuit did not help his disguise. A few more doors and a couple more turns and he would be out!

Suddenly, someone's handheld radio buzzed with activity around the corner, "We're going to need more help, the other patients are acting up..." the voice cut out and more footsteps came running towards Andy.

Stranded in the hallway he frantically looked for a place to hide, slipping into a closet at the last moment. After they passed, without wasting a second, Andy slid back out and jogged down the hallway, past a few cameras, which he simply smiled at, through two more doors, and he was in the main room of the Kay. Large brass doors of the entrance rose to the ceiling; Andy grabbed the wooden handle and put all his weight into pulling the door open.

"Hey! What do you think you're doing! Um...get back here!" a scrawny voice shouted from behind the front desk. The young man, who was the only staff member left to run the entire building, looked terrified.

Andy did not flinch, gave the man a wave, and said, "Thanks, but I'm better now!"

Earlier that morning Sean had come out of the daze, leaving confusion behind; the blanket of bewilderment the Conscious Whole had placed on him since he was a small being in utero was lifted after spending time with Jorge during breakfast. The interaction was subliminal as Jorge's energy connected to Sean's, covering him with balanced insight providing light. Sean's outburst was not due to noncompliance with medications as the staff members believed; he knew what he was doing and wanted to get out.

A unit of connected consciousnesses different from the Conscious Whole coalesced within the Kay; new light forms were taking shape; natural events would occur, viewed through the lens of the existing paradigm as miracles.

Andy tried to casually walk down the city block, hoping no one would notice his standard issue Kay uniform, including olive-colored slippers, topped off by a security guard's jacket. Despite looking like an escaped prisoner, all of the worries of living in the Kay left his mind and his only thought was of freedom. A strong cold breeze forced brown leaves from the few trees that lined the street, and Andy stopped for a moment, freely enjoying the sensation of moving air.

Within the sky above, it lurked, sensing a vulnerable prey.

Andy was relatively safe within the Kay Institute as its tall brass doors kept the different minds within, a temporary measure by the Conscious Whole to retain an intruder.

Low rolling clouds scraped the tops of the tall repetitive buildings, appearing to contain enough mass to knock them over, as heavy drops of rain began to fall, carrying so much volume Andy was instantly soaked. The people on the street were all prepared, propping up their umbrellas, cutting their awareness off from the world as the clouds sealed the city from any sign of the infinite sky above.

In between the pieces of matter, Andy began to feel the force he had fought while at sea, except now he was in its heart, and its strength was increasingly suffocating. Its long skeletal arms and fingers came out from the clouds and snaked their way towards Andy, winding around the buildings and people, snickering with excitement. Fifteen arms approached him from all angles and directions, and Andy was suddenly paralyzed.

Relentless in its efforts to reestablish Andy's form as it remembered, the long disgusting fingers grabbed him by every piece of physical matter that made up his body, multiplying as they seized hold of him. More and more fingers were born out of others and forced themselves into him, ferociously grabbing each particle of his being. The black, stagnant, opaque energy of the Conscious Whole resonated with Andy's dormant strings, bringing back the ones that once created his disease, the ones he had fought so hard to remove.

Andy slowly fell to the ground on the side of the street, ironically supported by the tentacles of the Conscious Whole. He was soaked as each finger, each drop of rain, covered him; lying in a pile of garbage he was helpless. He tried to get up but could not even lift his head out of the trash and struggled to breath as only a small amount of putrid air moved into and out of his lungs. Now covered in filth, he looked like a bum. People walked by, oblivious to his struggle, and passed judgments of repulsion and resentment, further cementing the belief of the Conscious Whole, strengthening the bonds of the fingers to Andy's physical body.

"Filthy drunk. The world would be better off without him," a woman muttered, splashing water on Andy as she trudged on by.

The cold rain battered his body, and he continued to lose sensation throughout his legs and arms. He could hear cars driving. People walking in the rain. His vision became fuzzy as buildings and people blended into one. His thoughts were less clear, as if entering a dream. Inside of his body the organs rapidly deteriorated, piece by piece, and the pain was excruciating. A few more breaths were all he had left.

The Conscious Whole had waited for the perfect opportunity to strike. Not weak as it was on the periphery, at its center the Conscious Whole was strong due to the summative force of millions of conscious clouds in Brave. They all believed Andy to be a man on the brink of death and that is what he was becoming.

Just before he let go, Andy felt a warm touch on the back of his neck, contrasting with the icy rain on this late fall day. Then, a bright light, like the sun, began spreading all over his body, starting at the nape of his neck and down his back following the contour of his spine. It coursed around his sides enveloping his entire back and chest before racing down his arms and legs. Finally, the light steadily covered Andy's face and scalp leaving a quarter-sized space at the top of his head untouched where the energy from Andy's conscious cloud entered. The light rested over his skin like a blanket, and its radiant warmth embraced him, slowly seeping into each pore of his being and into the space between matter. Andy began breathing deeper again and felt strength return to his body. The hand remained on his neck, and Andy looked to see who had brought him back to life!

Jeremy and Norman!

Just as Jeremy had known he was in trouble at sea, he knew Andy was locked up at the Kay as he peered through the gecko's eyes. Jeremy told Norman of Andy's imprisonment and they immediately left Meat Cove, following the same winds Andy took south and similarly encountered the force of the Conscious Whole but were able to evade its attempts to smother them. The power of their two consciousnesses, connected, allowed one to confirm the other's state of reality, providing strength.

Andy sat up in the pile of garbage, thankful to be alive, once again saved by his friends Jeremy and Norman. They exchanged hugs, excited to see each other but soaked to the bone and freezing; the cheerful reunion was abbreviated as they quickly ran for cover next to a nearby building.

"How did you find me!?" Andy exclaimed.

"Forget what I taught you?" Jeremy said, smiling at Andy from ear to ear. "Everything is connected. We had to come help you."

"It wasn't an easy journey…" Norman said revealing a fresh wound on the side of his face where a sharp fingernail of the Conscious Whole had left its mark, "…but it was worth it."

Both Jeremy and Norman looked at each other, waiting for the other to break the news, as excitement on their faces was replaced by concern.

"There's something else too, Andy. Things started changing right after you left," Jeremy said not hiding the trepidation in his voice. "We think a connection opened up between here and Meat Cove when you first came, allowing energy to follow you when you drove in. We fought them off in the past, but it's invading again. We came not only to save you but also to save our home. Meat Cove won't last long."

"I don't understand. I thought you were safe up there."

"We thought so too. Sandra is organizing a bigger group who are making their way here. We don't know what else to do." Jeremy looked around, overwhelmed by the pressure of the Conscious Whole.

They all knew what to do, but no one wanted to admit the daunting challenge that lay in front of them; to keep the lives they believed in, the Conscious Whole would have to be changed; the people would have to change.

The bleakness of Brave rode on their backs, sinking their feet into the cement sidewalk, making it physically difficult to move, but stagnation was not an option. Heading into the blowing rain, they maneuvered through the gray mass of people who all seemed to be going the opposite direction. Enemies deep in unfamiliar territory, with nowhere to go, the men were thankful to see refuge ahead: a shelter for the homeless.

44

A beating pulse set the course like a drum encouraging a crew to paddle forward; its strength grew as more and more gathered following its signal; all the while, morsels of energy peaked above the clouds, wondering what was approaching and how it would affect the known

FEAR. LITERALLY PARALYZING. SHE HAD STOPPED THE flow of energy to her legs, not on purpose but subconsciously; neglecting the vital life force, her legs had no guidance. Andy could not help but notice a gray and black vortex swirling at this woman's waist, where energy from her upper body pooled with no escape. He sat up in the cot where he spent the night, assessing his environment.

She had not walked since she fell eleven years ago; too scared to walk or to even try to stand again, all the while blaming other things. She blamed her body for not working. She blamed her past fall. She blamed the people around her for not helping. As Andy approached this very funny and outgoing woman she immediately smiled and gave him a quizzical look, as she was used to being ignored, sitting in her wheelchair next to her collection of prized garbage.

"Hi, my name's Andy."

"Oh, hello" a surprised and confused voice replied. "My name is Shelia."

Shelia was in her sixties and previously worked as a scientist in Brave, studying the evolution of insects. She had traveled throughout all of the known forests and discovered many new species; it was a devoted passion.

However, Shelia had fallen off of a twenty-foot cliff while on an expedition and almost lost her life. After a long and arduous recovery, she tried to walk but was unable to support her weight, despite being able to move her legs in every direction. Not limited by physical pain she blamed her body but never admitted her fear. Too scared to walk, the emotional trauma was burned into her being and Shelia withdrew inward, focusing on an inability to walk.

Shelia's body listened to her concerns and obeyed, the molecules resonating true with her intentions, manifesting as disease. Over time, Shelia's fears were confirmed by her body's new state, consciously validating the belief of a physical problem with her body. The doctors searched and searched for answers and finally found the nerves that were not working.

"It's a degenerative process. We will have to do more tests to find the exact cause," they said. Genetic tests on the cells in her body finally revealed the abnormality. "You see," the doctor said leaning forward with a sense of accomplishment, proud of finally discovering the **source**. "The **disease** is located in a certain part of your DNA related to the neuron's ability to stay alive," the doctor paused making sure Shelia understood. "In your neurons, the DNA does not code for a protein that keeps cells free of damaging effects from other molecules."

"Well, how did that happen?" Shelia innocently asked, blinded by the cloak of the Conscious Whole.

"A spontaneous point mutation. A random change in the DNA that now results in disease. It just happens," the doctors told Shelia, strengthening the weak groundwork they all believed in.

Spontaneous and random? No! All events are connected.

The spontaneous change was not random but related to a discrete event, Shelia's fear changing the outcome of her probability function by stopping the natural progression of essential energy to her legs. The specific electromagnetic frequencies she prevented flowing were at the same frequency as the strings that created a specific base in her DNA that built the protein that her neurons needed to stay alive. Without this energy, her DNA manifested as a mutated form, a not so random alteration.

Paralyzed further by a life that seemed out of control, she lost her job and eventually her home. Shelia's problem, like so many others in the Conscious Whole, did not begin in the physical body but was deeper. If Andy could help her change, even temporarily, it would give Shelia the opportunity to see the truth behind her illness, a physicality based on intentions that are no longer needed.

It would be an uphill battle as Andy's plan was in stark contrast to the theory so clearly shown to Shelia by her doctors. Once they found the faulty DNA, Shelia's technical mind felt satisfied her illness was due to something concrete and objective. Not knowing how damaging their misunderstanding would be to her psyche, the doctors confirmed the physical aspect of her disease on the laboratory report, exactly what Shelia was looking for: a source to blame. Masking her true intention, the miscoded DNA confirmed the illness belief, further rooting the future of her existence under the Conscious Whole. No one wanted to believe that *simple* fear created disease. That was not physical. There was no biological connection. DNA caused disease, and after finding Shelia's mutation, both she and the doctors had no reason to look for a more complete answer.

Everything stopped at DNA. It could not be reduced further. Disease did not lie deeper than DNA.

"You do not have to be scared anymore," Andy gently said in his baritone, husky voice. "Every single person is scared of something, but it's what you do with fear that determines who you become. Your true intention forms your body. Look for that and you will find health!"

Jeremy and Norman stood silently nearby, amazed by who Andy had become since he left Meat Cove. Shelia looked up, her conscious cloud churned confused currents, the heart of its reality altered by an outside force. Andy's conscious cloud knew the truth behind this woman's illness and sensed healing was possible. His thoughts, from his conscious cloud, transmitted into her conscious cloud and into her body as a rush of uneasiness ran through Shelia, her core being realizing it created illness and unconsciously relinquished control; it was ashamed to hear its mistakes and tried even harder to support its beliefs.

"It's my legs, they don't work," she said convinced of this truth. "It's genetic, there's nothing I can do about it!"

"I'm not asking you to become someone else. I'm saying you control your self."

Just as she had given it away, she took it back. One moment was all that was needed to induce a change of state.

Shelia began scooting the wheelchair around the room in short, bursting movements. The lock had been undone, and now she had to work in the physical realm to strengthen muscles and bones; she had a lot of catching up to do for the last eleven years. Shelia gave Andy a big smile, wondering who this man was who seemed to come from nowhere.

As quickly as they came to the shelter, they left; the Conscious Whole was not far behind, and all three men felt urgency on their shoulders. The rain had passed, and Andy got a change of clothes from the shelter, allowing him to be more inconspicuous. After a quick free bite to eat they marched down the dusky streets of Brave.

"Before we left, the plan was to meet at the northern end of the city. The group from Meat Cove will be coming by land, and we will be safer in numbers."

"When are they supposed to arrive?" Andy asked

"They were going to leave a few days after us, so we should start heading up there now," Jeremy replied.

Andy felt uneasy, sensing his plan was in contrast to Jeremy's and Norman's. They came to save Andy, but Andy came to save the people of the Conscious Whole and despite his near death encounters, he wanted to venture deeper.

"You know, we won't be able to stop this beast if we just keep running from it," Andy said trying to convince them of an alternative plan. "We need to get to the source."

Jeremy and Norman exchanged nervous glances, "We can't completely stop what is happening. We just have to prevent it from invading our town," Norman said, revealing the true scope of their intention.

"We have to run to it, not away," Andy bluntly replied; his frustration was becoming palpable.

"Listen, Andy. You can't, we can't, take on the energy here. It's too big. Trust us, we know," Jeremy pleaded.

"You know!?" Andy fired back, stopping his fast-paced walk, turning directly towards Jeremy and Norman. Andy showed them his thin, quivering left hand, a diseased piece of his being that held on tightly to the reality of the Conscious Whole. "It hasn't let go of me. Ever since I came back there has been an overwhelming force trying to change me, and here it is!" Andy pushed his atrophic hand closer to their faces.

The Conscious Whole held Andy's hand on his journey, even though Jeremy and Norman had released Andy from certain death, the ice cold, metallic, skeletal fingers dug their nails deeply into Andy's flesh and could not be removed.

The three men continued walking down the street in silence. Andy felt guilty for yelling at Jeremy and Norman but also knew his plan could not be carried out alone. *I almost died twice without them,* Andy thought.

"Listen, I'm sorry. But I'm not going to run back to Meat Cove with you. This is my home. This is where I belong. I truly appreciate all you have done for me, but now I have to do something for someone else. For everyone here," Andy's passion poured through his words. "I want...I need your help."

"But what are we supposed to do?"

"Change. One by one. If we show them what is possible they will see," Andy said, his hope and optimism impelling Jeremy and Norman.

"We still need to meet everyone," Jeremy replied, not giving Andy a straight answer, hoping he would eventually change his mind.

Jeremy felt it behind him as they walked westward deeper into the heart of the city and stopped for a moment, turning to look but fearing what he would see. The Conscious Whole was hunting them. It felt the change in Shelia and, even more than before, was out to destroy opposition. The plan was no longer a secret as the omnipotent force viscerally experienced perturbations in its field. Jeremy caught up and stayed close, knowing proximity added strength to their reality. They pressed on, walking past city blocks, all the while, lurking behind buildings, traveling through other conscious clouds, it followed, instilling a message in the people, its loyal supporters, to capture the men.

45

As they looked upon events occurring within the cloud mass, the beings were surprised by stinging tentacles that reached out towards them; they frowned upon the desperation and wept as upcoming events would bring out despondency no creature should bear

THE SITUATION AT THE KAY BOILED OUT of control, and police were called to help contain the patients. When the dust settled, one was missing.

"His name is Andy Fergus. A guy that's really out there, thinks he's from outer space or something," the round, red-faced supervising security guard said, who looked like a chuckling boiled beet. "But I'd be really careful," he continued more seriously, as he handed the police a picture of Andy. Nervous laughter was shared about the wild beard and hair, indwelling a false belief into their steadfast paradigm.

Miles away, a police officer recognized Andy from the disseminated image that flowed through the airwaves of the Conscious Whole. All of a sudden, Andy felt a numb sensation on the right side of his face, abruptly lost vision, and began falling backwards. The filthy hand of the Conscious Whole tugged at his head, its grimy sharp fingernails ripping his skin, the energetic intention of harm pushed ahead of the officer's physical body, overly eager to apprehend Andy.

He fell backwards, but fortuitously Jeremy and Norman dragged him onto a bus that was getting ready to depart. They quickly set off as the energy and officer were left behind.

"Sit down, you're bleeding," Norman said as blood seeped out of Andy's hair.

"I'll be fine...I'm fine," a confused Andy reassured Norman who was holding pressure on his head, while Jeremy haggled with the bus driver.

Andy slipped into and out of consciousness.

The entrance of a building lay in front of him, which appeared to be growing out of the hillside. Its large steel door was hinged open, and Andy peered inside; musty, warm air rushed into his nostrils, the stagnation luring him beyond the threshold, enticing him with the feeling this building had not been explored for years. *Hidden gems are inside*, it told him.

As he made his way inside, evening light shining behind him cast long shadows obscuring most of what was in front of him. A wide set of stairs led down into an atrium where there was another set of heavy steel doors. Andy was already beyond where he should be, and a rushing sense of fear closed in behind him, filling the space he had just traversed. Pushing his way through the doors, he ran through corridors and down sets of stairs for what seemed like hours, as he feverishly raced from the fear behind him. Passing through more and more dimly lit hallways, down more and more sets of stairs, he was inescapably going deeper and deeper into an evil abyss. The olive brown walls were covered in illegible graffiti, which spoke to Andy foretelling him of his doom. Lurking around every corner was an exponentially more malicious force filling every crevice. His only choice was to keep going, as the malevolence now snapped at his heels. He was truly trapped. There was no way out. He had chosen to enter, enticed by what he thought he could do.

46

The task was known when the being agreed, contended the orchestrator; they all knew choice was an obligatory condition but some doubted the duty would be carried through

SILVER HOLOGRAPHIC NEEDLES, EACH FOUR INCHES LONG, were all arranged within the boundaries of her energetic body, all in a different orientation with not one needle out of the millions pointed in the same direction, every one constantly battling for space.

She had extremely spastic movements as she walked down the aisle of the bus towards her seat, none of her limbs coordinated, each doing its own thing, on its own path. Her head was equally out of order, swaying from left to right and front to back, resulting in great difficulty in focusing her route, as she wildly swung a cane in her left hand, barely missing people near her.

Andy, trying to regain composure, externalized his healing energy and simply acted like a magnet as he sat near this woman. He focused on his feet, grounding them to the earth and then concentrated on his head, connecting it to the universe. Everything between his feet and head aligned with polarity created within his body; earth, where life is born into reality, contrasted with the infinite realm of space where all possibility lies, coalescing as subjective experience in the middle.

One by one, the needles in this woman's body became balanced by the nearby magnetic pole of Andy's body. Solidarity and clarity filled her mind like never before; parallel lines of energetic sinew drew into the ever-malleable structure supporting physicality; matter followed suit.

The bus clunked forward, deeper and deeper into Brave, westward through the heavily populated downtown. Hopelessness of the people in the Conscious Whole became deafening.

Andy turned his attention to the back of the bus where bright light accompanied the sound of running water. Soaking wet, like he had jumped into a lake fully clothed, Andy was surprised to see tears of white liquid light dripping off of a man's body. Running down his cheeks, chin, chest, arms, and legs, the quanta of liquid, each the size of a raindrop, were very bright like individual suns, burning Andy's eyes. As the drops splashed on the ground they disappeared into nothingness, where they had originated. Everything in the universe is both matter and light at the same time,[1] and in this man's body, Andy perceived the manifestation of water's matter, dihydrogen monoxide, and its energy, the white light, at the same time.

Wali's energy field mourned as an endless amount of anxiety and sadness poured from his being; anxiety for the uncertain future and sadness because Wali was forced to know he was sick everyday. The pill he took affirmed, three times daily, that he lived with a bodily disorder, a not-so-friendly reminder of the lack of control in his life, pressing his belief system further into the uncontrollable disease paradigm. Even if he was not sick, just taking the pill alone made him submit to illness.

The pill that collapsed the wave function was pink, rectangular, and very powerful, capable of perpetuating disease, if not entirely creating it.

Wali's parents believed he was never good enough, and he consequently grew up doubting himself and his abilities. They showed him how an unknown future was dangerous with malice lying around every corner. Never knowing what to do and apprehensive of everything, Wali's mind

---

1. Refer to wave-particle duality as previously cited.

spiraled into despair and anxiety. In his job, he felt useless, and in life, he was plagued by insecurities; fearful of taking a chance, the constant struggle became the clinical manifestation of depression and anxiety. Wali lost sight of life, and his thoughts reflected in his conscious cloud, carrying strings from the other side to build molecules that constructed DNA of a depressed man.

"What brings you in today?" Wali's family doctor asked.

After skirting around the issue complaining of a sore throat he admitted, "Well, I just feel run down."

"OK, how long has this been going on?"

"For a while, I guess. Ever since I started my job. I don't have any friends there, and whenever I'm not working I just sleep all the time."

"What kind of work is it?"

"Part-time, paper-pushing type of deal," Wali continued, physically retracting, regretting he brought up the issue.

"Do you not enjoy the types of things you used to enjoy?" the doctor predictably asked, trained well by the paradigm she practiced.

"Yeah, I guess."

"Are you eating well?"

"I just eat whatever is around the house."

"Do you seem to worry about nothing in particular?"

"Yeah, I've always been a nervous person."

"Can you concentrate well at work?"

"Nope," Wali replied, wondering how anyone could concentrate in the small cubicle he was confined within at work.

"Any thoughts of hurting yourself or others?" the doctor asked, briefly looking up from Wali's medical chart.

"No. Not at all."

"Well, Wali, you're clinically depressed. It's a medical condition. The good news is it's treatable. You also appear to have an anxiety disorder, but that's also treatable." The doctor gave him a pill for the anxiety and the depression, "You know, depression runs in families. It's genetic.[2] We can even do a blood test to confirm the diagnosis.[3] Were your parents depressed or anxious?"

"Well, yeah, my mom and dad dealt with anxiety and depression too," Wali unsurprisingly responded. "Mom was always worried about stuff. She couldn't let anything go. She seemed anxious about things all the time."

Both parents lived lives they did not enjoy, as if stuck in quicksand, afraid to move. They compared themselves to everyone surrounding them, choosing to see only misfortune and lost opportunities all the while fearful of stepping beyond their comfort zone. Obsessed with material existence, Wali's parents wrote anxiety and depression into the Conscious Whole, relinquishing responsibility over their existence, feeling as if life was out of their control. Luckily, the Conscious Whole had a penchant for permanence.

"See, that's where you get it from," the doctor consoled Wali, as if brilliantly finding the source of this man's depression. "These pills will help with your illness. It's not your fault," she said, further pulling the blanket of comfort and stability over Wali. "You're predisposed to this kind of mental state. It's permanently built into your DNA that your parents gave you. Your DNA can not make the appropriate chemicals in your brain, and this pill, with the chemicals inside of it, will correct the imbalance!"

Shown how to respond to life's everyday challenges, passed from parents to child, Wali learned depression, learned anxiety, and practiced these daily, becoming proficient, seamlessly blending them into his life and into his DNA.

Despite the doctor's vast knowledge of the truths within the Conscious Whole, she did not see the larger scope. Unaware that Wali's DNA was a product of his beliefs and his constantly changing, created, energetic

---

2. Sullivan, Neale, and Kendler. "Genetic Epidemiology of Major Depression: Review and Meta-Analysis." *American Journal of Psychiatry* (2000).

3. Papakostas et al. "Assessment of a Multi-Assay, Serum-Based Biological Diagnostic Test for Major Depressive Disorder: A Pilot and Replication Study." *Molecular Psychiatry* (2013).

field, the curative treatment was beyond the sight of what the good doctor could have ever imagined. Furthermore, not only was the correct solution to Wali's illness beyond the knowledge of the Conscious Whole, it was blasphemy! Speaking against the medical and scientific paradigm had become more damning than speaking against religious beliefs, for their science was paramount and had morphed into a religion of its own, far from the original intent of free discovery.

When the doctor conveyed that only the pill could help Wali's genetic illness,[4] responsibility for his own life was further relinquished to the Conscious Whole, deepening depression and helplessness. Wali had no reason to help himself or change his life as the pill would now do this for him. Everyday it reminded him of his predispositions, making depression reality, believing he had to live with it, thinking it was who he had to be. The energy of depression and anxiety flowed from Wali's conscious cloud and out of the seams of his being as Andy watched this man being destroyed from the inside out.

Andy's conscious cloud, brimming with hope, was a window into an unseen world; he opened the door just long enough for Wali to see beyond his present condition, plugging the porous leaking fissures of his conscious cloud. Just by being in close proximity, all of Andy's experiences were bestowed upon Wali, as if he was watching a film: driving through the rolling plains, the sublime landscape of Meat Cove, the realm of energetic manifestation with layer upon layer of depth built into the seemingly four dimensional world, the expansive ocean, and the Conscious Whole's vice-like grip on reality. Tucked away in spaces out of sight, Wali now saw the Conscious Whole hiding beneath his world like a frightened animal, strangely vulnerable to the slightest opposition, for its strength was gained from concealment.

---

4. Other treatments for depression include cognitive behavioral therapy, which works just as well as pharmacological treatment: DeRubeis et al. "Medications Versus Cognitive Behavior Therapy for Severely Depressed Outpatients: Mega-Analysis of Four Randomized Comparisons." *American Journal of Psychiatry* (1999).

The Conscious Whole

Looking into the beast was like looking into a mirror; derived from Wali's intentions, it fed on his depression, but now flooded with optimistic foresight, a privilege Wali was never allowed, he saw beyond the dense, soiled fog where infinity lay in front of his eyes. Wali needed a change of direction and a push down a path he did not allow to exist. The wrong treatment was a pill to make him even more unaware, more hopeless, and more dependent on a system that perpetuated disease and stagnation. Now, Wali could direct his life. He could put himself in control. His mind would seek new opportunity shaping his body; life would resonate with his core being.

47

How will he endure? the shy one asked; There's no way out! the astute one proclaimed; He's heading into its belly, the young one sighed; There is one way out, the teacher clarified; Will he go through the hidden door? they all inquired; He can't see the door but it will be upon him, the teacher said

WHOOSH! A YOUNG BOY WENT RUNNING PAST Andy on the bus, following in his wake was his mother's energy hurrying along, attempting to rein in the child. The boy's wild brown eyes glanced at Andy as he was now jumping from one seat to another, chancing injury, leaping over people as the mother's apologies paralleled the child's path.

A torrent brewed within the boy's conscious cloud, like massive storms stretching across alien planets, spinning slowly and destructively. Andy was drawn into the eye of the storm, sucked into this child's world, and fell through the sky closer and closer to the churning clouds as the storm grew in size beneath his feet. Andy descended through the source and entered the epicenter, a portal into a different realm, his body accelerating beyond the limits of terminal velocity. Blackness and solitude followed.

The energetic storm resonated with the child's entire body, bringing to life strings that made molecules that made different DNA base pairs producing changes in his brain resulting in hyperactivity. The people of the Conscious Whole were well educated on the pathology of overactive behavior; brain scans identified altered brain structure,[1] cementing their paradigm, proving the organic, unchangeable nature of the disease.

"There it is! The hyperactivity! Right there in the brain! We found it! The **SOURCE**!" The doctors proclaimed with overwhelming enthusiasm.

False. The source is deeper.

"It's called Attention Deficit Hyperactivity Disorder," the doctor told the boy's mother. "It often runs in families. Parents of children with hyperactivity often have the same disease. It can be genetic."

"Well that makes sense," the mother said, comforted by the doctor's words. "I was hyperactive as a child too, and I still feel out of control."

"There's a medicine we can give your son for his disease. In fact, we can also give you the same medicine," the doctor replied, happy to help two people instead of one.

Genetic? Well, DNA is involved with the behavior, but is it really a trait that is passed down without consideration for the behaviors of all involved?

Within the darkness, Andy had no orientation. He didn't even know if he was still falling or not. Then figures appeared, faintly at first but slowly becoming more vivid: a child within a circle of adults of all ages. Andy floated above them, suspended in space like a puppet held up by strings, observing the interaction between these people in a misty semi-permanent existence. The young girl's strong, passionate energy was suppressed by her controlling family and social norms, the silence of this moment was punctuated by the chaotic force of erupting energy, with no other outlet than to decompress through her conscious cloud.

Andy again fell deeper through the uncertain matter into the young girl's conscious cloud, turmoil tossed him in every direction, disorienting his senses until he finally felt solid ground beneath his feet. He had arrived back on the bus as the child now swung from luggage racks like a spider monkey.

---

1. Seidman, Valera, and Makris. "Structural Brain Imaging of Attention-Deficit/Hyperactivity Disorder." *Biological Psychiatry* (2005).

Connected through the timeless bridge of existence, strong roots planted the mother's expression in the norms of the past.

Within her conscious cloud the storm continued to smolder; deeply ingrained, larger, and moving more slowly than her son's, the bodily effects resulted in bounded mental energy mirroring her past. With no escape, the vortex in her cloud consumed energy, internalizing potential, only to be released at sporadic moments, severing her concentration.

One storm fed another. Her conscious cloud nourishing the child's. From the eye of her storm a tornado of energy tracked through space, in between matter, to the child's storm.

Providing not only physical matter but also energetic structure, sustenance, and life since the child was in utero, the mother and child were never released from each other's influence. As the son duplicated the behaviors of the mother, learning how to act by imitating without negative feedback, hyperactivity was reinforced, building stronger energetic pathways, allowing clear simple routes for the inherently high frequency energy to be bound and subsequently released.

Unconscious of her actions and subtle energetic transfer, the mother believed her son's condition to be genetic. Fate. Determined upon conception. Unstoppable nature not determined by nurture.[2,3] There was nothing she could do about DNA, she was told, but a medicine would make it better. A medicine would make her life better.

The child's brain is the manifestation of the parent's energy! Andy thought, seeing the complete process unfolding in front of his eyes.

Energetically, Andy reached his hand into the woman's conscious cloud and stuck his finger towards the outer rim of the storm. He winced

---

2. Human disease/behavior has been argued to originate from nature (i.e. inherited/deterministic causes) and/or nurture (i.e. environmental/external sources). Reviewed in: Ridley, *Nature Via Nurture: Genes, Experience, and What Makes Us Human* (2003).

3. However, DNA is all nurture and nothing is just "nature"! Nurture creates the DNA we measure, a manifestation of instructions from our mind/core and environment. Recall the world is built from quantum mechanics, where the observer creates reality and there is no such thing as objectivity!

like he was putting his finger into a spinning ceiling fan, feeling the sharp bite. The pain coursed up his arm and reverberated throughout his body as the storm tried to escape and dissipate through Andy, but he resisted and pushed it back into the woman's conscious cloud.

It needs an escape route, he thought.

"Be yourself," Andy asserted. She gave him a puzzled look, with one hand on the child and the other on a railing so her son would not pull her away.

"You have suppressed your inner potential," he continued, relaying what he had seen. "The potential will manifest, but you choose how it comes into the world. You are living the results of that choice."

Becoming increasingly annoyed with the situation, the woman looked towards her son and for the first time perceived not only the materialization of her energy but the actual storms brewing within their bodies. A victim of the windstorm, she now had insight to behold her inner power and connected to her son's cloud by a thick strong red cord of energy. His storm dissipated, no longer fed by the mother, as she embraced the natural outlets of true inner greatness waiting to be born, no longer frustrated by the external bounds of the Conscious Whole. She asked her son to look out the window of the moving bus and despite his young physical age, posed a question not normally asked of such a young child.

"What does your inner greatness hold?"

"I want to explore, Mommy," he quickly replied, true to his inner will.

"Let's do it," she said as they exited the side door of the bus.

A daily pill, a small dressing on a gushing wound, would not solve the root of their problem. Medicine for either herself or her child would keep them bound, not only unable to express their potential but also reminded by the Conscious Whole potential is dangerous, necessitating a disease label, stunting their growth and power.

"Thank you," the woman politely said to Andy as the door closed. "He's free now."

Andy felt promise in their goal of helping the people of Brave as his mind flooded with incoming energetic tracings no matter where he looked; he could not help but see people in need.

Hank. A very large man sitting in the front of the bus was both tall and stout. A constricted flow of energy was trying to enter his body, like a bathtub of draining water; a vortex above spiraled into his mouth and sounded like rushing wind minutes before an impending storm. However, it was being blocked, barely able to enter no matter how hard it tried; with every breath Hank took, a small piece of energy snuck past his vocal cords, hardly sufficient to nourish and energize his body.

Just as the vortex above was trying to enter, there was an equal amount of energy inside of him that could not escape, bottlenecked by a narrow white ring of energy in his throat containing strong opposing charges.

The fast growing tumor in Hank's neck not only blocked air but also prevented energetic flow. Hank sat hunched over in his seat wearing a concerned look on his face; not only did every breath feel like his last, but he was perseverating on the test results about to be delivered to him by his doctor; he had been progressively getting worse and knew to not hold onto hope, as his doctor had instructed.

The tumor's energy had a stronger presence than Hank, despite his large physical stature; the thick, sinew-like circle of energy with black stripes spun rapidly, tightening with every revolution like a constricting snake coiling prey, filling the bus with its malevolence.

Andy was uncertain of taking action and looked towards Jeremy, who also saw Hank's energy and wanted to help. Jeremy eagerly did what seemed obvious, as he had seen Andy do before, and etherically reached his fingers inside of the spooling vortex prying open the ring of energy creating a larger bore.[4] Hank grimaced, unaware of Jeremy's intervention.

---

4. Radiofrequency ablation, microwave ablation, and high-intensity focused ultrasound are forms of "energy medicine" that can be used to destroy tumors by heating tissue. Reviewed in: Valji, *The Practice of Interventional Radiology* (2011), pgs. 729-731.

Simple! Jeremy thought, feeling good about his deed, gaining confidence in their mission. Yet, moments later, screams from the front of the bus startled Jeremy out of his trance.

"Help, help!" a bug-eyed woman who had been sitting next to Hank screamed.

The bus slammed on the brakes and everyone fell forward. Bodies swarmed around Hank's lifeless body attempting to revive him while others ignored the situation, unable to escape their unconscious stupor.

"What happened?" Andy asked.

"Well, I don't know…I mean he just collapsed, I think." Permeating dread filled Jeremy's body as he wondered if he had somehow caused the situation.

Not really wanting to see if Hank was alive or not, Jeremy slowly peered through the crowd and caught a glimpse of Hank's lifeless face.

A low hissing sound filled Jeremy's ears, increasing in amplitude, as a fossilized white humanoid creature crawled off of Hank on all fours, its claws clinking on the metal floor as it hid within the mob.

"Hey…" Jeremy tried to shout, but the words did not make it past his lips.

Jeremy frantically looked for this strange being and then saw it grasp onto another passenger! Out of the corner of its hollow, hungry eyes it teased Jeremy whilst feasting off of another's conscious cloud, ravenous for its next fix.

Paramedics rushed onto the bus and helped revive Hank's empty-appearing body. As they carried him away, barely hanging onto life, the white creature gave a piercing hiss at Jeremy and leapt back onto Hank, slowly seeping between his matter, disappearing beneath his skin like a reptile in the sand.

The Conscious Whole was embedded within the people, and they were more than just living under the Conscious Whole, they **were** the Conscious Whole. The path chosen by Andy, Jeremy, and Norman would not be without losses.

Andy tugged Jeremy's arm as they slid out the back door. The bus lurched onward and the gloom of Hank's situation stayed with the men as they walked down the street in silence. Andy's thoughts were now cluttered with doubt, and he wondered how they were supposed to accomplish such an impossible task.

"Andy, do…do you think I had anything to do with it?" Jeremy asked afraid of the answer.

"I'm not sure. I don't think there's anything that you could have done," Andy uncharacteristically replied seeing how selfishly the Conscious Whole operated, questioning his own intentions.

"We'd better get to the rendezvous," Norman nervously reminded everyone, wanting nothing more than to return to Meat Cove.

As they rounded a corner of the less developed western sector of Brave, trying to get oriented, downtown Brave showed itself in the distance between the buildings. The sky above tossed and turned, unstable, ready to fall onto the world. The Conscious Whole had been awoken, and like running from a disturbed beehive there was little safety to be found. A strong cold wind blew onto their faces as the low, dense clouds rolled closer sensing their presence; it had to deal with more than just these three men as others were awakening.

Andy sternly walked ahead of Jeremy and Norman and kept to himself, becoming more uncommunicative as each block passed.

"Let's go back home. We can fight it there." Jeremy confided to Norman, breaking the silence.

"Yeah, but I don't know what Andy's going to do. I don't think he wants to go back, and we can't just leave him here."

"Come on, hurry up," Andy yelled back as he began jogging towards a hospital hoping it was where they had brought Hank, leaving Jeremy and Norman no choice but to run after him. Andy burst into the waiting room full of people suffering from various acute and chronic issues: cuts, sprains, pain, disease.

"Is there a man that was just brought here from a bus?" Andy asked, out of breath, to an overworked, distracted, stressed out emergency room clerk, who in turn gave Andy an apathetic look as she juggled three different phones. "Huh? Bus? The bus schedule is over there." She pointed to a ripped up piece of paper tacked onto the wall.

"No. A man was brought here who collapsed on a bus. He's...my friend. I want to see him, please."

"Only immediate family can be with patients."

"It's really important that I see him," Andy pleaded.

The clerk sighed and rolled her eyes, "Wait over there and I'll try to get a hold of a doctor."

"Andy, what are you doing!?" Jeremy asserted as he grabbed Andy's arm, frustrated with his aberrant behavior.

Andy brushed him off and proceeded to sit down. "Seeing that man almost die, almost suffocate to death, brought back memories of when I was dying. When I struggled to breath. I didn't die, so there's no reason for him to die either," Andy stoically replied.

What's the endpoint? What are we doing here? Jeremy thought. "We can't let him continue on this selfless path. I don't think we can do this," Jeremy whispered to Norman, who quietly nodded.

48

Layered forms took shape outside of the sphere of influence, each relinquishing self-identity but in turn becoming a new self; more layers were added upon each journey with new selves formed; repeated over and over until there was seemingly no self but instead a summation of experiences; they carried the light of time

A SHROUD SURROUNDED HIS BODY, ITS COLOR outside the limits of visible perception, indescribable to a human brain, yet audible to a human body. The protective covering produced a distant sound as if it had traveled from the other end of time, diluted during its journey with only an echo remaining, barely discernable and hardly recognizable from its source.

Norman stood nearby, waiting for an opportunity to pull Andy away from his self-consumed goal but was distracted by a presence near him, the sound of pure love; unstoppable and everlasting.

Pain encased the man's body rendering him incapacitated, the agony worn on his face. His younger daughter's expression portrayed accumulated sadness while his older daughter anguished in fear of what may happen in the future without her father; fear of what life would be like and fear of how her mother would deal with the loss. The man's wife was filled with defeat for everything they tried had failed.

Every few minutes, the trio increased their focus on the man, redirecting their attention, and the noise increased in volume, becoming thicker in quality. For a brief moment his pain would be manageable, and they all shared fleeting bliss.

Yet, doubt and uncertainty would inevitably return, weakening the connection; pain, for all, recaptured the moment.

Running on autopilot, DNA relentlessly churned out a protein altering pain receptors on the man's cells, resulting in autonomous neuronal sparks. Chronic pain was the result, however, the pathologic cause evaded the doctor's diagnostics tests.

Norman thought back to Meat Cove, when he had first met Andy and how he had been freed from what he thought was an inescapable fate. Norman focused his energy through the micromatter of his cells, between the organelles of the neurons to the nucleus, where DNA resides.

Norman imagined DNA as a channel, a bridge, where potential awaits before traveling into the physical realm.

Physical pain originated from psychic pain the man subconsciously channeled through his DNA, believing he should suffer for past failures: dropping out of college, losing his job for not working hard enough, not spending time with his father before his death, and now withdrawing from his family. Waveforms of emotional energy were powerful, filling his conscious cloud and like a rising river flooding its banks, easily channeled through DNA, the path of least resistance.

Disease ensued.

Seizing the opportunity, Norman transferred his resilient, solid, rock-like waveforms through the man's DNA. Energy knows no mistakes and is pure potential, a master of creating the future. The man's DNA temporarily changed as it was cleansed with glassy sky-blue tones flowing through the matrix of matter, and his face instantly smoothed as the grimace faded and pain abated. Held strong by the shroud of love from his wife and daughters, relief quickly spread through their presence. Norman waited a few moments before approaching them.

"The creation of reality lies within your grasp," Norman bluntly stated. The family looked at him inquisitively.

Norman continued, "It's your perception of who you are that creates your body, made in an image of who you think you are and what you think you should be," his deep voice echoed. "Your illness is a manifestation of what lies within your subconscious. Seek this out, resolve it, and you will be healed."

Snapped into a conscious state and out of self-loathing, the man's eyes peeled off of his past and into the shroud he had been ignoring. Seeing forgiveness from the family surrounding him fostered strength in self-forgiveness allowing accumulated, now useless energy cathartic release.

The room suddenly became solid, like a pearl, smooth and matte white with subtle iridescence.

There is hope! He is hope!! Andy exclaimed to himself as he became aware of a tall man who walked into the waiting room.

His hope filled the room to the brim and left space for nothing else. Doubt, fear, regret, and even hatred could not squeeze their ugly heads into the space, it was simply impenetrable.

Mr. Giving was hope in its purest form, and his pearly white hair matched his energy field. Others told him not to have hope. Not to believe. Not to believe in such a thing as hope.

"It's false hope to think you'll get better," his brother told him. "It's better to accept the reality that you're sick. It's not good to have false hope. You'll let yourself down. You'll be disappointed."

Is disappointment the worst outcome of believing? Mr. Giving thought, never responding to his brother's remarks. He would not listen and knew with all his being there was no such thing as "false hope." *It doesn't exist,* he told himself. *"False hope" is an oxymoron, a made up, created word used for control.*

"False hope" assumes outcomes are already determined, an incorrect interpretation of reality as there are only unlimited possibilities in the future; the world path is not predestined, confirmed by experimental laws of physics.[1] "False hope" is simply not compatible with nature.

There is **only** hope, and Mr. Giving was its manifestation. Yet, any idea that is polluted by the mind, by doubt, by incorrect assumptions of nature, by the Conscious Whole is **not** hope. Hope is pure and cannot be tainted by other beliefs or ideals. Hope is hope. It is mathematically represented by the wave function, phi, demonstrating that all possibilities are indeed possible, and hope is the belief that one of those outcomes will become true.

Mr. Giving had big eyes that stretched wide open, magnified by large framed glasses that poked out under his winter hat-like coat of thick hair. His arms and legs were long and skinny and his face filled with promises of the future. Andy could not believe what he was seeing as each and every manifestation of potential appeared as a holograph on the surface of the white pearl of energy, with multiple layers, one on top of another. Andy could have spent centuries pouring through all the possibilities, all of the potential, yet there was no end in sight as the holographic landscape continually changed. Layer upon layer flashed before his eyes: a bright landscape with blue skies and rolling fields, a snowy night filled with warmth by a fire, people laughing at a dinner party, Mr. Giving working at an easel designing buildings. However, Andy was taken aback when one of the images was of himself in a dreary, rainy city! The imagery and associated empathic sensation tied a knot in Andy's stomach pulling him out of his trance-like state.

Mr. Giving walked forward to the reception desk and when asked to sign-in, explained he had lost the ability to use his arms as they lay dangling at his sides. The clerk took his name and instructed him to wait his turn, but despite his condition and being reminded of his inabilities, Mr. Giving's hope and resilience was out-of-this-world, from beyond the Conscious Whole, unsoiled, channeled directly from another source on an unimpeded path to his surroundings.

---

1. The core tenet of quantum physics is the non-determined nature of reality and dependence upon the observer, as previously cited.

Only yesterday, Mr. Giving had met Dr. Rubin at a friend's house. She was a friend of a friend and everyone wanted to know about what was happening at the Kay, as it was all over the news. The Kay had never been openly discussed in the Conscious Whole before, it was a place to be forgotten, to be pushed under the rug, and an institution all were in favor of but none would admit their allegiance. Now, openly covered by the media, dragged into conscious awareness of the whole, the Conscious Whole shivered in embarrassment and anger. Mr. Giving listened closely at the periphery of the group, about the upheaval, about the missing patient Andy Fergus, and how people were changing without a clear medical reason. They were being healed. One by one. So called "miracles" were occurring.

"The mental changes spread from one person to another.[2] Kind of like a virus...we don't know why," Dr. Rubin explained. "We have no reason to continue treating them, so we've actually discharged more patients in a week than ever before! But we are getting a lot of pressure from the administration to keep people despite them being mentally and physically cleared. Some incurable illnesses seem to have spontaneously resolved," Dr. Rubin explained, perplexed by the changes she was seeing that were in stark contrast to the paradigm she practiced.

Earlier that day Mr. Giving had felt helpless, hope was a lost cause. His disease was on a downward slope, accelerating, and just like Andy he was given a timeline of forthcoming bodily failures. Fatefully, Dr. Rubin's conscious cloud, hope, and energetic tracks now tied to Meat Cove took seed in Mr. Giving, and more than anyone else at the dinner party he needed her hope. He needed to hear that life was not a predetermined path towards a certain future. He needed to know that even the self-proclaimed omnipotent, shortsighted, exclusionary medical paradigm of the

---

2. Mass psychogenic illness is when a group of individuals develop similar symptoms that may be psychological, neurological, or physical; yet, it can also be applied to a group's positive attitudes spreading to other individuals: Colligan, Pennebaker, and Murphy, *Mass Psychogenic Illness: A Social Psychological Analysis* (2013).

Conscious Whole could not predict his future. He now believed he had a chance too, just like the patients at the Kay.

The powerful energy Andy had brought to Brave was spreading from one conscious cloud to the next; seeded at the Kay, hope grew and proliferated from the most unlikely location. As Dr. Rubin and discharged patients interacted with others outside of the Kay Institute, the energy disseminated and exponentially grew as hope begot hope, driving the creation of new positive energy from within Brave in addition to the channeled energy coming from Meat Cove, much to the disdain of the Conscious Whole.

"Patient Givinnnnnggg?" a male nurse said loudly over the background noise of the emergency room. He motioned with his index finger for Mr. Giving to sit on a hospital bed near the front desk, and then pulled a white curtain around the bed.

Andy could no longer physically see Mr. Giving but marveled at the pearly white hope that was now cemented in the cube of space created by the thin curtain, like a solid block of ice wrapped in thin plastic. The doctor approached Mr. Giving's less than private room and had to squeeze his body around the block of hope, as it would not be penetrated.

"What brings you in today?" the veteran doctor said through his neatly trimmed white beard.

"I'm getting better!" Mr. Giving exclaimed as his bushy eyebrows jumped above the frames of his glasses like a set of jumping-beans, his voice sounding like a child wildly opening birthday presents. "I can move my arms just a little more!" His right arm barely flickered at his side as he motioned with his head for the doctor to look. Despite his limited mobility, he moved around as much as he could, dancing in contained joy.

The doctor pessimistically looked back at his patient, as a specific list of medical ailments rolled through his mind. *Psychiatric disease: acute mania, psychosis, delusional disorder. Drug use: amphetamines, hallucinogens…*

After testing Mr. Giving and not finding a medical cause for his bizarre behavior the doctor squeezed back into the room, "Well, I can't find a cause for you…feeling better…I mean most patients don't come to the hospital because they...feel better..." he trailed off, not knowing how to continue. "...so, you still have near-complete paralysis of your arms, and it's unlikely you will get better," he cautioned, trying to implant doubt as a self-fulfilling prophecy.

"I met Dr. Rubin. She's at the Kay Institute," Mr. Giving couldn't speak fast enough. "She said her patients are getting better and you know what? I think I am too! That's why I came. To see if I really am getting better!" Rays of light shot out from his eyes like headlights of a car.

Consternation covered the doctor's face, as he thought about rerunning the drug test for other stimulants. The Kay was not a place where people improved. Shaking his head he warned his patient, "You will hear wild things, you know. Things you shouldn't believe. It's not good. I haven't heard of people getting better there, and if I did, then I would be out of a job!" he laughed heartily, patronizing Mr. Giving's hope.

Mr. Giving heard the doctor's words, but they would have no effect. Unbroken, he sat smiling, knowing he had a chance to get better. His unlimited vision of the future, which everyone else in the Conscious Whole forced into one preset reality, allowed untapped solutions to break the horizon. His conscious cloud was changed by Dr. Rubin and now overflowed with infinite colors of endlessness, a pearly matrix enveloping his space.

"Well, it's good to reach for the stars, but you must be honest with yourself and not have false hope," the doctor said contradicting himself as he handed Mr. Giving his discharge orders.

Trying to reach for a star is considered an impossible task and would represent an example of false hope, since the doctor purportedly **knows** the outcome: failure. What the doctor did not consider, however, was Mr. Giving's height. His tall stature was not only a physical characteristic of his body but also an independent dimension of his core being, able to stretch beyond the stars towards infinity to touch the most distant possibility and make it real.

There's no such thing as false hope. There is only hope! Mr. Giving thought as he walked out the automatic glass doors exiting the emergency room, carrying his conscious cloud of promise, impenetrable to the Conscious Whole.

49

The underworkers turned their attention downward, coring through deposits of rock, burrowing through the past, seeking what lay within; they fought time, as events above accelerated; more workers were called and even those whose tasks were not completed dug side-by-side with the underworkers for without the source, their journey would be futile

THE INFANT WAS LIMP, A THREE-DIMENSIONAL puzzle floating in space with all of the pieces disassembled, each one a hologram containing the encoded, prismatic colors of the newborn, a complete image of the whole, yet, vibrating at disparate frequencies. As the units came into contact they would become one, a larger hologram, but the union was temporary, and they would again cleave into separate puzzle pieces. The smaller pieces would break apart into even smaller ones and then come together again. A constant dance. An ebb and flow of energy.

The instinctive maternal grasp rallied to bring every tiny piece back into order, to complete what she had started. Every part of the whole was present, ready for life but dispersed and lacking harmony.

Her languid body was unable to control itself, too thin for her age and without the vigor possessed by most to continue forward, her black thin hair seemed to dance in the wind as her arms and legs lay loosely at her side. The depth of her hollow eyes revealed a timeless uncertainty that no one should possess.

As Andy waited to hear about the condition of the man on the bus, the puzzle pieces floating past distracted his attention. *Her pieces need to be put back together*, he thought. *She needs a unifying force.*

This child formed in the womb by instructions from the energy force of the whole,[1] manipulating formation of the embryo. The energetic blueprint of space around and within the child created the physical manifestation of disarray and self-abandonment. Andy allowed his mind to sift through deeper and deeper layers of reality, seeing past experiences this child had lived worn intimately in its energy. Crimes in a time of war, orders passed from general to soldier, obedient following. It died serving a purpose not worth a cent, it thought. Andy viscerally felt pain still written into the collectiveness as the baby's hollow eyes drew him even deeper into its lonely depths.

Drops of water falling from the ceiling were ear ringing. Seemingly irrelevant subtleties of experience carried the heaviest sensory information. Clanking of chains and ripping of flesh on the prisoner's wrists. Muffled words bore no language but only meaning of ill-purpose. Haunted by its actions, the core being thought it did not deserve life and kneaded this principle seamlessly into subconscious beliefs, then written into the Conscious Whole.

Darkness pervaded the space, and Andy peered around the corner of a cave, accidently slipping into a ravine, perilously sinking to the bottom of a lightless ocean. Without sight, he could only sense what surrounded him, a horror pushed into the cavernous subterranean realm of the collective consciousness, stored by a being still tormented by the past. So distant in time and no longer bearing a form, the atrocities attempted to pull Andy through the cold soft silt on the bottom of the ocean floor.

He fought to drag himself from this basal coating of existence, struggling to pull himself out of a nightmare. Beliefs the very young child car-

---

1. A holographic energetic framework mediated by DNA may, in part, create the body: Miller and Webb. "Embronic Holography: An Application of the Holographic Concept of Reality." *DNA Decipher Journal* (2012).

ried into its life served no purpose, nor did they in the prior. The Conscious Whole predictably and unconditionally stored these memories and ideals, using them as a lattice to build the child. Yet, despite the magnitude of the previous actions, the connection to the Conscious Whole looked as thin as a bubble, coursed with brittle red streaks of energy. The bubble-like leaves flickered in the child's conscious cloud like a dying flame.

Andy worked to separate the beliefs from their tether to the Conscious Whole, as if cutting them with a sharp knife, removing unnecessary and unneeded input from past experiences, allowing the future, not the past, to be seen.

"Mr. Fergus?" a young doctor called as his voice cracked.

Andy towered above the fresh intern as he cleared his throat and anxiously looked back and forth between his papers and Andy's stern face, trying to figure out how to break the news.

"You're Mr. Fergus? OK...well, you know Hank Kopek? I mean... you're family?" he said continuing to ruffle through his papers.

"A friend," Andy flatly replied feeling like he wanted to shake the words out of the young doctor.

"Oh. So...I'm sorry. But Hank died, I mean Mr. Kopek didn't make it. He passed away."

Andy was furious. Not at the inexperience of the doctor's bedside manners but instead at himself. He did not want to let anyone down. He came back to show people that healing is possible, and he failed.

The fossil-like being that lurked within the material body of Hank was still present, feeding off of every last droplet of despair still residing within the physical corners of existence. Andy saw the being peeking between curtains containing Hank's body, sneering at Andy's attempt to change the world. The reason for Hank's recurrent tumor was not his lack of effort, for he unfailingly went to every treatment prescribed; it was not the fault of the medicine, for each round of treatment shrunk the tumor; it was not the lack of scientific progress, as the medicine was as strong as needed to kill the cancer cells. The disease, however, was a pact Hank signed with a being that sought protection and shelter for it could no longer live without bodily vices and in turn, the being brought Hank riches through its perception of the future. The medicine would have eliminated all of the tumor cells, but it continued to return from the over-stimulating radiant energy the cells received from the gluttonous being crawling through Hank's body.

Beneath the anger, motivation boiled inside of Andy. When others would quit, he pressed on. Andy's illness was more than a random event inside of his body that churned out proteins resulting in disability; it was a lesson in perseverance. In holding out hope. In never giving up. In doing **whatever** it takes to change the future.

With more drive than before, Andy gained clearer insight into his goal and admitted to himself that Jeremy and Norman would not agree with his intention. He knew what had to be done but would wait to disclose his thoughts.

"Let's go. We have a rendezvous to make," Andy conceded to Jeremy and Norman as all three left the hospital.

Fearlessness is truly an unheard of quality as even the strongest person has fears. Nevertheless, on the crowded street in front of the hospital, Marvin went whizzing by the three men, a vortex of fearless energy, a tornado without wind or rain protecting him from physical dangers.

A true one in a million, Marvin was moving faster than everyone around him, easily but harshly making his way past others walking on the sidewalk, weaving in and out. Busy, too. Everyone walking by seemed to be busy, but Marvin had ten times as many things happening in his life, taking a dozen different phone calls about dinner plans, class work, meetings, and scheduling other meetings.

However, it was difficult for him to speak, let alone breath. A machine was doing the breathing for him, and in between its breaths, he spoke with a dry, air-like voice telling others what to do. Yet, just by looking at Marvin, you would think he would be told what to do: what to wear, what to eat, where to go. His machine even told him when to breathe! None-

The Conscious Whole

theless, Marvin seemed not to care and did not need a perfect body to live his life. Despite not having legs and only one small arm, nothing got in his way as he expertly drove his agile motorized wheelchair around any person or thing in his path.

When Andy had sailed from the Three Tombs into the Conscious Whole, a tunnel was formed in his wake; a cylinder deforming light on its surface, like water rushing around a rock in a river, invisible from the outside, veiled from the Conscious Whole. However, within its interior was like being within a glass tube with only a hint of reflective coating. It acted as a low resistance passage for energy to freely follow Andy's trail and as a viewing corridor for those venturing within.

Far across the ocean, in the temperate churning waters of the Three Tombs, the beings anxiously watched through the tunnel, as if through a telescope. They saw Andy enter into the Conscious Whole and witnessed every event, emotionally sensing every encounter, feeling proud when he overcame the black beast and angry when he was wrongfully detained. The world they saw awakened their minds to reality beyond the archipelago, directly tuning in like radio receivers.

Incredibly intrigued by the alien land, they scoured through pages of the saga written by the people, and in particular they were attracted to Marvin's story. The empathic beings of the Three Tombs shuddered as they felt this boy's life; doubt and pity from family and society, doom from the doctors, sorrow from the teachers, but entombed within, wrapped tightly in protective layers, coveted by Marvin was a delicately woven vessel held strongly within his core. Pride, determination, and love.

Energy only parents could bestow upon a child, given to him at his earliest age but concealed from the outside world. Fearful to show others for what they would think, fearful to empower the inner energy for it may be taken, and fearful to manifest into the reality the energetic form he needed to succeed, Marvin hid the vessel from all of those around him, succumbing to the pervasive pitiful energy draped over his body.

When the beings of the Tombs saw Marvin and the vessel within, they were perplexed. "Why doesn't he release his vital life force?" they thought. Empathically forced into action, the beings instead bestowed their own sense of pride, determination, and love into Marvin's space, which resonated with his inner vessel and showed him not to hide his true self and to live his potential. Effortlessly flowing through the channel, emotional certainty filled Marvin's space and acted like a mirror for him to see his core.

Snapped out of the deterministic worldview of what he was "supposed to do", Marvin was awoken to an entirely new reality with ever-present possibilities within his reach. He quickly transformed into the man that always lay within and immediately went into action, starting his own business. He planned on making devices that would enable others like him to be more independent, now using unique perspectives gained from his condition instead of harping on the problems it created. Marvin was going to change the world.

"Everything you say, do, and think is literally created around you. Change how you think, and you will change the whole world!" Marvin's voiced cracked into the phone as he furiously spoke with a potential client who was frustrating him.

Andy could not believe what he was hearing: the message he carried from Meat Cove, heresy that raged the Conscious Whole.

As Andy, Jeremy, and Norman watched Marvin fly by, a trail was left behind for others to follow, tainting the Conscious Whole's once perfectly operating world. Like graffiti on the side of a "clean" oil refinery, it displayed the courage required to be fearless in order to advance society.

Suddenly, Norman collapsed, drawing Andy and Jeremy to his side.

"What happened!? What's wrong!?" Andy asked trying to revive Norman.

"I...I feel weak. Like when I was sick before."

"We have to get him back to Meat Cove," Jeremy asserted, frustrated by being at the whim of Andy's path.

"Let's get him up and walking," Andy replied, not wanting to stop and be vulnerable to the ever-present Conscious Whole.

Like Andy, Norman was tied to his old home by connections working behind the scenes; their time was limited as long as the beast lurked in the background.

"There's a train station this way," Jeremy said pointing to a sign. "We can make up some ground if we can catch one of the northbound trains."

"OK," Andy agreed, going along with Jeremy but knowing their paths would soon diverge.

50

No one wanted to be first, but after the most courageous being above leaped into a crevice of the cloud mass, others followed; a journey through memories of time, stored in an electric lattice; static shocks stunned the beings as they fell through space landing on earth below; covered in a coat of the cloud they traversed, their true form was masked, camouflaged by the existing framework of reality

THE WORN-APPEARING MEN WERE OUT OF place in the symmetric, well-groomed neighborhood of Pleasant Ferry, an oasis in a depressed region of Brave, where they took a shortcut to the train station.

On one of the porches of a house, a squadron formed a tactical unit, a unified fleet ready for battle, but the small porch was only big enough for three bodies, Mrs. Gentry and her two friends, Darlis and Dawn. However, there were countless others separate from the three physical forms that occupied every dimension, all focusing healing energy towards Mrs. Gentry. A cup of energy rested a few feet below the women, supporting them in the world, isolating them from the rest. Energy spilled from the porch heating the surrounding space contrasting the cool evening air, snapping the men back into the moment.

A light rose-colored undulating energy stretched out to Andy, Jeremy, and Norman on the sidewalk, its rhythmic motion mesmerizing, like docile waves crashing on a beach.

"Watch out ladies, this one is mine!" the computer generated voice stuttered unnaturally from the device on Mrs. Gentry's lap. She was looking directly at Andy, and he was caught off guard, not knowing what to say.

A stroke had destroyed her ability to talk but did not slow her down, and the rest of the ladies followed suit, making comments as well, not excluding Jeremy and Norman. The men felt overwhelmed as the squadron showed no mercy with their rapid-fire remarks! Andy's face turned bright red, which only added fuel to the fire.

They eventually settled down and retreated, allowing the men to continue down the street. The women and surrounding beings returned to their loving energetic flow state, providing Mrs. Gentry with all they could offer, siphoning infinite forms from a hole in the Conscious Whole's web. Limitless energy passed through the squadron and into their inter-matter space; previously blocked from the endlessness of the dark matter, Mrs. Gentry had no reserve to recover from her stroke and was forced to live with her damaged brain.

"Neurons don't just grow back like other cells in the body.[1] There's a scar in your brain, and that function is gone," the doctor explained to Mrs. Gentry. There would be little if any recovery and most importantly, no possibility of a cure.

The small cell of powerful energy was a unique space created by the ladies; they poked a hole through the destabilized Conscious Whole's thin shield like a hot iron rod through wax, channeling the strings needed to begin rebuilding Mrs. Gentry's brain; mental conditioning would then bring forth physical manifestation.

They exited the quaint community onto a single lane road, still feeling awkward from their encounter with the squadron; abandoned warehouses flanked the street and were overcome by an encroaching, eerie forest

---

1. Neuronal growth and regeneration are not nearly as prolific as with other cells (e.g. hair, skin) and had been thought to not occur in adults. However, there is evidence supporting neuronal growth in adults: Lee, et al. "Dynamic Remodeling of Dendritic Arbors in GABAergic Interneurons of Adult Visual Cortex." *PLoS Biology* (2005).

that seemed to watch the men as they walked. Night was enclosing their space, removing contrast from the surroundings; shapes blended together as their confused brains frantically computed insufficient input from their eyes, walking closer together, not wanting to mention the increasing unease overcoming their bodies.

No more than a mile down the road, a column of sun-colored light rose vertically towards infinity over the tall, now black buildings and trees, emanating from within the train station. Despite the infinite range this light sought, it was finite, dissipating as it approached the bounds of the sky, burning out with each photon released as a fiend fed from above.

Energy left Mr. Pillar with such voracity that there was nothing left for him. He was being emptied; pockets turned inside out.

Jeremy rushed to the ticket counter after entering the train station, hoping the next train was leaving shortly, now more focused on getting home than accomplishing their goal of helping the people of Brave. Andy stood nearby, captivated by Mr. Pillar, who on the surface was put together very well: sharp haircut, fashionable pink dress shirt, and well-groomed. Yet, he looked disconnected, removed, not present as his son sat next to him, wringing his hands over and over, eyes twitching back and forth looking through cracked glasses, long greasy hair hanging to the side. The two were headed to the Kay Institute as Mr. Pillar's son had heard about the healings and was seeking hope. His father, his hero, the one who once took care of him, was now in need of care himself.

Mr. Pillar was increasingly unable to recognize his environment and other people, even his own son, resulting in painful isolation. Disease was removing him from reality, sending him away like a castaway on a raft in the middle of an ocean, never to speak or interact with anyone again.

Once nourishing healthy strings, Mr. Pillar's energy was escaping, taking with it the vibrational support to stay in existence. With loss of the strings, molecules followed, and his matter was literally being thinned out, most noticeably in his brain where he could no longer store new memories and past experiences were being erased.

"Why is his energy leaving?" Norman nervously asked, "Can that happen to us?"

"I don't think he's losing it forever. Energy is always conserved, but as strange as it sounds, it seems like he's dissolving."

Norman gave Andy a look of disbelief and fear as they stood in the main hall of the train station, waiting for Jeremy to buy tickets.

"He's being diluted. His energy is still around, but it's not tightly packed. He can't hold onto what he had created of himself because the reality he once believed in is no longer real to him. It's like his core being discovered that the physical world, which it put its entire stake into, is nothing more than a creation. It's confused and giving up on everything," Andy said, fearing for Mr. Pillar's future, realizing the severity of the situation. "But his core is mistaken. The physical world is a creation, but creation is what gives us life!"

As the layers of matter peeled away in three-dimensional sheets right before Andy's eyes, Mr. Pillar's core, his true self, was being unmasked. Its large, hazel brown, infant-like wide eyes emerged first, looking into the world through a now semi-transparent physical male body. It despised what it saw and eagerly awaited the final moments when it could escape the disgusting reality it once loved. Like a caged animal, the core bounced around the body as its shell became thinner.

"What can be done?" Norman tensely asked.

"Show him there are people here who love him and want him around. Show him he can contribute to life, and that physical reality *is* reality. He doesn't need to leave," Andy said assertively.

The Conscious Whole fervently sucked the life force out of Mr. Pillar's weakly bound physical form, gaining strength, and the core happily conceded, eager to escape.

Rusty wheels screeched on the metallic track as a train entered the station, startling Andy. Innumerable clouds of consciousness poured off the train that had just arrived from downtown Brave and gray colors flooded the train station with thoughts of anger, frustration, unhappiness, and despair. Mr. Pillar's core reacted to the energy permeating the station, solidifying its belief that it wanted to break away.

After the last person stepped off, the Conscious Whole slyly slipped out the train door as it closed, jumping from one conscious cloud to another, snaking its way closer to Andy, as he and Norman walked towards Mr. Pillar.

"*You* can heal him. You don't need to go anywhere to accomplish that," Andy said to Mr. Pillar's son.

The young man looked straight through Andy and Norman, confused. "Those miracles can only happen at the Kay. That's what everyone is saying. And it's true too because my dad is still sick." The Conscious Whole dined off of troubled minds converging into its center, exploiting weakness and uncertainty.

"They aren't miracles," Andy insisted. "What you perceive as 'miracles' are true aspects of reality that are not yet understood because science has yet to describe how they work.[2] Logical explanations will describe how 'miracles' come to form when the understanding of reality has advanced. Then, what are 'miracles' today will be fundamental aspects of nature in the future."

Mr. Pillar's son gave the men a bewildered look.

"In order for the 'miracles' you speak of to come true, you must tear down barriers within your mind."

Shaking his head, focused on getting to the Kay, Mr. Pillar's son was weighed down by the Conscious Whole, now whispering in his ear dissuading his belief in the trueness of 'miracles'.

"We come from a place where reality is not restricted. Just see for yourself," Andy said as a pure yellow energy radiating from his hand turned into a solid ball encasing the lower part of his arm. He moved it above Mr. Pillar's head, the energy an exact copy of that fading from Mr. Pillar.

---

2. Similar concept discussed in: Green, *The Keys of Jeshua* (2004), pg. 162.

Norman was shocked by what he saw. "What are you doing!?" He struck Andy's arm, trying to get him away from the man he was supposedly helping.

Andy was draining, not replenishing Mr. Pillar's sun-like energy and continued, unfazed by Norman's assault, like a man possessed and controlled by the malevolent Conscious Whole.

Norman pushed his big frame into Andy, knocking him down, but the damage had already been done; the core being, now only contained by a few bodily molecules, was moments away from liberation. Yet, it paused as sadness rolled through its eyes seeing a world no longer obscured by the meaningless reality it had created, providing clarity it had not experienced in ages.

The core had forgotten why it created Mr. Pillar, and what its purpose and goals were. Now able to see past its materially focused house, its true and important intentions resurfaced; the core being saw why it needed the physical body of Mr. Pillar and began reclaiming energy from above to rebuild the material form. A fake self no longer masked the core's eyes while it prepared the physical body, its vehicle, for the journey it was about to embark upon. Mr. Pillar looked towards his son.

"Dad, we need you here. There are still things for you to do. For us to do…" the words were barely audible; Mr. Pillar's son was overcome with emotion from seeing his father's face return to the world. Mr. Pillar nodded and smiled, as life around him came back into focus.

"I got three tickets on the northbound train. From there it won't be far to the rendezvous," Jeremy excitedly interrupted.

Andy looked at his ticket. The black letters spelled out his future. **Train N3. North platform. Departure: 8:00 p.m. Arrival: 11:00 p.m. Non-stop.**

Frustration seeped into Andy's mind, annoyed by Jeremy's eagerness to leave behind all of the progress they had initiated. He shoved his ticket into his pocket, breaking it into pieces, self-destructing his escape.

51

They crouched in the corner, born into a world unlike any other; their senses were overwhelmed as they adapted; air burned on inhalation; noise was deafening; their feet froze to the ground; they feared to look into the surroundings, already overwhelmed by their other senses; once again, the most courageous one was first; its eyes watered from the cosmically bright light, but its form quickly acclimated and encouraged the others to see

THE PARENTS HELD HER BODY CLOSE TO their own, her energy ancient, one of the first to be part of the whole, yet her body was as small as tangible reality could hold. Wrinkled skin hung loosely on her bones, as if exposed to decades of radiation from the sun. Worn down over the ages by the Conscious Whole's ways, she followed the paradigm religiously and knew of no other, energetically aged, this poor young girl, no older than others still in the womb, reached out into the world with her elderly-like hands attempting to grasp what had left her. Yet, just as a person before death sees their past as a vehicle into mortality, this girl also saw her long journey through the Conscious Whole in the context of aging, developing into the smallest and youngest ninety-one year old looking woman alive. The parents encircled their little old lady, also waiting for the train to the Kay, as the Pillars were, seeking a cure.

The Conscious Whole

The child's early birth was a misconception of time, as time for this child progressed at a different pace. Time is relative:[1] the faster an object physically moves, the slower its time progresses[2] and the slower an object moves, the faster its time progresses. There is no fundamental, absolute existence of time.[3] Time: a creation of the subjective observer, a creation of the individual, a creation of the Conscious Whole.

The child carried with it a code, weakly connected by thin, fragile strings of energy, containing information about how to perceive time. Garnered over its lives and based upon the fast-paced and abrupt transitions of the early Conscious Whole, its sense of time became less and less relevant over generations. It was not absolutely wrong about time, but the convention it followed resulted in asynchronicity in relative time between the child and mother. The mother thought the child should be in the womb longer; the child thought its time was ready. Molecules that induce labor were formed and released. Premature birth resulted. An infection took hold. Death was in the future.

Yet, deeper within her, simmering in a dimension without moments, a peculiar energy stirred. Intertwined with burrowing depth as complex as the lives she had lived and rooted into primordial soil was a parasitic energy with solid, long, burgundy bands interwoven, braided impeccably into the core. Using small, thorn-like hooks, it grasped tightly, perfectly incorporating itself into the current materialization of whom the infant thought she was, an add-on picked up during the transition into birth.

It knavishly spoke to the core, coaxing its way into the inner sanctum, perpetuating the belief that it was naturally part of who she was.

"She's as much herself as I am her," the energy arrogantly stated, refusing to move from its home. "I'm good for you and will give you what you need," it vaguely promised.

---

1. Born, *Einstein's Theory of Relativity* (1965).

2. Einstein's theory of relativity experimentally proven in: Hafele and Keating. "Around the World Atomic Clocks: Predicted Relativistic Time Gains." *Science* (1972).

3. Barbour, *The End of Time: The Next Revolution in Physics* (1999).

The core embraced the energy, unknowingly believed the lies, thought support would be provided, and finally molded the burgundy cords into the final template of her DNA for this life. Antagonizing the core to follow the clock of time it had established, the ravenous parasitic energy yearned for its accelerating needs. The path for manifesting into reality was established as the infant adopted her identity, acknowledged it, held onto it and would not let it go, as that would abandon who she thought she was.

Time had taken its toll; the infant was aging despite the potential immortality of her physical cells,[4] which innately carried the ability to simply live on without end. Yet, mortality was never so evident in the infant's life, put in motion by her brain,[5] which collapsed the wave function at every instant into a finite form, over and over again, creating the perception of time.[6]

The Conscious Whole happily played each moment, each frame like on a reel of film, simulating a progression of events that when viewed in sequence resulted in the subjective creation of time, a subjective experience of reality determined by the brain.[7] The core watched the play unfold, confused by the rapid passage of events and bodily changes initiated by the brain, while DNA transformed within displaying the genetics of aging.[8] The brain aged the infant while the Conscious Whole aged its people; immortality coaxed into a destiny of aging, contrary to the core's existence in infinity. To compensate, the core formed many bodies, many lives.

---

4. Irfan-Maqsood et al. "Immortality of Cell Lines: Challenges and Advantages of Establishment." *Cell Biology International* (2013).

5. Similar notion mentioned in: Green, *The Keys of Jeshua* (2004), pg. 250.

6. Influence of the brain and consciousness on time perception discussed in: Walker, *The Physics of Consciousness: The Quantum Mind and the Meaning of Life* (2000), pgs. 205-208.

7. "Quantum units" of consciousness in relation to brain activity discussed in: Oschman, *Energy Medicine: The Scientific Basis* (2000), pgs. 114-115. Could the moments in between quantum units of consciousness be where all possibilities exist before the observer chooses one?

8. Murabito, Yuan, and Lunetta. "The Search for Longevity and Healthy Aging Genes: Insights from Epidemiological Studies and Samples of Long-Lived Individuals." *Journals of Gerontology Series A: Biomedical Sciences and Medical Sciences* (2012).

The Conscious Whole

The burgundy energy compelled the infant to look towards the future, never allowing it to live in the present where time goes to infinity. Life moved more quickly for her, hastening not only the perception of time but also physical time and ultimately the body's aging process.

The beings nestled in a corner of the train station and could not believe their eyes, as within cemented reality a pervasive hope floated in bliss. On the spectrum between blue and green, it had an audible, pulsating ring, like a living being taking in surrounding energy for its vitality while expelling forms no longer of use. Expanding. Contracting. It floated by the infant and her parents like a simple multiple cell creature living in the abyss of an endless ocean without light, its unawareness of the happenings in the Conscious Whole seemed ignorant, but that disregard was its strength for it did not accept unimportant baggage so easily forced onto others; the green pushed out while the blue breathed in. A simple, pure cycle that provided solidarity and health.

The beings felt the cool breeze in its wake like the ice-cold waters of its sunless world and one asked, "Why is this form visible in their world?"

"It's seeping from the pores of structure and coming from within, precipitating into matter."

The beings did not expect to see such strong hopeful perseverance coming from the people and wondered if their task needed to be carried out at all.

Unexpectedly, another sign streaked through their vicinity, a ray of hope like a jet high in the sky, almost touching outer space. The ceiling of the train station was translucent revealing sheet-like pearly clouds pushing forward with the tenacity of a glacier through the dark sky. Ten times as long as wide, the clouds looked as if you could run on them and leap from one to the other.

Even higher were clouds in the uppermost regions of the atmosphere where space and earth seamlessly blended into one. Thinner and longer than the lower clouds, they glowed brilliantly, radiating light from the retreating sun wrapped beyond the horizon.

The ray of hope beamed across the planet moving faster than light,[9] giving the perception that everything around it was flowing in reverse.[10] An arrow with a feathery long tail, the leading edge of which was an extraordinarily intense sun-like light, too bright to look at, that became softer further from the lead point.

It was not big, nor did it fill the room with its promises; its voice was not loud but silent in fact, you had to be looking at the ray to notice it. Yet, it provided a route, like a sign deep in the forest directing a lost traveler towards liberation, pointing to a place in the future that was masked by the Conscious Whole. Its knowledge was beyond what any scientist could have ever known, and its celestial understanding was without doubt, displaying endlessness.

In spite of the ray's unwavering sentinel knowledge, it was exceedingly delicate. An ancient, precious form of light that rarely surfaced, one that not even those of Meat Cove or the beings had ever witnessed. Both given an opportunity to arrive and the space to materialize, the ray showed itself to the people. Handling the ray, however, was an entirely different task, like trying to pick up a single strand of a spider's web; despite the vast strength of spider's silk, manipulating it with a clumsy hand would destroy the intended structure.

The beings held their breath, as they knew interacting too much with the ray would result in dissolution, but the opportunity needed to be seized for the ray would certainly return to the remote binding sinew of space.

The spectral code of formation spun within the infant and contrasted the ray's infiniteness. The beings sought harmony for the infant, as its state of existence was out of touch with the surrounding course of nature. One of the beings stepped forward, decisively taking action.

---

9. Tachyons are particles that travel faster than light (a yet to be definitively discovered entity). Theoretical and experimental (but controversial) evidence of tachyons reviewed in: Glinka. "Towards Superluminal Physics: Compromising Einstein's Special Relativity and Faster-Than-Light Particles." *Applied Mathematics and Physics* (2014).

10. Faster than light travel would theoretically allow particles to go backwards in time: Gribbin, *Schrodinger's Kittens and the Search for Reality* (1995), pgs. 80-82.

"No, we can not interfere," another one said.

"But she could be helped!"

"There's a reason the ray is showing itself, and we shouldn't muddle its presence. The energy of formation is unsewing itself from the background, and I fear we have entered a world of impending instability. The power of hope is revealing itself, and despite its fragile appearance it is not as weak-hearted as we may think but in fact can bring with it violent upheaval," the courageous being said, revealing its own trepidation about their one-way journey.

Part VII

"Be fearless!"

ELIZABETH J. SUSMAN, PH.D.[1]

---

1. Elizabeth J. Susman, Ph.D., Emeritus Professor of Biobehavioral Health, Pennsylvania State University. Dr. Susman showed by example and taught others how to be fearless researchers.

52

Hidden between two seemingly unimportant entities, the source was found; the underworkers delivered it with great care to the ante site and glanced above, wondering if they were too late

Two trains squealed into the station, filling it with a surge of stagnant warm air as if just unearthed from being trapped for generations below ground. Andy, Jeremy, and Norman approached the trains trying to figure out which one to board.

Andy rubbed his eyes, which burned from dust spit up by the trains, and through his blurred vision felt nauseated as he looked at the train that had just arrived from the southern region of Brave. An overflowing, torrid, midnight black river rushed past his feet as he stood at the bank of an eternally deepening and perpetually widening expanse of barely visible but viscerally penetrating water. Bottomless darkness contained violence and sinister energy with directed and intense purpose. The smell of the river filled Andy's nose, which at first smelled fresh but then burned like hot oil; bitter water sprayed onto his face, as he tasted it running onto his lips. The river relentlessly pulled at Andy's feet with its undertow intending to take him below.

Anywhere but here. I want to be anywhere but here, Norman thought, nearly opening the automatic train door himself, eager to get back to Meat Cove as soon as possible. Jeremy followed closely behind, but Andy remained on the platform, drawn in by the other soon-to-be departing train headed to the south of Brave.

He knew where his arrow pointed as intuition softly spoke the words Andy's mind did not want to hear: fleeing back to Meat Cove was not the answer, but instead resolution lay within the deep recesses of Brave.

Jeremy peeked his head out the train door, expecting to see Andy close behind but was shocked to see him walking onto the southbound train!

"What are you doing!?" Jeremy cried out.

Andy gave a blank look back at Jeremy as a frown appeared from beneath his beard. "We both know going back, running away from this, isn't the answer for me."

"No! We're getting help. We'll be back!" Jeremy pleaded, now running towards Andy.

Norman stuck his head out the window, "Come on! It's leaving!"

The trains slowly began rolling in opposite directions, but Jeremy was not in time, forced to look at Andy through a small glass window of the closed door as he stood on the platform. Tears were rolling down Jeremy's face, and Andy thought of how he had never seen Jeremy cry, feeling his own throat tighten with sadness. Jeremy stumbled back to his departing train in shock and tried to get another look at Andy, but instead he saw an orb of light, no bigger than a foot in diameter, floating behind the train. Completely sealed off and contained, Andy cut himself from all ties, closing the strands connecting him to all others. The network was severed that had kept him alive at sea, that had allowed Jeremy to see into the Kay, and that had permitted the beings of the Three Tombs to see within other worlds.

Andy tore a seemingly unbreakable bond between himself and the nourishing support built throughout his journey, a task he felt necessary to delve further than anyone else dared to travel; he feared the Conscious Whole was capable of tracing the path they paved and erasing all they had done by traveling faster than light and snaking its way upside-down in time, influencing each step he took, each person helped by their change, and each new consciousness formed.

The train sped through the underworld of Brave, into the dungeon of the Conscious Whole; hot dry air blew through small slats on the roof, containing barely enough oxygen to support life, and Andy felt nauseous and dizzy as the jerking of the train invoked a dry heave or two. He closed his eyes, concentrating on not being ill.

The train burrowed deeper into the underground, further and further away from the life Andy had built, while closely behind, menacing webs of gray energy closed off the tunnel, masking its path, like a spider building a trap. Amongst the swaying, sometimes violent motion of the train, Andy was drawn to an area with a paucity of physical movement, a void, a portal into another realm. His consciousness fluxed into a semi-dream-like world, ever so slightly removed from the physical rules of the Conscious Whole.

"Rosemarie? Rosemarie!?" Margaret struggled to yell from her seat in the corner of the train, hopelessly looking back and forth through opaque eyes for her caretaker, who had just abandoned her at the previous station.

The amorphous, sublime void grew in size, slowly filling Andy's vision and extending into his periphery. He looked into its center and saw shapes spontaneously forming out of blackness, people outlined by velvet texture who spoke but not in words; yet strangely, he understood what was being said.

"I want something that will make this go faster. Make me die faster."

"We can't do that, you know…we've been through this," her doctor explained, detaining Margaret's control over her body. "The medicine…"

"That doesn't work!" the energy shuttered throughout the void, reverberating it like a bronze cymbal.

Death was her purpose. To leave a body she had found herself in; frustrated, she wanted to move on. A flow of crystalline spikes appeared from the borders of Andy's vision permeating the field, pushing Margaret towards her future, creating destiny.

Her family and friends had given up and to make the situation much worse, her caretaker, Rosemarie, had just quit after sitting her down and stepping off the train. Life was judged and graded in importance, which is why everyone had given up on Margaret, including herself. Once an infant with infinite potential, her endless possibility seemed to have dissipated in flagrant disregard to its own definition. When does infinity, innate to a child, become finite? If she were a one-year-old baby in the same predicament, she would be cared for. Yet, this was not the case for this poor, old woman as her time was up, and everyone had counted her out. Her life was no longer revered and as such, a respectable death was not honored or bestowed.

The void was morphing as Andy had difficulty deciphering dream from reality. Like a siphon, the Conscious Whole was funneling off Margaret's energy as the indistinct figure in the void was stretched towards the center, as if in a black hole, being reclaimed by the maker. The contract Margaret had signed was being cashed in and fulfilled as per the request written into its paradigm.

Suddenly, shapes blended and unwillingly became tangled with one another as the complex, soft signals formed back into one, disappearing from existence like colors coalescing and vanishing into homogenous light.

Andy was shaken awake by the shrieking brakes and a fast series of left and right turns. He felt embarrassed because he had been judging Margaret, treating her as inferior because of her seemingly pending demise, betraying his normal values, and he waited for the relief that comes after waking from an unpleasant dream but instead felt the exponentially more powerful Conscious Whole continuing to cloud his mind.

Andy looked towards Margaret, trying to latch back onto reality, and felt an increasing uneasiness. Margaret slowly turned her head towards him and despite being blind stared right into his eyes with her menacing, dark, fixed pupils in the middle of maroon globes, which were buried deep beneath her wrinkly skin and over-exaggerated facial features. Andy's hair stood up on end, now blatantly aware he had crossed an unseen line and realized he was looking directly into the eyes of the Conscious Whole!

Andy pressed his body against the back of his seat, feeling terrified of the harsh environment he dove into headfirst. *What am I doing? This is crazy!* Andy questioned his purpose. *Why didn't I get on the train with Jeremy and Norman!?*

The train began slowing, but blackness outside did not reveal the environment. A row of dimly lit lights began passing the windows, outlining a train station platform. Andy squinted and focused on the word Greymouth, the southernmost district of Brave, written onto the exterior of a small wooden building. The train jerked to a stop, and he rushed off, never more uncertain of where his next step would lead.

Thick, heavy fog partially masked the surroundings, as yellow light fought to illuminate the world where the Conscious Whole had buried its roots. Andy found it difficult to move when he walked off the train and onto the uneven cobblestone street, ever aware of the Conscious Whole's compressive force pushing on his chest, as if he were lying at the bottom of the sea. The streets were deserted, but he felt like he was being watched. Wasting no time, the train began lurching backwards, returning into the tunnel; Andy ran back, panicked that he was being left alone, but the train sped beyond his reach and a sooty-looking conductor hung halfway out the window, tracking him with his yellow eyes, cackling unintelligible words through a sparsely toothed mouth.

Near completely overcome by fear, Andy turned to the only thing he had left, himself. He closed his eyes for a moment and looked inward, first feeling then seeing the churning fiery red energy within his core, continually weaving pieces of matter together, maintaining his desired form, a vessel which carried precious cargo: hope. At all costs, the core would not let Andy fail.

He opened his eyes and felt magnetized to his destination; a force beyond the train station radiating a deep hollow pulse, glowing above the shallow buildings no more than a few blocks away, but as he began walking he felt resistance, like wading through tidal waters.

Several sublime forms began appearing out of the mist, paralleling his trajectory, as he weaved through crooked streets. The homes lining the street were narrow and warped, looking near collapse, with peaked, overhanging roofs looming, hardly holding onto thick shingles that threatened to fall at any moment. A man, seeming to come out of the ether, bumped shoulders with Andy as he hurried past and turned his head completely around like an owl watching Andy walk closer to the source.

At the street corner, there was a person who was allowed to rot on the side of the road, left as if no longer a worthy addition to society, a drag on the functionality of the whole. A child, dressed in a long black rain jacket and boots, briefly looked at the homeless man as his mother tugged his arm, hurrying him along so his perception would not be tarnished, so the Conscious Whole's thoughts could remain unbroken. A fleeting glimpse for the child and a forcefully forgotten thought for the mother. *Like a piece of garbage*, the Conscious Whole reminded its followers.

As Andy approached, the man's energy field emanated worthlessness from the conscious cloud floating above his decrepit body. *There's nothing I can do*, the homeless man believed, parroting the voice of the Conscious Whole.

With everyone treating him as such and self-confirming their world, his state of molecular reality was solidified, collapsing his already unstable wave function to near zero potential.

He looked up through matted graying hair with emotionless eyes and sunken cheeks. Andy gazed within and walked in the light that no one else chose to see, grasping the infinite potential laden within this man and in the world of the Conscious Whole. Andy's large frame physically shielded the influx of energy pinning the man to the ground.

He knelt down and opened up his palm, holding it near the homeless man's field and lifted him from the street corner, simply showing him that hope was real and a meaningful future existed. The child that had passed turned back to look, momentarily escaping his mother's reach and saw for the first time generosity and hope. Even for a person considered beyond help, the homeless man was given a chance, more than he was ever offered before.

53

Covered in layers of accumulated debris and nearly fossilized, light was shined upon the source; the sacrifices of the underbeings were atoned, their service fulfilled

LONG, LOW FREQUENCY, PRIMORDIAL VIBRATIONS EMANATING from the origin carried a thick viscosity making it increasingly difficult to walk forward, the density paralleling the Conscious Whole's presence, strong within each being, a base for its dogma, a solid foundation to create collective reality. The molecules coming into and out of existence were moving at such a slow rate that Andy physically saw reality being formed around him.

This is creation, he thought.

As he rounded a corner, an open desolate area lay before him. Garbage littered the streets and outlines of abandoned, petrified buildings bounded the edges of the fog. Two figures were standing under a bridge and huddled around a burning fire, causing shadows to dance on the underside of the bridge extending ten times further than expected.

Clivus had a long, black beard with coarse, long, stringy hair to match. He wore an oversized brown coat and only his fingers could be seen coming out of the sleeves.

It looks like he doesn't have palms, Andy thought.

His dirty fingernails were sharp and knife-like, reminding Andy of the fingers of the Conscious Whole he periodically encountered during his journey. Clivus waved his fingers above and within the flames, intently looking into the heart of the blaze. Within, Clivus could see the whole of his world, easily controlling it by manipulating the flames with ritualistic movements, grabbing strands of energy and moving them from one place to another. His eyes glowed with the colors of the flames feeding his hungry core.

Clivus's conscious cloud ravenously circled above his head with dark purple and metallic shiny black energy, which looked like serpents swimming in a bottomless pool. Periodically, a serpentine band of energy dove into the center of his conscious cloud, coursed through his body, out his fingers, and was then magnified in the flames, producing solid, low frequency energy emitted in a spherical distribution from beneath the bridge. This was the energy Andy experienced as he approached the center of Greymouth, what he felt when he first entered the Conscious Whole by boat, what laid the foundation of the paradigm, what people based their reality upon, and what shaped their lives and created their illnesses.

Clivus's cloud was intimately connected to the conscious cloud of Zoris, who sat nearby. She was a short woman, hunched over with a hooded cloak draped over her whole body and covering the ground surrounding her; all that could be seen was her mouth and nose that stuck out far in front of the hood. She sat next to the fire, rhythmically rocking back and forth, stirring an energy field that looked like an impermeable shell enclosing the two of them; the last layer of the immune system. Isolated, Clivus and Zoris were left alone to create as they pleased, allowed to manipulate the Conscious Whole.

Born into an era filled with insecurity and the unknown, they had difficulty in their lives. Treated poorly and left in the dark by the privileged of society, jobs and food were scarce and for Clivus and Zoris the future was uncertain, with unpredictability leaving many without clear foresight or guidance. Countless people suffered under this reign, however, the duo spearheaded an uprising against the existing powers, formed the resistance, and eventually became leaders of the new world.

Over time, their power grew, and they yearned for more control, more predictability, and a stronger dogma that made everything knowable, taking their paradigm to the extreme. They went as far as ensuring even the unknown could not exist, and to accomplish their goal, physical rule would not suffice, they desperately needed energetic control.

Clivus and Zoris were early officers of the Conscious Whole, which was born from an elemental energetic template that bound consciousness. Having found such a basic underpinning of nature, they seized the tool and first united their conscious clouds followed by those of their immediate circle. Their ideals and laws grew, spreading like a wildfire, until each person under their influence accepted the reality that Clivus and Zoris perpetuated. To keep it alive was surprisingly simple, as everyone only experienced one reality, ensuring few questions would be raised. All contributed to this system, cementing the laws of nature into a seemingly separate world, apart from the people. They lost sight of what had been formed, why it had formed, and who formed it. It became the accepted truth. They were all happy living within the Conscious Whole as it seemed to give everyone what they wanted: stability and a finite, known quality to life. Surely they were better off than before.

However, the inherent nature of the Conscious Whole had a predilection to become a constrictive force, and when taken to the extreme, its structure could not change and became out of control. Just as the privileged controlled the people before, the Conscious Whole now controlled in the same way.

Then came Andy. He, like many others, had a predictable world that was not in his favor. For those with health, success, wealth, and power, predictability was a golden ticket, and they would fight to the death to sustain the unsustainable. Andy though, suffered from the created reality, albeit in a different way than Clivus and Zoris had before.

Andy stood at the other end of the street, partially hidden by a stone pillar supporting the bridge. After having come this far, he did not know what to do and frankly was unimpressed by Clivus and Zoris. He imagined an enormous beast at the heart of the energetic field of the Conscious Whole, but these two feeble people were no more than half his size.

As he planned his next move, Clivus was reading the signals within his cauldron, the flames portraying what had happened, what is happening, and what has already been set in motion. Seemingly one step behind Andy at all times, Clivus's eyes lit with fervor at what he saw burning before him. Deep red and dusk orange swirled in the blaze, and Clivus's eyes grew wider, not believing what was encoded in the energy shapes taking form! A figure danced out of the fire, a message so clear Clivus looked more intently, nearly pressing his face in the blaze as saliva hissed, dropping from his gaping mouth into the flames.

From between the stones holding the buildings together, from beneath the cobblestone streets, and from the pores in between the mist, it crawled out, manifesting into existence and approached Andy from behind. Slithering in the shadows, creeping in the darkness, peering around the corners, its intent was palpable.

Andy was so focused on the task before him he did not see it coming. He did not even know what happened.

Confusion. Disorientation. Regret.

The grin on Clivus's face grew larger and larger followed by a high-pitched laugh. He methodically toiled in the flames with callused, blackened fingers tying up loose ends, sealing Andy's fate.

The man who took Andy's life followed a path spawned by Clivus but disguised in circumstance. Seen to no others, the true murderer worked behind the scenes, through a medium. The body of Andy lay on the street corner as rain began falling, filling the air with intermittent pings as drops bounced off metal roofs.

His journey was not over. His intent to help the people of the Conscious Whole would be followed through. All of his effort would not be lost. His core being would not fail.

54

Reverberations echoed throughout the underworld, sending a shockwave, alerting all to Andy's physical death; plans would be altered as they hastily deciphered the last part of the code garnered from the source

Laced between molecules of Andy's body, the core began coalescing, detaching from matter, peeling away the small barb-like hooks from the body it worked so hard to create and fought so hard to change. It did not immediately leave Andy's body but sat in wait, composing itself after an unexpected, traumatic jolt out of material existence. Awakening and becoming lucid of the surroundings took a few minutes as it felt disoriented and confused, not sure of what had happened. It also felt naked, no longer encased by a body. Yet, it was not long until the vastly important task Andy had put into motion rose into the core's awareness, churning strongly within.

Clivus and Zoris continued to meld the world, distracted by their most recent victory. Feeling more powerful than before, Clivus pushed the powers of the Conscious Whole to the maximum, systematically reverting what Andy had done, infiltrating the hope he had spread with disappointment, and ensuring the future of change Andy had promised would bear no fruit. Jorge would be recommitted, Mr. Giving's doctor would find disease progression, and the premature baby would succumb to infection. All predictable outcomes laid out by the Conscious Whole's impenetrable dogmatic science, showing no leniency for the expected course. Andy's dream of showing people that healing was possible would just be a brief fluctuation from the norm in the Conscious Whole's otherwise flawless paradigm of birth, disease, and death modulated by the unchangeable course of DNA.

Andy's core gained composure and clarity as it perched on the outermost boundaries of the body it once lived within. Seeing Clivus and Zoris tear down the hope and change it brought to the Conscious Whole strengthened the core's motives. In a dimension with vibrations five orders of magnitude higher in frequency than within the Conscious Whole's energetic field where the shiny black serpentine fingers worked, Andy's core circled around Clivus and Zoris with unimaginable stealth.

Yet, sadness reverberated throughout the core, for it knew the task at hand would not be favorable for all. A quantum superposition of the core spanned multidimensional space around the sphere of energy Zoris created and effortlessly penetrated gaping holes in the field, which now looked more like a porous spider web than an impenetrable shell; gaps Zoris could not fill, existing outside of her breadth of energetic work, in a higher dimension than she knew to exist. The core shimmered, flickering between forms of light, converting from a translucent soft white to a deep blue and purple sheen like a soap bubble.

Immediately below the surface of the earth, the beings gathered, knowing their purpose was imminent and aligned in a row, acting as nodes spaced at the requisite frequency for the upcoming energy transfer. The ancient, massive workers were handed the now unraveled code that had been secretly encrypted and buried; this ancient formula was then used to release primordial energies that had been stored for millennia. Like miners, they formed shafts in the bedrock above while the Shapemakers pooled the whirling, erratic energy that finally felt freedom, coaxing it into discrete units. The golden channels, bridges from the underworld, focused the energy to the event occurring above through the nodes, forming a single unit of transforming power and fought to push the energy level high enough to allow an immediate and total change.[1]

Andy's core received the energy, which carried weight, amassing matter[2,3,4] as it permeated empty space and spawned a new physical existence. For a fleeting moment, Clivus and Zoris saw depth in the world they had never experienced before. The wave function stayed open, and true infinity existed for an instant, however, it would not remain for Clivus and Zoris as they decided to limit reality to maintain their control. They saw all possibilities but denied them in self-interest; overwhelmed with the influx of higher-order energy, they preferred to succumb to death rather than to change.

The old ways of the Conscious Whole continued to flow through their veins, imprinted on their sinew, and the energetic framework maintaining Clivus and Zoris's molecular composition dissipated as their core beings retreated due to dissonance with the new, emerging worldview. Subatomic particles essential to the existence of their DNA withdrew into the darkness from which they came, once again potential in dark matter.

Clivus and Zoris died under the overpass, their fire extinguished. They held on so tightly to their created world, the world they believed in, that the change Andy, Jeremy, and Norman brought was too much to bear. It was too different. Death was ***chosen***.

The remote creature from distant space had finally arrived, heard by all as the chains of loneliness dragged behind. None of the beings knew how to react to this moment as the creature's existence was thought to be a

---

1. Transforming to a higher dimensional level discussed in: Tombazian, *The Path to the 5th Dimension* (2012), pg. 11.

2. The Higgs boson is responsible for giving mass to elementary particles.

3. CMS collaboration. *Precise Determination of the Mass of the Higgs Boson and Studies of the Compatibility of its Couplings with the Standard Model (Technical Report)*. CERN (2014).

4. Aad et al. "Measurement of the Higgs Boson Mass from the H$\rightarrow \gamma\gamma$ and H$\rightarrow$ Z Z*$\rightarrow$ 4 ℓ Channels in p p Collisions at Center-of-Mass Energies of 7 and 8 TeV with the ATLAS Detector." *Physical Review* (2014).

myth, or at least an overstatement by those who believed. Gnarled proportions made its presence even more shocking, but its purpose was not to do harm. It acted as a guide, mindfully showing and doing but not judging, as no other known being could inscribe the source code back into matter of the nascent world. The creature spoke softly to Andy's core with sounds unrecognizable to human ears.

Andy's core carefully heeded the information from the creature while channeling the seeds of creation. The remote being methodically replaced the code back into the scaffold of the world being formed, but the code would no longer be hidden; like filling in empty puzzle pieces, it placed the code within the real world that was self-assembling by the moment, sewn into the infrastructure, available for all to access. However, to be seen, the code would have to be sought.

With the demise of Clivus and Zoris, the caretakers and curators of the Conscious Whole, came the birth of the New Conscious Whole and a quantum leap into a new collective consciousness[5] that was truly a ***conscious*** Conscious Whole.

By removing the functionally uninodal source of the Conscious Whole and establishing a sentient multi-nodal collective connection, the entire whole transformed and covered more distance than the old, spanning across Brave and included Meat Cove, all basing reality on the new paradigm. The previously unreachable connection to the energetic world was now accessible to all, even bringing those in Meat Cove to a heightened level of awareness. The New Conscious Whole gave hope and freedom to create life on a framework once thought to be omnipotent and awakened minds to the underpinnings of reality.

The group of beings that had traveled to the physical plane of earth stood in wait, as Andy's core completed its purpose. They saw what had been done, and some of the young ones wept, while the courageous one

---

5. Shift of a large portion of consciousness and the idea of an interconnected brain discussed in: Laszlo, *Quantum Shift in the Global Brain: How the New Scientific Reality Can Change Us and Our World* (2008).

stepped forward entering the ash-like remains of a long fought battle. Eventually, they all gathered around Andy's core and guided it away from its physical life into a white brick house, which sat in a cluster of nearby trees, a passageway allowing them to slip into an interconnected web-like realm, behind the scenes of the New Conscious Whole. They all stayed close together, none knowing what would ensue, but the uncertainty turned towards purpose as they saw a series of events unfolding before their eyes, each grasping onto a different arrow of time that would take them separate ways, onto their next journey, incarnating into new forms.

As Jeremy and Norman met up with Sandra and the people of Meat Cove, they all felt a tsunami-like wave of elevated consciousness blanket the landscape from the south. Hoping to have returned in time to help Andy with his undertaking, Jeremy and Norman intuitively knew what had happened and felt their stomachs turn. They would return to Brave seeking their friend, but knowing they were merely looking for their own closure.

Walking the streets of downtown Brave provided solace for the two men, fruits of their effort now openly displayed as people navigated the world no longer unconscious of their actions.

Consciousness was advanced.

However, over time, the newness of the New Conscious Whole became routine, and it was not long before an individual found hardship within the new. For this person, another change needed to occur, and the quietness that followed would not last. A new force was going to rise up against what had become the old.

"A new scientific truth does not triumph by convincing its opponents and making them see the light, but rather because its opponents eventually die, and a new generation grows up that is familiar with it."

MAX PLANCK, PH.D.[1]

---

1. Planck, *Scientific Autobiography and Other Papers* (1949), pgs. 33-34.

Acknowledgments

Writing this book has been a project of passion and humility, and it could not have been done alone. Beyond the gratitude I owe to the innumerable researchers and authors who compiled a mountain of literature that this book is based upon, there are four very special people that were instrumental to this project.

I would like to thank Kathleen A. Kilmer for publishing this book through Circle of Friends Press and for her fastidious copy-editing. Her support and belief in this project has brought it into print for you to read. Beyond the professional scope of editing and publishing, Kathleen has contributed to a large portion of the content of the book through many of our conversations and queries of the abstract. Her mind can bridge worlds, and she has shown me that anything is possible.

I would also like to thank Megan A. Randazzo, M.D. for her valuable copy-editing and contextual input for this book. She has provided tremendous encouragement for me to complete this project and has given me insight that I could never have seen. Her vision of the future is a gift to this earth.

I would also like to thank R. Brad Abrahams, D.O., DABR for his cover art and Circle of Friends Press imprint design. After only a brief conversation about the book, he produced an ethereal piece of art that perfectly symbolizes the Conscious Whole. He can produce a blend of realism and abstraction that fuses our world with other realms. Please visit his website to see more of his work at: www.bradabrahams.com.

The Conscious Whole

Lastly, I would like to thank Kenneth W. Kilmer. He introduced me to the world of physics and showed me how our mind can act as an instrument to see beyond the world in front of our eyes. I am forever grateful for the passion we shared.

Bibliography

Aad, G., B. Abbott, J. Abdallah, S. Abdel Khalek, O. Abdinov, R. Aben, B. Abi et al. "Measurement of the Higgs Boson Mass from the H→ γ γ and H→ Z Z*→ 4 ℓ Channels in p p Collisions at Center-of-Mass Energies of 7 and 8 TeV with the ATLAS Detector." *Physical Review D* 90, no. 5 (2014): 052004-1-35.

Ade, Peter AR, N. Aghanim, C. Armitage-Caplan, M. Arnaud, M. Ashdown, F. Atrio-Barandela, J. Aumont et al. "Planck 2013 Results. XVI. Cosmological Parameters." *Astronomy & Astrophysics* 571, no. A16 (2014).

Aguilar, M., Giovanni Alberti, B. Alpat, A. Alvino, G. Ambrosi, K. Andeen, H. Anderhub et al. "First Result from the Alpha Magnetic Spectrometer on the International Space Station: Precision Measurement of the Positron Fraction in Primary Cosmic Rays of 0.5–350 GeV." *Physical Review Letters* 110, no. 14 (2013): 141102.

Adler, Lawrence E., Ann Olincy, Merilyne Waldo, Josette G. Harris, Jay Griffith, Karen Stevens, Karen Flach et al. "Schizophrenia, Sensory Gating, and Nicotinic Receptors." *Schizophrenia Bulletin* 24, no. 2 (1998): 189-202.

Arndt, Markus, Olaf Nairz, Julian Vos-Andreae, Claudia Keller, Gerbrand Van der Zouw, and Anton Zeilinger. "Wave–Particle Duality of C60 Molecules." *Nature* 401, no. 6754 (1999): 680-682.

Aspect, Alain, Philippe Grangier, and Gérard Roger. "Experimental Realization of Einstein-Podolsky-Rosen-Bohm Gedankenexperiment: A New Violation of Bell's Inequalities." *Physical Review Letters* 49, no. 2 (1982): 91-94.

Aspect, Alain, Jean Dalibard, and Gérard Roger. "Experimental Test of Bell's Inequalities Using Time-Varying Analyzers." *Physical Review Letters* 49, no. 25 (1982): 1804-1807.

Aspect, Alain, and Philippe Grangier. "Wave-Particle Duality for Single Photons." *Hyperfine Interactions* 37, no. 1 (1987): 1-17.

Aspect, Alain. "Quantum Mechanics: To Be or Not to Be Local." *Nature* 446, no. 7138 (2007): 866-867.

Bach, Edward, and F. J. Wheeler. *The Bach Flower Remedies*. New Canaan: Keats Publishing, Inc., 1979.

Barbour, Julian. *The End of Time: The Next Revolution in Physics*. Oxford: Oxford University Press, 1999.

Barefoot, John C., Beverly H. Brummett, Redford B. Williams, Ilene C. Siegler, Michael J. Helms, Stephen H. Boyle, Nancy E. Clapp-Channing, and Daniel B. Mark. "Recovery Expectations and Long-Term Prognosis of Patients with Coronary Heart Disease." *Archives of Internal Medicine* 171, no. 10 (2011): 929-935.

Bek, Lilla and Philippa Pullar. *Healing with Chakra Energy: Restoring the Natural Harmony of the Body*. Rochester, Vermont: Destiny Books, 1995.

Bell, John S. "On the Einstein-Podolsky-Rosen Paradox." *Physics* 1, no. 3 (1964): 195-200.

Bickford, Paula C., Vera Luntz-Leybman, and Robert Freedman. "Auditory Sensory Gating in the Rat Hippocampus: Modulation by Brainstem Activity." *Brain Research* 607, no. 1 (1993): 33-38.

Bischof, Marco. "Biophotons - The Light in Our Cells." *Journal of Optometric Phototherapy* (March 2005).

Born, Max. *Einstein's Theory of Relativity*. Mineola, New York: Dover Publications, Inc., 1965.

Born, Max, and Emil Wolf. *Principles of Optics: Electromagnetic Theory of Propagation, Interference and Diffraction of Light*. 7th edition. Cambridge: Cambridge University, 1999.

Brabham, Daren C. "Crowdsourcing as a Model for Problem Solving: An Introduction and Cases." *Convergence* 14, no. 1 (2008): 75-90.

Braden, Gregg. *The Spontaneous Healing of Belief: Shattering the Paradigm of False Limits*. Carlsbad, California: Hay House, Inc, 2008.

Bridges, Bryn A. "DNA Turnover and Mutation in Resting Cells." *Bioessays* 19, no. 4 (1997): 347-352.

Buhner, Stephen Harrod. *Plant Intelligence and the Imaginal Realm: Beyond the Doors of Perception into the Dreaming of Earth*. Rochester, Vermont: Bear & Company, 2014.

Carslaw John H. "Abstracts from Current Medical Literature: Heredity of Tuberculosis." *Glasgow Medical Journal 37* (1892): 73-74.

Chetty, Sundari, Aaron R. Friedman, Kereshmeh Taravosh-Lahn, Elizabeth D. Kirby, Christian Mirescu, Fuzheng Guo, Danna Krupik et al. "Stress and Glucocorticoids Promote Oligodendrogenesis in the Adult Hippocampus." *Molecular Psychiatry* 19, no. 12 (2014): 1275-1283.

Choi, Ch, W. M. Woo, M. B. Lee, J. S. Yang, K. S. Soh, J. S. Yang, G. Yoon, M. Kim, C. Zaslawsky, and J. J. Chang. "Biophoton Emission from the Hands." Journal-Korean Physical Society 41 (2002): 275-278.

Chopra, Deepak. *The Essential Ageless Body, Timeless Mind: The Essence of the Quantum Alternative to Growing Old*. New York: Harmony Books, 2007.

Church, Dawson. *The Genie in Your Genes: Epigenetic Medicine and the New Biology of Intention*. 3rd Edition. Fulton, California: Energy Psychology Press, 2014.

Close, Frank. *Antimatter*. New York: Oxford University Press, 2009.

CMS collaboration. *Precise Determination of the Mass of the Higgs Boson and Studies of the Compatibility of its Couplings with the Standard Model (Technical Report)*. CMS-PAS-HIG-14-009. CERN. https://cds.cern.ch/record/1728249 (2014).

Cohen, S., and F. A. Popp. "Biophoton Emission of the Human Body." *Journal of Photochemistry and Photobiology B: Biology* 40, no. 2 (1997): 187-189.

Colligan, Michael J., James W. Pennebaker, and Lawrence R. Murphy (Eds.). *Mass Psychogenic Illness: A Social Psychological Analysis*. New York: Routledge, 2013.

Cooper, Vernon. Lumbee Tribe. *White Bison Elder Meditation of the Day*. July 25, 2011.

Cromwell, Howard C., Ryan P. Mears, Li Wan, and Nash N. Boutros. "Sensory Gating: A Translational Effort from Basic to Clinical Science." *Clinical EEG and Neuroscience* 39, no. 2 (2008): 69-72.

Davies, Paul CW. "Does Quantum Mechanics Play a Non-trivial Role in Life?" *Biosystems* 78, no. 1 (2004): 69-79.

De Broglie, Louis. "XXXV. A Tentative Theory of Light Quanta." *Philosophical Magazine Series 6* 47, no. 278 (1924): 446-458.

Deisseroth, Karl. "Controlling the Brain with Light." *Scientific American* 303, no. 5 (2010): 48-55.

DeRubeis, Robert J., Lois A. Gelfand, Tony Z. Tang, and Anne D. Simons. "Medications Versus Cognitive Behavior Therapy for Severely Depressed Outpatients: Mega-Analysis of Four Randomized Comparisons." *American Journal of Psychiatry* 156, no. 7 (1999): 1007-1013.

d'Espagnat, Bernard. "The Quantum Theory and Reality." *Scientific American* 241, no. 5 (1979): 158-181.

Dossey, Larry. *Space, Time, & Medicine*. Boston: Shambhala Publications, Inc., 1982.

Duff, M. J. "String and M-theory: Answering the Critics." *Foundations of Physics* 43, no. 1 (2013): 182-200.

Dunne, Brenda J., and Robert G. Jahn. "Experiments in Remote Human/Machine Interaction." *Journal of Scientific Exploration* 6, no. 4 (1992): 311-332.

Einstein, Albert, Boris Podolsky, and Nathan Rosen. "Can Quantum-Mechanical Description of Physical Reality be Considered Complete?" *Physical Review* 47, no. 10 (1935): 777-780.

Ersche, Karen D., P. Simon Jones, Guy B. Williams, Abigail J. Turton, Trevor W. Robbins, and Edward T. Bullmore. "Abnormal Brain Structure Implicated in Stimulant Drug Addiction." *Science* 335, no. 6068 (2012): 601-604.

Esser, James K. "Alive and Well After 25 years: A Review of Groupthink Research." *Organizational Behavior and Human Decision Processes* 73, no. 2 (1998): 116-141.

Fernyhough, Charles. *The Voices Within: The History and Science of How We Talk to Ourselves.* New York: Basic Books, 2016.

Flobots. "We are winning." Fight with Tools. Detroit: Motown Record Company, L.P., October 16, 2007.

Fosar, Grazyna, and Franz Bludorf. "Vernetzte Intelligenz: Die Natur Geht Online." *Omega-Verlag, Dusseldorf* (2001).

Freeman, Ken, and Geoff McNamara. *In Search of Dark Matter.* New York: Springer, 2006.

Freedman, Stuart J., and John F. Clauser. "Experimental Test of Local Hidden-Variable Theories." *Physical Review Letters* 28, no. 14 (1972): 938-941.

Freitas, Renata, GuangJun Zhang, James S. Albert, David H. Evans, and Martin J. Cohn. "Developmental Origin of Shark Electrosensory Organs." *Evolution & Development* 8, no. 1 (2006): 74-80.

Gage, Fred H., and Alysson R. Muotri. "What Makes Each Brain Unique." *Scientific American* 306, no. 3 (2012): 26-31.

Gerber, Richard. *Vibrational Medicine: The #1 Handbook of Subtle-Energy Therapies*. Rochester, Vermont: Bear & Company, 2001.

Glinka, Lukasz Andrzej. "Towards Superluminal Physics: Compromising Einstein's Special Relativity and Faster-Than-Light Particles." *Applied Mathematics and Physics* 2, no. 3 (2014): 94-102.

Goswami, Amit. *Quantum Doctor*. Newburyport: Hampton Roads Publishing Co., 2004.

Green, Glenda. *Love Without End: Jesus Speaks*. Sedona: Spiritis Publishing, 2002.

Green, Glenda. *The Keys of Jeshua*. Sedona: Spiritis Publishing, 2004.

Grey, Alex. *Sacred Mirrors: The Visionary Art of Alex Grey*. Rochester, Vermont: Inner Traditions International, 1990.

Gribbin, John. *In Search of Schrodinger's Cat: Quantum Physics and Reality*. New York: Bantam Books, 1984.

Gribbin, John. *Schrodinger's Kittens and the Search for Reality*. Boston: Back Bay Books, 1995.

Griffiths, Anthony JF, Susan R. Wessler, Richard C. Lewontin, and Sean B. Carroll. *An Introduction to Genetic Analysis*. 9th Edition. New York: W. H. Freeman and Co., 2005.

Gubser, Steven S. *The Little Book of String Theory*. Princeton: Princeton University Press, 2010.

Guedj, Eric, Serge Cammilleri, Jean Niboyet, Patricia Dupont, Eric Vidal, Jean-Pierre Dropinski, and Olivier Mundler. "Clinical Correlate of Brain SPECT Perfusion Abnormalities in Fibromyalgia." *Journal of Nuclear Medicine* 49, no. 11 (2008): 1798-1803.

Hafele, Joseph Carl, and Richard E. Keating. "Around the World Atomic Clocks: Predicted Relativistic Time Gains." *Science* 177, no. 4044 (1972): 166-168.

Hameroff, Stuart, and Roger Penrose. "Orchestrated Reduction of Quantum Coherence in Brain Microtubules: A Model for Consciousness." *Mathematics and Computers in Simulation* 40, no. 3-4 (1996): 453-480.

Harrington, Anne. *The Placebo Effect: An Interdisciplinary Exploration.* Cambridge: Harvard University Press, 1997.

Harrington, Cynthia R., Tracy C. Beswick, Michael Graves, Heidi T. Jacobe, Thomas S. Harris, Shadi Kourosh, Michael D. Devous Sr, and Bryon Adinoff. "Activation of the Mesostriatal Reward Pathway with Exposure to Ultraviolet Radiation (UVR) vs. Sham UVR in Frequent Tanners: A Pilot Study." *Addiction Biology* 17, no. 3 (2012): 680-686.

Herbert, Nick. *Quantum Reality: Beyond the New Physics.* New York: Anchor Books, 1987.

Hoeft, Fumiko, John DE Gabrieli, Susan Whitfield-Gabrieli, Brian W. Haas, Roland Bammer, Vinod Menon, and David Spiegel. "Functional Brain Basis of Hypnotizability." *Archives of General Psychiatry* 69, no. 10 (2012): 1064-1072.

Hogg, Christopher, Magella Neveu, Karl-Arne Stokkan, Lars Folkow, Phillippa Cottrill, Ronald Douglas, David M. Hunt, and Glen Jeffery. "Arctic Reindeer Extend Their Visual Range into the Ultraviolet." *Journal of Experimental Biology* 214, no. 12 (2011): 2014-2019.

Hölzel, Britta K., James Carmody, Mark Vangel, Christina Congleton, Sita M. Yerramsetti, Tim Gard, and Sara W. Lazar. "Mindfulness Practice Leads to Increases in Regional Brain Gray Matter Density." *Psychiatry Research: Neuroimaging* 191, no. 1 (2011): 36-43.

Home, Dipankar, and Rajagopal Chattopadhyaya. "DNA Molecular Cousin of Schrodinger's Cat: A Curious Example of Quantum Measurement." *Physical Review Letters* 76, no. 16 (1996): 2836-2839.

Horwitz, Allan V., and Jerome C. Wakefield. *The Loss of Sadness: How Psychiatry Transformed Normal Sorrow into Depressive Disorder*. New York: Oxford University Press, 2007.

Howes, Oliver D., and Shitij Kapur. "The Dopamine Hypothesis of Schizophrenia: Version III—The Final Common Pathway." *Schizophrenia Bulletin* 35, no. 3 (2009): 549-562.

Irfan-Maqsood, Muhammad, Maryam M. Matin, Ahmad Reza Bahrami, and Mohammad M. Ghasroldasht. "Immortality of Cell Lines: Challenges and Advantages of Establishment." *Cell Biology International* 37, no. 10 (2013): 1038-1045.

Jacobs, M. Todd, Donald P. Frush, and Lane F. Donnelly. "The Right Place at the Wrong Time: Historical Perspective of the Relation of the Thymus Gland and Pediatric Radiology." *Radiology* 210, no. 1 (1999): 11-16.

Joos, Erich, H. Dieter Zeh, Claus Kiefer, Domenico JW Giulini, Joachim Kupsch, and Ion-Olimpiu Stamatescu. *Decoherence and the Appearance of a Classical World in Quantum Theory*. Germany: Springer, 2003.

Jung, Carl G. *The Archetypes and the Collective Unconscious*. Princeton: Princeton University Press, 1981.

Just, Marcel Adam, Vladimir L. Cherkassky, Augusto Buchweitz, Timothy A. Keller, and Tom M. Mitchell. "Identifying Autism from Neural Representations of Social Interactions: Neurocognitive Markers of Autism." *PloS One* 9, no. 12 (2014): e113879.

Kabir, Zubair, Gregory N. Connolly, and Hillel R. Alpert. "Secondhand Smoke Exposure and Neurobehavioral Disorders Among Children in the United States." *Pediatrics* 128, no. 2 (2011): 263-270.

Kaku, Michio. *Hyperspace: A Scientific Odyssey Through Parallel Universes, Time Warps, and the Tenth Dimension*. New York: Anchor Books,1995.

Kamm, Laura Alden. *Unlocking Your Intuitive Power: How to Read the Energy of Anything*. Audiobook. Louisville, Colorado: Sounds True, Inc, 2007.

Kant, Immanuel. *Religion Within the Limits of Reason Alone*. New York: Harper & Row Publishers, 1960.

Khan, Sajjad A., and Stephen V. Faraone. "The Genetics of ADHD: A Literature Review of 2005." *Current Psychiatry Reports* 8, no. 5 (2006): 393-397.

Kiecolt-Glaser, Janice K., and Ronald Glaser. "Psychological Stress, Telomeres, and Telomerase." *Brain, Behavior, and Immunity* 24, no. 4 (2010): 529-530.

Kirlian, Semen Davidovich, and V. Kirlian. *Photography and Visual Observation by Means of High-Frequency Currents*. No. TT 62 1549. Foreign Technology DIV Wright-Patterson AFB Ohio, 1963.

Knickmeyer, Rebecca C., Jiaping Wang, Hongtu Zhu, Xiujuan Geng, Sandra Woolson, Robert M. Hamer, Thomas Konneker, Weili Lin, Martin Styner, and John H. Gilmore. "Common Variants in Psychiatric Risk Genes Predict Brain Structure at Birth." *Cerebral Cortex* 24, no. 5 (2014): 1230-1246.

Kuhn, Thomas S. *The Structure of Scientific Revolutions*. 3rd Edition. Chicago: The University of Chicago Press, 1996.

Kurtsiefer, Ch, T. Pfau, and J. Mlynek. "Measurement of the Wigner Function of an Ensemble of Helium Atoms." *Nature* 386, no. 6621 (1997): 150-153.

Lamoreaux, Steven K. "Demonstration of the Casimir Force in the 0.6 to 6 μm range." *Physical Review Letters* 78, no. 1 (1997): 5-8.

Langer, Nicolas, J. Hänggi, N. A. Müller, H. P. Simmen, and L. Jäncke. "Effects of Limb Immobilization on Brain Plasticity." *Neurology* 78, no. 3 (2012): 182-188.

Laszlo, Ervin. *Quantum Shift in the Global Brain: How the New Scientific Reality Can Change Us and Our World*. Rochester, Vermont: Inner Traditions, 2008.

Lee, Wei-Chung Allen, Hayden Huang, Guoping Feng, Joshua R. Sanes, Emery N. Brown, Peter T. So, and Elly Nedivi. "Dynamic Remodeling of Dendritic Arbors in GABAergic Interneurons of Adult Visual Cortex." *PLoS Biology* 4, no. 2 (2005): e29.

Lipton, Bruce H. *The Biology of Belief: Unleashing the Power of Consciousness, Matter, and Miracles*. Carlsbad, California: Hay House Inc., 2008.

Liscovitch-Brauer, Noa, Shahar Alon, Hagit T. Porath, Boaz Elstein, Ron Unger, Tamar Ziv, Arie Admon, Erez Y. Levanon, Joshua JC Rosenthal, and Eli Eisenberg. "Trade-Off Between Transcriptome Plasticity and Genome Evolution in Cephalopods." *Cell* 169, no. 2 (2017): 191-202.

Loew, Patty. *Seventh Generation Earth Ethics: Native Voices of Wisconsin*. Madison: Wisconsin Historical Society Press, 2014.

London, Fritz, and Edmond Bauer. *La Théorie de l'Observation en Mécanique Quantique*. Paris: Hermann & Cie, 1939.

Matloff, Gregory L. "Can Panpsychism Become an Observational Science?" *Journal of Consciousness Exploration & Research* 7, no. 7 (2016): 524-543.

Mayberg, Helen S., J. Arturo Silva, Steven K. Brannan, Janet L. Tekell, Roderick K. Mahurin, Scott McGinnis, and Paul A. Jerabek. "The Functional Neuroanatomy of the Placebo Effect." *American Journal of Psychiatry* 159, no. 5 (2002): 728-737.

Mayburov, S. N. "Photonic Communications and Information Encoding in Biological Systems." *arXiv preprint: 1205.4134* (2012).

McFadden, Johnjoe, and Jim Al-Khalili. "A Quantum Mechanical Model of Adaptive Mutation." *Biosystems* 50, no. 3 (1999): 203-211.

McTaggart, Lynne. *The Field: The Quest for the Secret Force of the Universe.* New York: HarperCollins Publishers, 2008.

McTaggart, Lynne. *The Intention Experiment: Using Your Thoughts to Change Your Life and the World.* New York: Simon and Schuster, 2008.

Miller, Richard A., and Burt Webb. "Embronic Holography: An Application of the Holographic Concept of Reality." *DNA Decipher Journal* 2, no. 2 (2012).

Murabito, Joanne M., Rong Yuan, and Kathryn L. Lunetta. "The Search for Longevity and Healthy Aging Genes: Insights from Epidemiological Studies and Samples of Long-Lived Individuals." *Journals of Gerontology Series A: Biomedical Sciences and Medical Sciences* 67, no. 5 (2012): 470-479.

Myatt, Christopher J., Brian E. King, Quentin A. Turchette, Cass A. Sackett, David Kielpinski, Wayne M. Itano, C. W. D. J. Monroe, and David J. Wineland. "Decoherence of Quantum Superpositions Through Coupling to Engineered Reservoirs." *Nature* 403, no. 6767 (2000): 269-273.

Nakamura, Kimitsugu, and Mitsuo Hiramatsu. "Ultra-Weak Photon Emission from Human Hand: Influence of Temperature and Oxygen Concentration on Emission." *Journal of Photochemistry and Photobiology B: Biology* 80, no. 2 (2005): 156-160.

Narby, Jeremy. *The Cosmic Serpent.* New York: Penguin, 1999.

Neese, R. A., L. M. Misell, S. al Turner, A. Chu, J. Kim, D. Cesar, R. Hoh et al. "Measurement in Vivo of Proliferation Rates of Slow Turnover Cells by 2H2O Labeling of the Deoxyribose Moiety of DNA." *Proceedings of the National Academy of Sciences* 99, no. 24 (2002): 15345-15350.

Nelson, Fred RT, Carl T. Brighton, James Ryaby, Bruce J. Simon, Jason H. Nielson, Dean G. Lorich, Mark Bolander, and John Seelig. "Use of Physical Forces in Bone Healing." *Journal of the American Academy of Orthopaedic Surgeons* 11, no. 5 (2003): 344-354.

Nestler, Eric J. "Hidden Switches in the Mind." *Scientific American* 305, no. 6 (2011): 76-83.

Nielsen, Holger B., and Masao Ninomiya. "Test of Effect from Future in Large Hadron Collider: A Proposal." *International Journal of Modern Physics A* 24, no. 20n21 (2009): 3945-3968.

Null, Gary. "The Gary Null Show." *Progressive Radio Network*. PRN.FM. August 8, 2013.

O'Connell, Aaron D., Max Hofheinz, Markus Ansmann, Radoslaw C. Bialczak, Mike Lenander, Erik Lucero, Matthew Neeley et al. "Quantum Ground State and Single-Phonon Control of a Mechanical Resonator." *Nature* 464, no. 7289 (2010): 697-703.

O'Connell, Aaron D. "Making Sense of a Visible Quantum Object." TED Talks, Long Beach, CA, March 2011.

Oschman, James L. *Energy Medicine: The Scientific Basis*. New York: Churchill Livingstone, 2000.

O'Shea, Jacinta, and Vincent Walsh. "Transcranial Magnetic Stimulation." *Current Biology* 17, no. 6 (2007): R196-R199.

Papakostas, G. I., R. C. Shelton, G. Kinrys, M. E. Henry, B. R. Bakow, S. H. Lipkin, B. Pi, L. Thurmond, and J. A. Bilello. "Assessment of a Multi-Assay, Serum-Based Biological Diagnostic Test for Major Depressive Disorder: A Pilot and Replication Study." *Molecular Psychiatry* 18, no. 3 (2013): 332-339.

Pauling, Linus. *The Nature of the Chemical Bond and the Structure of Molecules and Crystals: An Introduction to Modern Structural Chemistry*. Vol. 18. Ithaca: Cornell University Press, 1960.

Pearce, Joseph Chilton. *Evolution's End: Claiming the Potential of Our Intelligence*. New York: HarperCollins Publishers, 1992.

Penrose, Roger. "On Gravity's Role in Quantum State Reduction." *General Relativity and Gravitation* 28, no. 5 (1996): 581-600

Peres, Julio Fernando, Alexander Moreira-Almeida, Leonardo Caixeta, Frederico Leao, and Andrew Newberg. "Neuroimaging During Trance State: A Contribution to the Study of Dissociation." *PloS One* 7, no. 11 (2012): e49360.

Petrie, Keith J., and John Weinman. "Patients' Perceptions of Their Illness: The Dynamo of Volition in Health Care." *Current Directions in Psychological Science* 21, no. 1 (2012): 60-65.

Petty, Richard George. *Healing, Meaning and Purpose: The Magical Power of the Emerging Laws of Life*. Lincoln, Nebraska: iUniverse, 2007.

Piaget, Jean. *The Construction of Reality in the Child*. Vol. 82. London: Routledge, 2013.

Planck, Max. *Scientific Autobiography and Other Papers*. New York: Philosophical Library, 1949.

Powers III, Albert R., Megan S. Kelley, and Philip R. Corlett. "Varieties of Voice-Hearing: Psychics and the Psychosis Continuum." *Schizophrenia Bulletin* 43, no. 1 (2016): 84-98.

Prigogine, Ilya, and Isabelle Stengers. *Order Out of Chaos: Man's New Dialogue with Nature*. New York: Bantam Books, 1984.

Priyadarshy, Satyam, David N. Beratan, and Steven M. Risser. "DNA Double-Helix-Mediated Long-Range Electron Transfer." *International Journal of Quantum Chemistry* 60, no. 8 (1996): 1789-1795.)

Radin, D. I., and R. D. Nelson. "Meta-Analysis of Mind-Matter Interaction Experiments: 1959-2000." *Healing, Intention and Energy Medicine*. London: Harcourt Health Sciences (2003): 39-48.

Raleigh, Michael J., Michael T. McGuire, Gary L. Brammer, and Arthur Yuwiler. "Social and Environmental Influences on Blood Serotonin Concentrations in Monkeys." *Archives of General Psychiatry* 41, no. 4 (1984): 405-410.

Ramachandran, Vilayanur S. "Blind Spots." *Scientific American* 266, no. 5 (1992): 86-91.

Randall, Lisa. *Warped Passages: Unraveling the Mysteries of the Universe's Hidden Dimensions.* New York: HarperCollins Publishers, 2005.

Rattemeyer, M., Fritz-Albert Popp, and W. Nagl. "Evidence of Photon Emission from DNA in Living Systems." *Naturwissenschaften* 68, no. 11 (1981): 572-573.

Reimann, Michael W., Max Nolte, Martina Scolamiero, Katharine Turner, Rodrigo Perin, Giuseppe Chindemi, Paweł Dłotko, Ran Levi, Kathryn Hess, and Henry Markram. "Cliques of Neurons Bound into Cavities Provide a Missing Link between Structure and Function." *Frontiers in Computational Neuroscience* 11 (2017): 48.

Ridley, Matt. *Nature Via Nurture: Genes, Experience, and What Makes Us Human.* New York: HarperCollins Publishers, 2003.

Rieper, Elisabeth, Janet Anders, and Vlatko Vedral. "Quantum Entanglement Between the Electron Clouds of Nucleic Acids in DNA." *arXiv preprint: 1006.4053* (2010).

Roberson, Debi, Jules Davidoff, Ian RL Davies, and Laura R. Shapiro. "The Development of Color Categories in Two languages: A Longitudinal Study." *Journal of Experimental Psychology: General* 133, no. 4 (2004): 554-571.

Robinson, Mark T., and O. S. Oen. "The Channeling of Energetic Atoms in Crystal Lattices." *Applied Physics Letters* 2, no. 2 (1963): 30-32.

Rohan, Kelly J., Jennifer N. Mahon, Maggie Evans, Sheau-Yan Ho, Jonah Meyerhoff, Teodor T. Postolache, and Pamela M. Vacek. "Randomized

Trial of Cognitive-Behavioral Therapy Versus Light Therapy for Seasonal Affective Disorder: Acute Outcomes." *American Journal of Psychiatry* 172, no. 9 (2015): 862-869.

Rosch, Paul J. *Bioelectromagnetic and Subtle Energy Medicine.* 2nd Edition. Boca Raton: CRC Press, 2015.

Rudd, Richard. *The Gene Keys: Unlocking the Higher Purpose Hidden in your DNA.* London: Watkins Publishing, 2013.

Seidman, Larry J., Eve M. Valera, and Nikos Makris. "Structural Brain Imaging of Attention-Deficit/Hyperactivity Disorder." *Biological Psychiatry* 57, no. 11 (2005): 1263-1272.

Sha, Zhi Gang. *Power Healing: Four Keys to Energizing Your Body, Mind and Spirit.* New York: HarperCollins Publishers, 2003.

Shalev, I., Terrie E. Moffitt, K. Sugden, B. Williams, Renate M. Houts, A. Danese, J. Mill, L. Arseneault, and Avshalom Caspi. "Exposure to Violence During Childhood is Associated with Telomere Erosion from 5 to 10 Years of Age: A Longitudinal Study." *Molecular Psychiatry* 18, no. 5 (2013): 576-581.

Sheffield, Julia M., Lisa E. Williams, Neil D. Woodward, and Stephan Heckers. "Reduced Gray Matter Volume in Psychotic Disorder Patients with a History of Childhood Sexual Abuse." *Schizophrenia Research* 143, no. 1 (2013): 185-191.

Sheldrake, Rupert. *Morphic Resonance: The Nature of Formative Causation.* Rochester, Vermont: Park Street Press, 2009.

Sheldrake, Rupert. *The Presence of the Past: Morphic Resonance and the Memory of Nature.* Rochester, Vermont: Park Street Press, 2012.

Sherman, Rachel, and John Hickner. "Academic Physicians Use Placebos in Clinical Practice and Believe in the Mind–Body Connection." *Journal of General Internal Medicine* 23, no. 1 (2008): 7-10.

Shih, Chi-Tin, Stephen A. Wells, Ching-Ling Hsu, Yun-Yin Cheng, and Rudolf A. Römer. "The Interplay of Mutations and Electronic Properties in Disease-Related Genes." *Scientific Reports* 2, no. 272 (2012).

Simons, Daniel J., and Ronald A. Rensink. "Change Blindness: Past, Present, and Future." *Trends in Cognitive Sciences* 9, no. 1 (2005): 16-20.

Solomon, Jane, and Grant Solomon. *Harry Oldfield's Invisible Universe: The Story of One Man's Search for the Healing Methods that Will Help Us Survive the 21st Century*. London: Thorsons, 1998.

Spalding, Kirsty L., Ratan D. Bhardwaj, Bruce A. Buchholz, Henrik Druid, and Jonas Frisén. "Retrospective Birth Dating of Cells in Humans." *Cell* 122, no. 1 (2005): 133-143.

Stapp, Henry Pierce. "S-Matrix Interpretation of Quantum Theory." *Physical Review D* 3, no. 6 (1971): 1303-1320.

Stapp, Henry Pierce. "The Copenhagen Interpretation." *American Journal of Physics* 40, no. 8 (1972): 1098-1116.

Stapp, Henry Pierce. *Correlation Experiments and the Nonvalidity of Ordinary Ideas About the Physical World*. No. LBL-5333. California University, Berkeley (USA): Lawrence Berkeley Laboratory, 1976.

Stapp, Henry P. *Mindful universe: Quantum Mechanics and the Participating Observer*. Verlag/Berlin/Heidelberg: Springer, 2011.

Steptoe, Andrew, and Jane Wardle. "Positive Affect Measured Using Ecological Momentary Assessment and Survival in Older Men and Women." *Proceedings of the National Academy of Sciences* 108, no. 45 (2011): 18244-18248.

Stoneham, A. Marshall, Erik M. Gauger, Kyriakos Porfyrakis, Simon C. Benjamin, and Brendon W. Lovett. "A New Type of Radical-Pair-Based Model for Magnetoreception." *Biophysical Journal* 102, no. 5 (2012): 961-968.

Sullivan, Patrick F., Michael C. Neale, and Kenneth S. Kendler. "Genetic Epidemiology of Major Depression: Review and Meta-Analysis." *American Journal of Psychiatry* 157, no. 10 (2000): 1552-1562.

Sun, Daqiang, Lisa Phillips, Dennis Velakoulis, Alison Yung, Patrick D. McGorry, Stephen J. Wood, Theo GM van Erp et al. "Progressive Brain Structural Changes Mapped as Psychosis Develops in 'At Risk' Individuals." *Schizophrenia Research* 108, no. 1 (2009): 85-92.

Tawa, Elisabeth A., Samuel D. Hall, and Falk W. Lohoff. "Overview of the Genetics of Alcohol Use Disorder." *Alcohol and Alcoholism* 51, no. 5 (2016): 507-514.

Taylor, Ann Gill, Lisa E. Goehler, Daniel I. Galper, Kim E. Innes, and Cheryl Bourguignon. "Top-Down and Bottom-Up Mechanisms in Mind-Body Medicine: Development of an Integrative Framework for Psychophysiological Research." *Explore: The Journal of Science and Healing* 6, no. 1 (2010): 29-41.

Tolle, Eckhart. *The Power of Now: A Guide to Spiritual Enlightenment.* Novato: New World Library, 2004.

Tomasetti, Cristian, and Bert Vogelstein. "Variation in Cancer Risk Among Tissues Can be Explained by the Number of Stem Cell Divisions." *Science* 347, no. 6217 (2015): 78-81.

Tombazian, Jacques. *The Path to the 5th Dimension.* E-book. Castlegar, British Columbia: Alchemy111, 2012.

Tomes, Nancy. *The Gospel of Germs: Men, Women, and the Microbe in American Life.* Cambridge: Harvard University Press, 1999.

Ulmer, W., Germaine Cornelissen, Franz Halberg, and Othild Schwarzkopff. "Theory of Coupled Electromagnetic Circuits, the Connection to Quantum Mechanical Resonance Interactions and Relevance to Chronobiology." *arXiv preprint: 1110.2637* (2011).

Valji, Karim. *The Practice of Interventional Radiology, with Online Cases and Video E-Book: Expert Consult Premium Edition-Enhanced Online Features*. Philadelphia: Elsevier Saunders, 2011.

Van Wijk, Roeland, and Eduard PA Van Wijk. "An Introduction to Human Biophoton Emission." *Complementary Medicine Research* 12, no. 2 (2005): 77-83.

Vedral, Vlatko. "Living in a Quantum World." *Scientific American* 304, no. 6 (2011): 38-43.

Volkow, Nora D., Dardo Tomasi, Gene-Jack Wang, Paul Vaska, Joanna S. Fowler, Frank Telang, Dave Alexoff, Jean Logan, and Christopher Wong. "Effects of Cell Phone Radiofrequency Signal Exposure on Brain Glucose Metabolism." *JAMA* 305, no. 8 (2011): 808-813.

Walker, Evan Harris. *The Physics of Consciousness: The Quantum Mind and the Meaning of Life*. New York: Perseus Publishing, 2000.

Wigner, Eugene P. *The Collected Works of Eugene Paul Wigner*. Vol. 6. Berlin: Springer-Verlag, 1997.

Zabelina, Darya L., Daniel O'Leary, Narun Pornpattananangkul, Robin Nusslock, and Mark Beeman. "Creativity and Sensory Gating Indexed by the P50: Selective Versus Leaky Sensory Gating in Divergent Thinkers and Creative Achievers." *Neuropsychologia* 69 (2015): 77-84.

Zimmerman, J. E., Paul Thiene, and J. T. Harding. "Design and Operation of Stable rf-Biased Superconducting Point-Contact Quantum Devices, and a Note on the Properties of Perfectly Clean Metal Contacts." *Journal of Applied Physics* 41, no. 4 (1970): 1572-1580.

Zimmerman, J. E. "Josephson Effect Devices and Low-Frequency Field Sensing." *Cryogenics* 12, no. 1 (1972): 19-31.

Zurek, Wojciech H. "Decoherence and the Transition from Quantum to Classical." *Physics Today* 44, no. 10 (1991): 36-44.

Zurek, Wojciech H. "Decoherence and the Transition from Quantum to Classical-Revisited." *Los Alamos Science* 27 (2002): 86-109.

www.ingramcontent.com/pod-product-compliance
Lightning Source LLC
Chambersburg PA
CBHW020048170426
43199CB00009B/205